D0338298

Other
Creations

Other Creations

REDISCOVERING
THE SPIRITUALITY
OF ANIMALS

Christopher Manes

Doubleday
NEW YORK   LONDON   TORONTO
SYDNEY   AUCKLAND

Published by Doubleday
a division of Bantam Doubleday Dell Publishing Group, Inc.
1540 Broadway, New York, New York 10036

Doubleday and the portrayal of an anchor with a dolphin are
trademarks of Doubleday, a division of Bantam Doubleday Dell
Publishing Group, Inc.

Book design by Jennifer Ann Daddio

Library of Congress Cataloging-in-Publication Data

Manes, Christopher, 1957–
Other creations : rediscovering the spirituality of animals / by
Christopher Manes. — 1st ed.
p.   cm.
Includes bibliographical references and index.
1. Animals—Religious aspects—Comparative studies.   2. Spiritual
life.   I. Title.
BL325.A6M36   1997
291.2'12—dc21   96-40430
CIP

ISBN 0-385-48365-1
Copyright © 1997 by Christopher Manes
All Rights Reserved
Printed in the United States of America
May 1997
First Edition

1   3   5   7   9   10   8   6   4   2

To Stanley Douglas, a teacher

Contents

Part III: The Gospel of Beasts

Part IV: The Soul's Other Kingdom

Preface and Acknowledgments

In writing this book, in casting about for words and physically putting them on paper, I came face to face with the issue the work seeks to address. Despite the fact that the waning years of the twentieth century have seen a resurgence in the political power of religion, we seem painfully bereft of a vocabulary adequate to express our spiritual beliefs and longings. Our religious discourse is alternately scolding and fainthearted, abstract and tradition-bound, doctrinaire and clouded. It no longer seems to embrace an inner life, but only the references of texts to texts to texts. Our spiritual vocabulary in particular creaks and cracks, so that the word "spiritual" itself has for many become suspect, often for good reason.

No doubt this has resulted in part from the long exile devout, committed reflection has experienced from the mainstream official institutions of modern culture, where people actually work and think and dream. To discuss spiritual matters in public, except in the most superficial and bland manner, has become a terrible breach of etiquette, akin to talking loudly about the hazards of flight in an airport lobby.

Not all cultures suffer equally from this dissociation of faith from everyday life. When I was studying in Iceland, a friend of mine who helped build the first road around the island—the "Ring Road" as it's called—told me this story, which is well known among Icelanders. A construction crew, following the path flagged by the surveying team, came upon a large mound in the landscape marked for grading by a bulldozer. The night before the crew was scheduled to flatten the mound, the foreman had a dream. A figure known to Icelanders as an *alfur* (loosely translated as "elf," but a more august being than the English word implies) appeared before the man and pleaded for a halt in the construction. It seems the *alfur* and his family lived in the mound, as spirits are wont to do in Northern folklore, and they needed twenty-four hours to find a suitable new home. The next day the foreman told his crew about the dream, instructing the men to hold off on bulldozing the mound to honor the *alfur*'s request.

The men did just that. After a day's respite to give the *alfur* family time to move, the project continued as if nothing unusual had happened.

And nothing happened to the foreman, who was not in any way disciplined or questioned about his decision. Ask the Icelanders, even the stodgiest Lutherans among them, and many if not most say the foreman did the right thing. Perhaps they remembered the reason it took a thousand years to build the Ring Road was a common belief that a highway around the island might somehow offend the land spirits, who according to tradition have always protected their country.

Now consider what would have happened if the foreman were working on an American road. Not only would he have probably been fired, he might have received a strong recommendation to see a psychiatrist.

The difference here comes not only from temperament—the Icelanders are probably a little more superstitious than Americans and a little less enamored with economic efficiency—but from language. Iceland has ancient narratives that explain the existence of mound-dwelling spirits, connecting them to the well-being of the nation. This had tangible meaning for an agriculture people living just below the

Arctic Circle, where every square foot of arable land is precious. People didn't capriciously tear up the landscape in Iceland, at least not if they wanted to survive the coming winter. Their vision of life and their way of life met in tales of *alfur* and land spirits.

For us, a modern technological giant, standing with one foot in urban ennui and the other in cyberspace, all this is just a charming fairy tale. Our skepticism may do no harm where minor folk beliefs are concerned, but we have also become estranged from our central religious visions, because the living, organic world from which they arose is no more. The texts we hold sacred, the Torah, the Bible, the Koran, gave birth to ideas embedded in a landscape of animals, both real and metaphoric, where lions stalked the highways of Judea, and a good shepherd evoked sentiments of mysterious divine love. Alienated from that living world, we should hardly wonder that modern faith, for all its garrulousness, popular support, and political agitation, seems adrift in a culture that lacks the robust spirituality of men and women who know their sacred stories in their hearts.

"In a wonderful and inexpressible way," wrote the medieval philosopher John Scotus Erigena, "God is created in his creatures." The question we face, in a geography increasingly creatureless and artificial, an environment more and more derivative and mechanical, is how can we again embody our spirituality in the living, organic world of bird wings, coyote music, and the inexplicable migrations of frogs under the garden gate. We start, I am convinced, with stories about them, which is what this book attempts to tell.

Many thanks to David Abram, Jessie Hardin, Mike Roselle, and Dan Rinnan, whose profound conversations over sherry and cups of ale rang in my ears as I wrote this book; to Kathy Doerksen, for her research assistance; to Howard Sanger, for his encouragement; to Maria Rodriguez, for her moral support; Tracy Benedict, for her enthusiasm; and to Patricia Van der Leun for her patient nurturing of ideas.

Introduction

The first metaphor was animal.
—JOHN BERGER

A Saint Bernard, despite its name, is unwelcome in church. Every breed of dog or cat, sheep, bovine, terrapin, or bird, faces this same unspoken prohibition. Nor are you likely to find any fauna, except for *Homo sapiens*, invited into the marble, brass, and burnished wood world of a synagogue, mosque, or Mormon temple.

The complete absence of animals in our places of worship normally goes without notice, based as it is on obvious good sense and the customs of our time. But there is something disturbingly symbolic about this fugitive menagerie. Like the missing man on the stairs in the Hugh Mearn doggerel—"I met a man who wasn't there / He wasn't there again today / I wish, I wish he'd stay away"—the nonappearance of animals in our spiritual life is a nagging paradox, especially in light of a worldwide religious history in which animals play such a prominent part. Modern mainstream religious institutions have become, above all else, exclusively human affairs, distanced both physically and psychologically from the burgeoning, unruly world of living things surrounding us. It is as if we have built our houses of worship as glorious and immaculate temples to zoophobia, as if religious devotion and the repudiation of animal life occupied the two sides of the same coin.

There are, of course, exceptions. Some Catholic dioceses—mostly in southern Europe and Latin America—still celebrate an annual "blessing of creation," a ritual that throws open the church doors to a parade of livestock and pets brought before a priest for benediction. A few years ago, I attended one such blessing ceremony, not in São Paulo or Turin, but in, of all places, judicious, mostly Lutheran Minneapolis, at the Basilica of St. Mary. As it does every year on the October 4 Feast of St. Francis, the great church resounded not with the usual solemn cadences of the liturgy, but with the squawking of cockatoos and the yelping of dachshunds, as children brought their pets to receive a blessing. The incongruity of allowing the living sounds and colors of animals within a space so meticulously stylized and turned inward away from the natural world is irresistibly peculiar, which was the reason I came (not having my cat with me at the time), and probably the real reason that draws most everybody else.

But as a matter of fact, until the fourteenth century, pets regularly accompanied their owners to church services, a situation that ultimately attracted the condemnation of religious authorities. Bishop William of Wykeham, a contemporary of Chaucer's, rebuked the nuns of Romsey Abbey in Hampshire for their inordinate love of pets: "we strictly forbid you . . . that from henceforth you do not presume to bring to church any birds, hounds, rabbits or other frivolous creatures that are harmful to good discipline." As might be expected, the rich and powerful did not always abide by these proscriptions. One distraught nun wrote in the eighteenth century that "Lady Audy . . . has a great abundance of dogs, insomuch that whenever she comes to church, there follow her twelve dogs, who make a great uproar in church, hindering the nuns in their psalmody, and terrifying them."

These colorful anomalies, however, only prove the rule about spirituality in modern Western culture. We prefer to worship, it seems, not in the richness of physical creation with its "frivolous creatures," but rather in what Yeats called the "artifice of eternity," the purely human spaces of our own making.

Or do we? Enter the church that prudently shuts its door to the dog, and there may stand a priest whose very title comes from the Sanskrit *purugava*, meaning "the leading bull in a herd." If it is a Catholic church, a ciborium and chalice might rest on an altar, from the Latin *altus*, "high"—an allusion to the elevated platforms on which animal sacrifices were once performed in pre-Christian times. And near the altar, water used for sacred purposes might stand in a piscina: Latin for "fish pond."

If the church is like the one I attended as a boy, the pastor (from the Latin word for "shepherd") might refer to the parishioners as his "flock." High above in a stained glass window glows the image of a white dove, symbol of the Holy Spirit, one third of Christianity's sacred Trinity. In an adjoining scene, Jesus, called in the New Testament both the Lamb of God and the Lion of the tribe of Judah, might carry a lost sheep on his shoulders back to the fold in metaphorical tribute to his role as the divine Good Shepherd. As the service ends, the minister asks for God's blessing: from the Anglo-Saxon *bledsian*, "to consecrate by sprinkling with blood." Originally, the blood of a sacrificed animal.

Or perhaps a synagogue is celebrating Passover, and the rabbi rekindles in the imagination of those assembled the ten plagues of Egypt (including swarms of frogs, lice, flies, and locusts), and how the angel of death took the firstborn of both men and beasts, except for those in houses with lintels marked with the blood of a lamb without blemish.

And ultimately, in places of worship everywhere, all religions acknowledge a common concern for the condition of our souls, and the word "animal" itself traces back to the same Latin root as *anima*, meaning "spirit" or "soul."

Try as we might, we cannot bar the doors of religion to the world of animals; in a figurative sense they were already inside while the edifice was being built. (And sometimes in a whimsically literal sense too: mice have silenced the mighty organ in the Basilica of San Marco, Italy, at least twice in recorded history, by gnawing at the reeds.) Like a hologram, our religious institutions turned one way show nothing but humans, human concerns, human history. Turned another, and the ghost of some long-extinct Palestinian lion leaps out at you. Every religion, even those that seem consciously to distance themselves from the world of nature, has not only a human and divine history, but a *natural* history involving a bestiary of sheep, serpents, cats, wolves, dragons, and unicorns. And yet, modern people rarely ask about the source of this tacit relationship between their spiritual lives and the animal world, an affinity so close that it mostly remains hidden from view. Almost, one might say, taboo.

My interest in the connection between animals and religion came out of an unanswerable question most parents sooner or later face: my five-year-old daughter's pet rabbit died and she ask me what happened to it. Like most parents, I felt inadequate to the task of explaining the mysteries of life and death to a child. And so, like most parents, I answered awkwardly that her animal had gone to "rabbit heaven" or "pet heaven" or something of the sort. It struck me later that I had once had a very similar conversation with my father when I was a boy, and no doubt his father with him, and so on back countless generations, perhaps even to that moment of illumination when our ancestors first perceived the grim reality of death. The words that passed between my daughter and me were less a conversation than an ancient ceremony, one perhaps critical to becoming a fully conscious human being.

Upon reflection, I began to sense that the "where do pets go when they die" liturgy is merely the tip of a vast interior iceberg concerning our spiritual relations with animals. In *The Geography of Childhood*, naturalist Paul Nabhan tells a story from his boyhood about an occasion when he and his friends caught a racerunner lizard, strapped it

to a model airplane, attached a cherry bomb—and blew the poor reptile to smithereens. The young Nabhan immediately regretted his part
in this casual slaughter, and looking back years later, considered it a
"loss of innocence." His choice of words is instructive, as it suggests
a rite of passage, an initiation into another level of understanding the
world, a religious stirring. Most of us as children probably had similar, if less gruesome, introductions to the sanctities of life and death
through animals, whether it involved the birth of a litter of puppies
or the loss of a pet rabbit.

The concern and affection children have for animals is no acci-
dent of culture. We live in a world awash with sensations, from the
slight buzzing of a gnat to the lashing downpour of monsoons. Most
of nature's operations remain hidden to us, beyond the limit of our
senses, unless augmented by technology. Ultraviolet rays fall invisibly
before our eyes; radio waves from distant galaxies constantly break
over us without ruffling a sleeve; the shrieks of bats nightly fill the air
and do not stir a human eardrum. Nonetheless, like a finely crafted
musical instrument, the human body is attuned to the natural world,
and specifically to the presence of animals. As our common biological
legacy we have a thousand generations of intimate communion with
the animal kingdom, with the eerie magic of howling wolves, the crazy
flights of swallows, the terrible rush of some unseen carnivore. Our
very capacity to perceive the world and ourselves in all their sensual
complexity was influenced through a constant dialogue with other
forms of life.

It should come as no surprise, then, that some of the most prominent thinkers in Christian theology—St. Augustine, Boethius, Ælfric,
Calvin—have seriously considered my daughter's very question.
And, moreover, a few of them have even come down on the side of
evasive parents like myself. St. Francis of Assisi, the twelfth-century
monk and patron saint of animals (and the saint honored at St. Mary's
blessing of creation), preached the gospel to swallows, wolves, and
other creatures out of concern for their souls. His love for God's cre-

ation went so deep that he once refused to put out the fire burning his robe, admonishing his concerned fellow monks that the flame was a creature of God and should not be harmed. Francis for one had no trouble believing that animals had souls as valuable to God as his own.

The important thing is not whether I, or St. Francis for that matter, reached the correct conclusion about the nature of animal souls. As I say, the question is in an ordinary sense unanswerable, if not absurd. None of us can provide convincing evidence that our next-door neighbor has a soul, much less whether crocodiles can look forward to an afterlife. When speaking about faith, we are simply not in the realm of proof, but of personal experience. Common sense leads us away from the two missionaries in Forster's *Passage to India*, who argue over whether God has provided a heavenly mansion for monkeys. Yes, says the younger, more liberal missionary. The older man asks the same questions about jackals, and so on down the animal kingdom, all to the younger evangelist's approbation. Until he reaches wasps. "No, no, this is going too far," the young missionary finally concedes. "We must exclude someone from our gathering, or we shall be left with nothing."

Straining at a wasp's soul, we may, like Forster's missionaries, overlook the more interesting riddle that hovers before us: the fact that animals raise spiritual themes for us, about the nature of the soul, the moral life, and the afterlife, not only among schoolchildren but among philosophers and saints. The pervasive presence of animals in religious history and thought says something in its own right about the architecture of our spiritual sense, quite distinct from the various conclusions people might reach.

What would human spirituality be without animals? The Bible portrays Satan as a snake, a dragon, a roaring lion, a beast. Yahweh tempers the steel of Daniel's faith in a lion's den. Historical Christianity populated heaven and hell with zoomorphic forms, and produced a rich medieval literature called bestiaries, which interpreted the fauna of the world in spiritual terms. The great cathedrals of Europe teem with stone eagles, stags, and other symbolic animal statuary. Until the destruction of the Temple in Jerusalem in 70 A.D., both Jews and early Christians practiced ritual animal sacrifices. From a religious perspective, Jesus' most revolutionary act, the expulsion of the money changers from the Temple, was also directed at the merchants who sold the doves, sheep, and oxen required for blood sacrifice, an act that struck at the heart of Jewish religious law. One can imagine, as he turned over tables and the birdcages burst open on the ground, that in his wake a flock of liberated birds rose to the heavens—a symbol of this new faith embodied in their animal forms.

Our spiritual vocabulary contains a menagerie of real and imagined beasts, though we rarely consciously take notice of the imagery. So deeply woven are animals into many of our sacred texts and myths that the religious significance would come unraveled without them. Probably no document better embodies the Judeo-Christian understanding of the relationship between God and humanity as the Twenty-third Psalm, instantly recognizable to people of every creed for its fusion of simple pastoralism and profound theology: The Lord is my shepherd; I shall not want. But if we take out the references to animals and animal husbandry, and replace them with synonyms from modern culture, the famous first lines become hollow shells of doctrine:

The Lord is my [leader, protector, guide];
I shall not want.
He [gives me food]
He [gives me drink] . . .

Obviously, the change here is more than stylistic. The relationship between a shepherd and his flock is at the heart of the psalm's meaning, and it arises out of a real and unique experience. As a central sacred metaphor in the Judeo-Christian worldview, it cannot adequately be replaced with modern equivalents. From this experience flows a profound religious sensibility we can barely reconstruct today. For a pastoral people like the ancient Hebrews, the drifting of their flocks over the landscape at some point suggested humanity's spiritual wandering through this inexplicable world of ours, with the constant possibility of becoming lost, straying from God. In the Twenty-third Psalm, the sheep still wander, but through faith they move under God's direction, and this dependence is ecstatically transformed from a weakness into divinely inspired power.

In a very tangible sense, then, much of Western theology rides on the back of a small domesticated ruminant that cannot fend for itself. (The point is coincidentally highlighted by the fact that the first Bibles in Europe were written on parchment, that is, sheepskin. Who knows what course Christianity would have taken, what now lost oral traditions would have crept into its doctrine, had the church fathers been forced to wait until the rise of the paper industry in the twelfth century before they could get adequate stationery to write the Bible down?) In *The Great Code: The Bible and Literature*, Northrop Frye invites us to see the Bible as a vast, complex symbolic text in which "metaphor is not an incidental ornament of Biblical language, but one of its controlling modes of thought." If Frye is right, a fundamental question arises for believers about how we relate to these references to a bygone world as a foundation of religious faith. Most modern Christians and Jews have never even touched a living sheep, much less seen a shepherd, a profession all but extinct in modern industrial societies. The metaphor may be almost dead, but we still seek it out, as if we realize that we have no equivalent to replace it.

The natural history of religion overflowed the Bible and for centuries invigorated the spiritual imagination of popular culture. It would only be a slight exaggeration to say that the conversion of England to Christianity in the early Middle Ages was due in large part to a common house sparrow. When Paulinus, one of the first bishops on English soil, began his evangelizing, the pagan king Eadwin challenged him to prove the correctness of this new faith. Paulinus responded with a story about a bird. Human life on earth, said the bishop, can be likened to a situation where a king is sitting in his hall on a winter's night, the room warmed by a bright fire, while outside it rains and snows, when suddenly:

in flies a sparrow, which flutters through the hall, comes in through one door, and exits through the other. Lo, during the time the bird is within, he isn't touched by the storms of winter. But that lasts only a little while, a twinkling of an eye, before he soon returns to winter from winter. Just so this life of man appears only for a short time; what went before and what follows, we know not.

Lif is laena—"life is transitory" (literally, "loaned")—is how the Anglo-Saxons expressed the lesson of Paulinus' story. The flight of the sparrow through the hall so impressed Eadwin that he become one of the first English converts to Christianity (given the times, virtually assuring his subjects would do the same), and Christian England eventually changed the course of Northern European religious history. It's hard to imagine that any medieval Englishman familiar with this tale could see a sparrow's flight across a field without contemplating this loaned life and the importance of cultivating his spiritual life, not just the soil. We, however, see just a bird.

Not only Judaism and Christianity, but also Islam turned toward the world of animals to embody some of its central teachings, especially in the mystical Sufi tradition. One of the most beautiful Sufi stories is about a woman at a well and a thirsty dog:

The Prophet told of a woman who was considered to be a transgressor. While proceeding in the desert, she came upon a well by which was standing a dog, panting with thirst. Moved by pity, she abandoned her work, made a bucket of her shoe and a rope of her head-covering to draw water for the dog. For this God blessed her in both His worlds. The Prophet said that on his mecrāj [Journey of ascent] he saw her, radiant as the moon, with the whole paradise of Eden at her disposal.

In another story, the Sufi teacher al-Shibli appeared to a friend of his in a dream after his death. Al-Shibli related that when he came before God, God forgave his sins and asked if he knew the reason why. The Sufi pointed to his good works, prayers, fastings, and pilgrimages. God answered: "Do you remember when you were walking in the lanes of Baghdad and you found a small cat made weak by the cold creeping from wall to wall because of the great cold, and out of pity you took it and put it inside a fur you were wearing so as to protect it from the pains of the cold? Because of the mercy you showed that cat I have had mercy on you."

A number of medieval Christian narratives develop a similar theme of redemption for a sinner who shows mercy to a beggar, leper, or other outcast. But by using a dog or a cat as the object of sympathy, this Islamic tradition makes an even more radical point: spiritual rewards await those who bestow kindness on any part of creation, human and nonhuman alike. This deep sense of reverence for God's creation could not be expressed if the stories only involved human actors.

Similar parades of spiritual fauna appear in all the major religions of the world. Classical paganism revolved around animal images and animal sacrifice. The ancient Egyptians not only deemed many animals divine, but organized their rituals in almost an obsessive manner to care for the remains of dead beasts. Various ancient Egyptian burial sites have yielded over a million mummified carcasses of cats, ibises, and other creatures, after thousands of years still waiting for the resurrection anticipated by their devout embalmers. While certainly less pious, the early Romans sealed almost every important business deal with the sacrifice of an animal, presumably to discourage swindling by making the gods a party to the agreement. Pagan Greece engaged in the slaughter and burning of large numbers of cattle at important religious festivals, a practice that gave us the now familiar word "holocaust," to burn whole.

Finally, at the prehistoric heart of both ancient and modern institutional religions lies the practice of animism, humanity's oldest religious worldview. Animistic cultures see animals as inspirited beings that can be invoked for wisdom, success, insight in life's mysteries, and to do harm. Traveling back to the source of humanity's attempts to articulate spiritual sentiments, we find ourselves in the caves of Lascaux or Altimara, places Joseph Campbell called "the landscape of the soul," gazing not at portrayals of white-robed deities, but at the images of giant Ice Age beasts.

On a more experiential level, it is difficult to imagine a rich internal life for a people totally cut off from the creative energy of salmon swimming up white-water rivers, tigers hunting in the forests of the night, geese filling the air with their nomadic music. Different religions and denominations have their own distinct theological views of these expressions of natural diversity. But putting doctrine aside, no one can doubt that our spiritual imaginations as a whole respond in a special way to the shapes, sounds, and behaviors of living creatures. This doesn't mean animistic tribes or premodern Europeans have a special claim on being kinder or more responsible toward animals than we are. The facts in many cases indicate the contrary. But unlike us, these societies place their moral and religious existence in a universe oriented toward other living things, while we increasingly turn our minds toward an abstract and inert realm of human artifacts, texts, and machines.

The existence of an ancient link between religion and animals begs the question of how our spiritual lives have been influenced by the urbanization of the world and the violent exclusion of nature from our culture. There is a widespread sense that mainstream religions are no longer satisfying people's spiritual needs, and that society as a whole has fostered a culture of disbelief in its exaltation of secular knowledge and technology. This religious drift has many causes. But one among them remains largely ignored: the continuing loss of the central metaphors that breathe life into faith, as our mechanized, domesticated, and digital culture increasingly distances daily life from animate nature.

If you want to see a society without living metaphors for its spiritual convictions, just read the *New York Times.* Our religious values seem not so much discarded as disembodied, inorganic. Americans believe in God and practice their faith in greater numbers than any other Western nation, but for all our religiosity we somehow cannot refrain from murdering one another at a rate that would shame the most warlike tribe. Our society talks about Judeo-Christian ethics, but worships at the shrine of market economy and the endless pursuit of profit. The disjunct between our religious institutions and our spiritual lives has caused many people to look elsewhere for a medium to express their spirituality. Perhaps for this reason, pets and wildlife (rare though face-to-face contacts with undomesticated animals have become) seem more than ever to have attracted to themselves spiritual connotations. In researching this book, I have spoken with dozens of persons. Virtually all of them talked with conviction and gratitude about particular animals that somehow—often in a manner they cannot articulate—struck an inner chord with them. Here is a typical example:

"Chela was an orange-white cat with white whiskers and golden eyes. She and I were closest companions for thirteen years. We were completely bonded. I would walk around my home with her either draped over my shoulder or stretched out across my back. After I had to have her put to sleep because of her severe arthritic condition in her final year, I had many very lucid dreams about Chela.

"One of the most memorable: I was sad, thinking of how lost I was feeling without Chela. But then I knew to reach into a pocket over my heart, where there was an envelope. I pulled out the envelope and it had a picture of Chela in it. But when I went to take the photo out of the envelope, instead she walked right out of the envelope, big and vital as ever! As if to say, 'Don't mourn me; I am right here with you.'

"Then, a couple nights later another dream: I am visiting Chela in a colorful, woodsy, and meadowlike area. She can communicate with me. She takes me to this large, spacious clearing, where many animals of all sorts are relaxing together. At the front of the clearing is a small platform. She goes up onto the platform and speaks to the animals there, introducing me to all of them! It was a wonderful, heartfelt spiritual experience which I shall never forget."

I would guess that many if not most people have had experiences not too dissimilar to this, ones important enough to stick in the memory. Depending on their background, people might explain them as profound visions or idle fancies. We have no way of judging which is true. But whatever their status, the fact remains that animals seem mysteriously to haunt our houses of worship, our sense of the supernatural, our dreams of paradise, our visions of hell. That presents a riddle we can explore.

The riddle is as old as religion itself. Everyone familiar with the Bible knows that within the first couple pages of Genesis, two versions of the creation narrative are recounted. In Genesis 1, God makes animal life and declares it good, with Adam and Eve created later. In Genesis 2, animals come into existence almost as a kind of afterthought in God's search to find an appropriate mate for an already created Adam, alone and separated from the rest of creation in his garden paradise. For modern biblical scholarship, this seeming contradiction shows that Genesis as we have it was the work of an editor who brought together two separate creation stories, perhaps one version taking God's perspective, and the other seen from Adam's. Whatever its literary history, the contrast is startling. It is as if the Bible offers us a choice right from the start: either we can see ourselves embedded in the living animal world as participants in the larger unfolding of creation, or we can view ourselves as unique and isolated beings at odds with other living things, civilization versus the wilderness, man against the elements, art over nature.

Needless to say, modern culture chose the latter. It is a tribute to the enduring vitality of the Bible that after several thousand years the story still confronts us with this fundamental spiritual decision, even as our culture would probably prefer to avoid the whole issue.

We do not appear to have that luxury. The naturalist E. O. Wilson has theorized that humans have a fundamental interest in and attraction to other animals that is at the core of human identity. Wilson's "biophilia thesis" argues that bred in our bones is a need to interact with the living things around us, and that our thinking, imagination, and creativity become impoverished without this participation. Following this argument, it may be that we are creatures with brains destined to create the religious visions that govern our lives, while those visions, vast and mysterious as they are, emerge from the simple play of children chasing dragonflies near a pond. The fact that the first religions were apparently religions of the hunt confirms that the biophilia thesis describes something fundamental about the spirituality of animals.

In his groundbreaking book on totemism, Claude Lévi-Strauss described the way in which the world of animals provides a model and mirror for human self-definition and self-reflection with the evocative phrase "Animals are good for thinking." We are all aware of the economic importance of animals. Even in this technological age, much if not most of the food, clothing, and fuels (such as petroleum) that sustain our way of life come from fauna. With the rise of environmentalism, most enlightened people have also recognized the ecological significance of animals. The animal rights movement and new scientific research showing the deep-seated similarities between humans and other primates have for many even broken the barrier of moral superiority arrogated to *Homo sapiens*. But the *metaphysical* importance of animals, the idea that they may be significant not just to our physical existence, but to our spiritual well-being and the cultivation of our humanity, that possibility has eluded serious discussion.

This book attempts to explore the implications of Lévi-Strauss' epigram that animals are good for thinking, taking "thinking" to include the quest for spiritual growth and wisdom. For millennia, animals were at the center of humanity's religious beliefs, and only gradually, and recently, have they vanished from view, becoming the "marginal creatures of childhood, nightmare and dream."[9] Animals of flesh and blood have become invisible or absent in our society, reduced to geometrical shapes bought in supermarkets for food, or the two-dimensional images transmitted via wildlife documentaries and nature magazines. But unlike so many corporeal animals, our spiritual fauna has not completely left the scene. We still have a bestiary of our own, hidden in the underbrush or at the margins of our popular and religious culture, anxious to appear every time we watch a monster movie, speculate on the ethical life, recite a psalm, or answer our children's questions about the meaning of death. So important are animals to our spiritual lives that we do not merely use animal imagery to embody religious themes; rather, we *discover* spiritual values through animals.

When Paulinus told the story of the winter sparrow in the hall, he wanted to emphasize how unknown and precarious seems the fate of the soul after death. He could have made a different point with the same imagery by slightly changing the perspective. Warm and secure in his stronghold, the king sees a bird fly in from the dark and back out again. In that instant, he realizes how the glow of his hearth forms only a small circle of the visible, which gradually fades into the vaster, invisible, unknown world outside. The swallow may be just an animal, driven by muscle and instinct, but it is also the only link the king has to what lies beyond his home. And if he pays close attention, if he follows its movement, listens carefully to its voice, notes its form, the bird might provide clues to the nature of that vaster realm before flitting back into the darkness again forever.

If only for a little while, let's turn our gaze away from the comfortable hearth of religious culture as we know it, and like Paulinus' nobleman, peer out toward the dark where the shadowy forms of birds and beasts gather round us, as if about to speak.

PART ONE

The Book of Nature

CHAPTER ONE

Bestiary of the Soul

The wild deer, wand'ring here & there,
Keeps the Human Soul from Care.
—WILLIAM BLAKE

"I am Mr. Ed!" Think about the theological problems raised by these words.

Almost every Sunday night during the early 1960s, my grandmother and I would watch a talking palomino named Mr. Ed swing open his stable doors onto our black-and-white TV screen, sing those words, and go on to solve the problems of his befuddled, stammering owner, Wilbur Post. Not only did Mr. Ed talk, he had better diction and seemingly a higher IQ than any of the humans around him. Even his name suggested a universal order turned on its head: he wasn't called Ed, but *Mr.* Ed; while his nominal master was just plain Wilbur.

I think my grandmother enjoyed the show so much because she grew up taking care of plow horses on her family's farm back in Europe. This was before mechanized agriculture, when people, especially country people, depended on the muscle power of big animals and therefore felt closer to them than we do today in our zoologically barren cities. In the lustrous new manmade landscapes of Southern California's Kennedy-era suburbia, *The Mr. Ed Show* was about as close to animal husbandry as my grandmother could hope to get.

My grandmother's farming background roused her every now

and again to point out some mistaken detail of equine grooming or behavior that appeared in the show. Strangely, however, her criticisms never included Mr. Ed's ability to speak, as if steeds with contrabass voices were the norm in Central Europe. Like most viewers, she suspended her disbelief and accepted the premise of the theme song (whose lyrics are probably better known to most Americans than the National Anthem): "No one can talk to a horse, of course. / Unless, of course, the name of the horse is the famous Mr. Ed."

But why could Mr. Ed talk? Leaving aside the technical magic of dubbing and the mastication of peanut butter Mr. Ed's trainer fed him to keep his mouth moving, the show never explained his gift of gab. He apparently wasn't supposed to be a freak of nature, like some equestrian Teenage Mutant Ninja Turtle. Often as not, Mr. Ed got Wilbur out of trouble through some piece of inside information wheedled from another horse (usually some love-smitten filly or a police mount), who was apparently just as clever as the star of the show, if less articulate. In Mr. Ed's world, all horses were intelligent, rational beings with more sense than the humans sitting in the saddles. That was the conceit played out in episode after episode, along with endless puns about horse sense.

Like most good jokes, it was hardly original. To see society from an animal's point of view is an ancient literary device for gaining distance and apparent objectivity about ourselves. Chaucer used it in *The Parliament of Fowls*, as did George Orwell over half a millennium later in *Animal Farm*. It is the basis of the tenth-century Arabic text *The Island of the Animals* (which ends with the surprisingly egalitarian note that "Man is accountable to his Maker for the way in which he treats all animals, just as he is accountable for his behaviour towards his fellow human beings"). But much more than a literary trope is at work here, something more fundamental and strange. In addition to Mr. Ed, our culture has created a whole universe of talking animals, from comic strips to cartoons to television shows, fairy tales, novels, and pull-string teddy bears. From our imaginations have sprung sentimental purple dinosaurs, wisecracking rabbits, cereal-selling tigers, lisping house cats, slang-ridden terrapins, bashful lambs, dogs with drawls and speech impediments, good-old-boy roosters, eagles that philosophize, pigs trying to be sheepdogs, and amorous skunks with French accents. We have surrounded ourselves with a conversational menagerie.

Not only that, this menagerie has a cultural resonance that goes beyond mere fantasy and play. Talking animals are important to us. Most readers can probably identify the zoological figures I just alluded to with an adjective or two. If I made a similar sketch of a dozen writers or political leaders, only a savant might get the references.

Mr. Ed himself comes from a long lineage of talking equines. His immediate predecessor was Francis the talking mule, who appeared in seven highly profitable movies by Universal, though this seems like double counting since the films' director, Arthur Lubin, went on to create Mr. Ed. A talking horse is central to *Animal Farm* as the allegorical voice of the long-suffering, easily led Russian proletariat. In the last part of *Gulliver's Travels* (the part of the book your high school teacher probably didn't have you read because of its disturbingly dark misanthropy), Swift lets the equestrian and highly rational Houyhnhnms look down their thoroughbred noses—literally—at the cultural pretensions of eighteenth-century Europeans. In the more distant recesses of European history, some Germanic tribes, according to the Roman historian Tacitus, kept sacred white horses, with whom priests purported to converse in order to obtain knowledge of the future.

Mr. Ed's pedigree even reaches back to the Bible, to recorded history's first and most unlikely spokesman of animal rights: Balaam's ass. In one of the most enigmatic and dreamlike passages in the Old Testament, Balaam—apparently a Moabite soothsayer who incongruously worships Yahweh and "knew the knowledge of the Most High"—is bribed by the hapless King of Moab to place a curse on the Israelite army advancing on his kingdom. Balaam departs on his donkey toward a place of sacrifice, but Yahweh sends an angel to block his path:

> And when the ass saw the angel of the Lord, she fell down under Balaam; and Balaam's anger was kindled, and he smote the ass with a staff.
>
> And the Lord opened the mouth of the ass, and she said unto Balaam, What have I done unto thee, that thou hast smitten me these three times?
>
> And Balaam said unto the ass, Because thou hast mocked me: I would there were a sword in mine hand, for now would I kill thee.
>
> And the ass said unto Balaam, Am not I thine ass, upon which thou hast ridden ever since I was thine unto this day? was I ever wont to do so unto thee? And he said, Nay. [Numbers 22:27–30]

Besides the wonderful pun of the last line (which appears only in the English translation), perhaps the oddest thing about this passage is Balaam's reaction to his newly articulate beast of burden. Except for the serpent in the Garden of Eden, this is the only instance in the Bible of an animal speaking. Yet, not taken aback in the slightest, Balaam enters into a conversation with his beast of burden, even conceding the justice of its complaints, which seem to be *cri de coeur* against the mistreatment of animals by humans everywhere. The angel, finally manifesting itself to Balaam, even criticizes the soothsayer for getting upset with his mount, pointing out that he would have perished at the angel's hand had the ass not shied away. The effect of the drama is to emphasize the moral stature of the animal, who ironically not only has deeper spiritual vision than the famous diviner, but who also bests him in an argument about ethics.

Balaam became one of the most frequently maligned villains in the Bible, though the reason is unclear. After the incident with his donkey, he listened to God's commandment, and much to the chagrin of the Moabite king, actually blessed the Israelites instead of cursing them. A millennium or so later, St. Peter found the incident interesting enough to fashion it into a serious moral point, just as Hollywood employed Mr. Ed for comic effect: "But [Balaam] was rebuked for his iniquity: the dumb ass speaking with man's voice forbad the madness of the prophet" (II Peter 2:16). Peter saw some spark of spiritual truth, the exact nature of which we do not quite understand today, but it was important enough for him to include a talking equine in Christianity's sacred text as a voice of morality.

The religious quality of talking equines has declined over the years, turning from divine spokesmen into sideshow draws and sitcom premises. The dressage of allegedly sentient horses through recent history mostly involves the performance of tricks, from the dice-counting of Morocco, a steed famous enough to be mentioned by Shakespeare (and supposedly burned at the stake in Rome for witchcraft along with his apparently very loyal owner), to the complex arithmetic of the *fin de siècle* wonder pony Clever Hans—not to mention Silver, Trigger, and a host of other cowboy movie horses who seemed to understand their master's every word. Nonetheless, the reason for Peter's or our interest in reports from the distant past, such as Balaam's verbal duel with his donkey, lies in the fact that the problems they pose remain, in an exemplary manner, the same we face today. The vast parade of wordy animals stretching back through our history suggests that, in the products of our imagination at least, we feel compelled to portray animals as being like us: conscious, rational, and possessing what can only be called a soul, even though we know their existence is mysteriously and silently different from our own. In our everyday lives, we may never expect animals to speak (though we cannot resist speaking to them as if they could articulate a response), but when we dream or play or tell stories that go beyond mundane existence, suddenly the dumb beasts we thought we knew rear up like Macy parade balloons into fantastic, unexpected forms. It is as if on some deep level, our inner creative lives drew strength from a kinship with animal life, if not among the beasts of the flesh, then among the more engaging fauna of the imagination.

So pervasive is this animal colloquy that we rarely even think about its implications. But it represents the lingering echo of an old and at times dangerous debate about the religious significance of animals.

John Scotus Erigena learned firsthand just how dangerous. Perhaps the most learned European in the ninth century A.D., and the first rigorous philosopher of the Middle Ages, the Celtic cleric was supposedly beaten to death by his own students in the year 847. They apparently became enraged when he proposed—the technicalities of medieval philosophical aside—that the divine spark dwelt not only in God and man, but in all of physical creation, including "dumb beasts." The elegant phrase that summed up his philosophy: "In a wonderful and inexpressible way God is created in his creatures." Not satisfied with simple homicide, Pope Honorius III took the trouble to officially condemn John's major work, *On the Division of Nature*, some two centuries after the philosopher's death.

Both Boethius and St. Augustine, the two most popular philosophers in the Middle Ages, concede that the soul, as the *anima*, as a life force, is possessed by animals. Boethius talks enigmatically about a "world-soul" that permeates creation. In a passage in his *Confessions*, Augustine alludes obliquely to some kind of connection between human spirituality and animals, between praising God and kinship with creation: "Thy whole creation speaks Thy praise—the spirit of every man by the words that his mouth directs to Thee, animals and lifeless matter by the mouth of those who look upon them." He even says about the nature of divinity that "animals great and small see it," but cannot learn about it through study and reason.

Ultimately (and it seems almost grudgingly) both these thinkers go along with the predominate teaching of the church as we know it today, that only humans have an immortal, rational soul or mind that can understand, participate in, or reject God's eternal plan for redemption.

The Anglo-Saxon clerics Alcuin and Ælfric also insisted that the soul is a rational, intellectual entity that distinguishes man from beasts, but they did not suffer from Augustine's misgivings. Ælfric was particularly vociferous on this point, interjecting the assertion that animals are "sawulleas" (soulless) at least a dozen times in his commentaries or translations of church authorities, even where such assertions are not particularly cogent. "Hund is sawulleas and on helle ne þrowað" ("A dog is soulless and does not suffer in hell"), declared Ælfric in one of his homilies, apparently unwilling to share even eternal damnation with such "lower" life forms. The fact that Ælfric felt compelled time and again to mention this indicates at least some of his Anglo-Saxon flock did indeed expect their pets might accompany them in the afterlife. For better or for worse.

Curiously, six hundred years later, Descartes began using a similar rhetoric about "thoughtless brutes," fused with the new imagery of animals as machines, for a totally different purpose. The French philosopher was less interested in humanity's spiritual preeminence in the plan of redemption than he was in justifying the scientific study of animals. Some justification was necessary, since for him study equaled vivisection, experimentation on living creatures, often in an unspeakably cruel manner.

Animals were a "problem" for medieval religion. Churchmen saw God's creation as a possible distraction from God's word, where ultimate truth resided. St. Bernard, founder of the twelfth-century monastery of Clairvaux, wrote the following diatribe against theriomorphic decorations on the facades of Romanesque churches, making the animal/book distinction:

What is the meaning of those absurd monstrosities, that astounding amorphous plethora of form, that formal opulence of shapelessness standing in front of the eyes of studious monks in the cloisters? What are those obscene apes doing there? Those savage lions? those centaurs and half-men? The striped tigers? . . . There we can see many bodies with one head and, conversely, many heads on a single body, here a quadruped with a serpent's tail, over there a fish with a quadruped's tail. Over there a beast, horse in front and goat behind, and again, a horned beast with a horse's rump. Everywhere is such a rich and amazing profusion of different shapes, that one would sooner learn from the statues than from books, sooner spend the whole day doing that alone rather than contemplate the commandments of God.

Against this current of spiritual zoophobia waded St. Francis of Assisi, the twelfth-century monk and patron saint of animals (did the creator of Francis the mule come up with the name as an homage to the saint?). Called by one historian an "animistic revolutionary," St. Francis expressed the belief that God's spirit dwells in all of nature, not just in the descendants of Adam and Eve. His views reached vaguely heterodox heights in his famous "Sermon to the Birds," which begins with this strikingly egalitarian invocation: "Oh, birds, my brothers, you have a great obligation to praise your Creator." For Francis, "God smiled on all creatures equally."

Church authorities were never comfortable with St. Francis. To say the least. As one medieval scholar noted, the prime miracle of his life is that he did not end up at the stake. St. Bonaventure tried to suppress Francis' "doctrine" of animal souls, but the patron saint of animals was too popular among the laity for a theologian even of Bonaventure's stature to censor the saint's teachings. In addition to his famous sermons to animals, Francis also urged the church to lend its authority in preserving the natural world, something unheard of at the time, by petitioning Rome to outlaw the capture and killing of songbirds. The petition failed, not surprisingly: the pontiff at the time was the very same Pope Honorius who denounced John Scotus Erigena.

The spiritual ambiguities of animals have a rich history in the Judeo-Christian tradition, a history often neglected both by those who condemn Western attitudes toward the nonhuman world, and by those who extol them. In 1967, the publication of a short essay called "The Historical Roots of Our Ecological Crisis" by Lynn White, Jr., crystallized a critical view of the Bible among many thinkers interested in the relationship between religion and nature. According to White, a historian and medievalist, our alienation from nature stems from the core theological teachings of Judaism and Christianity derived from Genesis, where Yahweh seems to give Adam and Eve dominion of all other living things. White dug the trenches for the mainstream battle over the usefulness of Judeo-Christian ethics in the Age of Ecology.

But even assuming White's conclusion is true, rather than indicting anything that actually appears in the Bible, it identifies a historical failure to ponder the nuances and possibilities of our religious heritage. One response to the malaise accurately identified by White has been the growth of the "creation theology" movement, an attempt to restore a Christian vision of humanity's responsibility to and participation in the rest of creation. Fr. Thomas Berry confronts the issue directly, stating that one of the most disturbing facts he had to contend with as a modern Catholic was the ease with which Christianity has been used to support ideologies that exploited and depreciated the natural world. The best-known and most prolific advocate of creation theology, Matthew Fox, calls on believers to redeem the Bible from patristic writers who have emphasized original sin and the fall of nature, and to explore the meaning of God's original blessing on humanity and the rest of creation. In a mild reprise of the unpleasantries visited upon John Scotus Erigena, ecclesiastical authorities censured Fox in 1988 for his alleged misreadings of church literature.

If we take up Fox's challenge, we find that the Bible does indeed reveal a deep sense of spiritual mystery about animals, belying the later tradition of Ælfric's soulless fauna. For example, the story of the Flood makes Noah and his family the protagonists, but the narrative focuses on the fate of creation. Many if not most cultures have myths about a calamitous deluge that sweeps away a corrupt world. We need look no further than Ovid's *Metamorphoses* for the same motif. But only the biblical version centers the story on the building of an ark and the preservation of the animal kingdom (curiously plants are completely omitted in Noah's elaborate attempt to preserve the world's biological heritage). And when the waters recede, we are told that Yahweh fashioned a rainbow as a token of his promise never to send another flood to devastate the world, a promise made not only to Noah, but to "every living creature of all flesh that is upon the earth." Unspoken is the idea that the animals understand the promise, a condition that would seem necessary for this covenant to have any meaning.

The story of the Flood suggests not only an intense metaphysical concern for nonhuman life, but a belief that animals are more than dumb beasts. If Balaam's conversation with his donkey does not confirm this, then the commandments given to Moses do. In Exodus, Moses receives from Yahweh not only the Ten Commandments, but scores of lesser laws never engraved on tablets, mostly relating to social mores. One of these laws involves a homicidal ox:

If an ox gore a man or a woman, that they die: then the ox shall be surely stoned, and his flesh shall not be eaten: but the owner of the ox shall be quit [i.e., excused]. [Exodus 21:28]

The passage can be rationalized, as it has, to mean nothing more than that a dangerous animal should be destroyed, and should not be eaten since it was not slaughtered for food. The possibility also exists that some obscure superstition involving demon possession is at work here. Nonetheless, the clearest, most obvious interpretation of this dictate is that the ancient Hebrews believed animals were legally and morally responsible for their actions. Strikingly similar mandates regarding oxen that gore appear in the Code of Hammurabi and the Laws of Eshnunna; in fact so similar are these three bodies of law that they may have all derived from a common source. Yet only the biblical version imposes capital punishment on the offending bovine. The other codes only require monetary compensation. The biblical law seems to be only a special case of God's instruction to Noah in Genesis 9:5–6 requiring capital punishment for the shedding of man's blood. The biblical treatment of the ox that gores seemingly points a finger of culpability at the animal, and culpability requires understanding, consciousness, or whatever term people use from time to time as descriptions for the soul.

The Bible even gives direct expression to its doubts about the spiritual preeminence of humans over animals. The writer of Ecclesiastes thunders against the arrogance of men who denigrate the spirituality of nature:

> I said in mine heart concerning the estate of the sons of men, that God might manifest them, and that they might see that they themselves are beasts.
>
> For that which befalleth the sons of men befalleth beasts; even one thing befalleth them: as the one dieth, so dieth the other; yea, they have all one breath; so that a man hath no preeminence above a beast; for all is vanity.
>
> All go unto one place; all are of the dust and all turn to dust again.

Who knoweth the spirit of man that goeth upward, and the spirit of the beast that goeth downward to the earth?
[Ecclesiastes 3:18–21]

This last question could be properly asked today of our culture, which has lost the sense of mystery about animal existence in the gross accumulation of zoological data.

But despite Francis' passion, Augustine's qualms, and the glimmer of animal spirituality that teases the careful reader of the Bible, White was correct to this extent: historical Christianity did indeed come down on the side of Ælfric and his soulless hound. On some unexplored level, however, our culture remains unconvinced. To bear this out, we merely have to turn on the Saturday morning cartoons or listen to a respectable citizen complimenting his dog. But what is this cultural *terra incognita* where animals appear as speaking subjects? And just as important, why has it remained neglected for so long?

In his comprehensive study of shamanism, the French anthropologist Mircea Eliade writes: "All over the world learning the language of animals, especially of birds, is equivalent to knowing the secrets of nature and hence to being able to prophesy." The reason animals can reveal the future is, he argues, "because they are thought to be receptacles for the souls of the dead or epiphanies of the gods." Eliade further suggests that in many primal traditions, communication with animals derives from a "paradisal syndrome," a belief that in a mythical dreamtime, when the basic patterns of the universe, such as male/female, light/dark, etc., were forged, "man lived at peace with animals and understood their speech." Many Native American myths recount an era when humans and animals could interchange forms, or when all humans had animal forms. Among the Alsea of western Oregon, for instance, there was a belief that the world was formerly peopled by the present animals and birds in human shape, and various groups of people were transformed into animals. Kalapuya myth speaks of a time when humans gave birth to animals or were transformed into them. In a Bororo (Brazil) myth about the cultural hero Meri, during dreamtime, human and animals changed form promiscuously, so that Meri visits the house of a man, who is actually a heron, while the birds that assault him are actually men. The Greek legend of Prometheus, at least as reinterpreted by Aesop, also assumes the divine transformation of animals into men, which according to the witty fabulist explains why some people have the forms of humans but the irrational souls of beasts.

In this inspirited universe of animism, the shaman's office is to solve problems in the physical world (sickness, lack of game, enemy attacks) by leaving his body and sojourning to the invisible realm of spirits where the root causes of worldly problems can be changed. To that end a shaman must seek the help of guiding spirits, almost always animal spirits. The "animal language" spoken by shamans, Eliade suggests, is only a variant of "spirit language," the language of magic, religion, mythology. The role of shamanism may help explain Balaam's curious reaction to his talking beast of burden. Instead of being startled by the creature's ability to speak, Balaam gets into a shouting match with it. Later, in Numbers, we learn that Balaam has the ability to fall into a trance and see future events unfold. Perhaps Balaam, like shamans in primal societies all over the world, grew so accustomed to conversing with spirit animals while in these altered states that his donkey's outburst struck him as impudent, but not especially unusual.

The shamanistic world of speaking, numinous animals described by Eliade exists against the backdrop of the religious worldview of animism. Animism is as complex and difficult to define as our worldview, but at its core lies the perception that all the phenomenal world—humans, animals, plants, and even nonbiological entities, such as stones, rivers, and cultural artifacts—is alive in the sense of being inspirited. Not only is the nonhuman world alive, but it is filled with articulate and at times intelligible subjects, able to communicate and interact with humans for good or ill.

Diamond Jenness' study of the Ojibwa Indians summarizes the threads of kinship that exist in an animistic worldview: "Not only men, but animals, trees, rocks, and water are tripartite, possessing bodies, souls, and shadows. They all have a life like the life in human beings, even if they have all been gifted with different powers and attributes." From an animistic perspective the world is filled with spirits constantly communicating, constantly interacting. This has both good and bad consequences, generating the possibility of prophecy and mystical knowledge (the "language of birds" mentioned by Eliade), but also the necessity to propitiate injured spirits, to defend against spiritual attack, to erect taboos against entities too spiritually charged to be handled safely. In his study of Iglulik (Eskimo) society, Knud Rassmussen quotes one of the native informants he interviewed on the dangers of living in an animistic world:

> The greatest peril of life lies in the fact that human food consists
> entirely of souls. All the creatures that we have to kill and eat,
> all those that we have to strike down and destroy to make clothes
> for ourselves, have souls, like we have, souls that do not perish
> with the body, and which must therefore be propitiated lest they
> should revenge themselves on us for taking away their bodies.

As this angst about killing animals suggests, Ælfric's statement that "Hund is sawulleas" contradicts the very heart of animistic culture and its practices.

The feeling that animal spirits must be treated with respect is so strong in some tribal cultures that it dominates their myth of origins. The Tsimshian-speaking tribes of the Pacific Northwest believed in an earthly paradise called Temlaham, which in one version came to an end when men treated with irreverence the bones of the salmon. In another version, Temlaham was devastated by an earthquake, caused by the spirits of mountain goats whom men had hunted and devoured without paying due respect.

Our most powerful narrative of origins, Genesis, also places the blame for the ruination of paradise on some discord between the human and animal worlds. Yahweh creates a vegetarian Eden, without predation, without animal death, but the serpent, "more subtil than any beast of the field," disrupts the relations among humans, animals, and heaven. Although later theologians identify the serpent with the devil, Genesis presents the creature as a real animal, endowed with reason and the genes for cunning. The fact is, Satan isn't even mentioned in Genesis, and the curse that God pronounces falls not on some infernal spirit, but on the flesh and blood animal of the order Ophidia: "Because thou has done this, thou art cursed above all cattle, and above every beast of the field, upon thy belly shalt thou go, and dust shalt thou eat all the days of thy life" (Genesis 3:14). Whatever else it may be, God's curse against the serpent is first and foremost zoological, not metaphysical.

Our inability to feel the connection between our religious narratives and real snakes in the landscape, as surely the Genesis writers did, describes our cultural dilemma in harmonizing spirituality with modern life. My grandmother's generation was probably the last in the West to grow up close to large domestic and wild animals. The plumes of white breath from a horse's snout in winter, the grunts of hungry livestock, the smell of sheep wet with dew—these palpable experiences vividly impressed the presence of animals onto human consciousness since the earliest times. The muscle power of horses, the herding instinct of dogs, the fecundity of hares were the source of well-being and the common vocabulary of our culture. Industrial economy, however, not only had no use for the physical power of animals, it humanized the landscape and drove fauna away from our daily lives until they have become for the most part mere two-dimensional images viewed on televised nature shows. We have lost the kinship my grandmother felt with animals, and with it the reference points to our religious metaphors. And, perhaps, to the root of truly deep religious experiences.

The images most of us feel comfortable with involve a humanized, rationalized, commercialized landscape whose angles and predictability leave little space for spiritual discovery, except perhaps the doleful insight mourned by writers for the past two centuries, that spiritual integrity has become difficult, if not impossible, in the wasteland of mechanized culture.

Our culture's reliance on reason has also diminished the quality of our relationships with the animal kingdom. The application of reason has succeeded tremendously in building a materially prosperous society, but it has also impoverished our frame of reference to the nonhuman world. Since Aristotle's time, animals have been defined in the West as creatures that lack rational thought. This, in fact, was the quality many philosophers fixed upon to distinguish humanity from the rest of the biological world. Hamlet uses the comparison to denounce his mother's hasty remarriage to his uncle, decrying that "a beast that wants [i.e. lacks] discourse of reason / Would have mourn'd longer." People have known from the earliest times that animals do not measure out their lives the way humans do. But to a culture like ours, transfixed by the power of reason and the material progress it brings, this trait means that animals have nothing of value to teach us. As a Tuscarora Indian put it, unlike the experience of primal cultures, in Western society, "the uncounted voices of nature are dumb."

This isn't exactly true. The animistic welter of faunal spirits may seem far removed from our technological society and its machine-like solidity. We are not, of course, an animistic culture, and have not been so for a long time. But that does not mean we live in a philosophically pure present, cut off from the anxieties and ecstasies that animism exerted over human society for uncounted ages. Expelled from the rarefied atmosphere of theology, pushed to the margin by an industrial economy, the spiritual sensibilities we have toward animals have gone underground. Into popular culture, into the names of sports teams and rock bands, into art, literature, film, and toys.

There may be economic or aesthetic reasons why the Detroit baseball team is called the Tigers, why Miami chose a dolphin to represent its football team, or why Minnesota has a basketball club named for the almost extinct *Canis lupus*. But when all is said and done, modern people favor zoological names for the same reason tribal people select a totem animal: to capture the animal's spiritual force. This is pure magic, whether we acknowledge it or not. Nothing else can explain the animal appellations of so many sports teams, or the fact that the world's most famous rock group is the Beatles (not to mention the Turtles, the Animals, the Monkees, and so on), or that political parties take animal mascots, or the number of automobile makes christened with such names as Mustang, Cougar, Jaguar, or Bronco.

We experience the persistence of animal spirituality every day. Children in our culture universally talk to stuffed animals and puppets without being considered mentally deranged. In fact, we encourage them to do so with fairy tales, which almost always involve talking animals, or people turned into animals, or beasts with magical powers. Respectable citizens shout curses at flies that land in their soup. Despite the technological world we inhabit, our deeper convictions about the meanings of animals take on such simple, familiar forms as a rabbit's foot kept in a glove compartment of a car, or a horseshoe hung over a door.

The animism observable in the earliest sources of Western culture has ceased to be a living belief, overwhelmed first by monotheism and later by modern zoology. Still, the spiritual force of animals seems deeply ingrained in the human psyche, lingering on as a "reflex," in the almost literal sense that when a snake is killed its tail continues to twitch. The animals of our cultural and religious past—the redemptive scapegoats, diabolical wolves, luminous doves—continue to wriggle about, making their presence known, and influencing the world of humans, as if driven by the irrepressible spirit of an earlier understanding of nature, now alien to our intellectual life. Alien, but not entirely outcast.

While we could dismiss the persistence of animistic themes in our lives as nothing more than a religious curio, an artifact of less sophisticated times, too much of our religious and cultural imagery is dedicated to speaking, teaching animals for such an easy explanation. Myths may take many forms, but one clear mythological function is to make life understandable, or at least coherent, by explaining apparent contradictions. Our many images and stories about sentient animals, while perhaps not rising to the level of full-blown myths, seem to play a similar role.

At the core of our society struggle two contradictory views of animals, and of nature in general. On the surface level, an unlikely union of religious doctrine and modern zoology has reduced animals to mere biological data, Ælfric's soulless dog and Descartes' mechanical brute, obediently and insensibly following modern humanity into a future of genetic manipulation and factory farms. This represents the official view of animals we hear in most universities, churches, and other institutions. But underneath this thin layer of language flows a deep, ancient, sometimes disturbing tradition that shimmers with the imagery of spirit animals. These animals of dreamtime and deep history have never left us.

Modern society as we know it, with its dependence on reason and the manipulation of the natural world, probably could not function under the full force of the animistic tradition. If, like Rassmussen's Iglulik informant, we consciously acknowledge that animals have souls, our technological way of life and its treatment of animals would suddenly become indefensible and obscene. But we also apparently cannot function without the energy of animism. It wells up into our culture, and so we direct it into areas that can be managed, into fictions and fairy tales, where real questions about the nature of animals never have to be discussed. We satisfy our need to envision animals as spiritual forces, without having to confront what that vision implies. To do so, to talk about the central role animals play in our exploration of religious meaning, might break the spell of material progress that justifies much of what we call modernity.

Zoology vs. St. Francis. The one directs our practical lives, the other kindles our mythic sensibilities, the dreamtime understanding that makes day-to-day existence meaningful. But for the St. Francis in us to keep pace with the explosion of scientific knowledge, for our spiritual lives to avoid becoming trivialized and dissociated from the past and from the breathing world around us, work and dedication are required. The scientific study of biology proceeds through diligent research; acquiring knowledge of what animals mean to our religious understanding of the world demands no less effort. This is not a new task. It has simply been neglected.

CHAPTER TWO

Holy, Intelligible Elephants

And perhaps just as God made man in his own
image and likeness, so also did he make the
remaining creatures after certain other heavenly
images as a likeness.
—ORIGEN

Eusebius Hieronymus—better known to the world as St. Jerome, the great theologian and church father—sits toward the back of his cramped study, engrossed in his writing. Presumably he is working on his Latin translation of the Bible, the Vulgate (from the Latin *vulgaris*, meaning "in common use"), a version that would serve as Christendom's central text for over a thousand years and give us such famous expressions as "paternoster," and "consumatus est." As he translates the verses, the saint also dictates to three monks seated around him, apparently emphasizing each sacred word with a thrust of his extended index finger.

But this momentous event in religious history (which actually took over twenty-five years to complete), this big bang in the formulation of the West's spiritual language, seems almost incidental to the strange drama taking place in the foreground. There sits a monk, and in front of him a lion. The monk holds a pair of tweezers and is carefully removing a thorn from the lion's right forepaw.

This scene appears in *St. Jerome in His Study*, a fifteenth-century painting by the Spanish painter Nicolás Francés. The theme is hardly original. The representation of St. Jerome working on his translation of the Bible in the presence of his tame lion (and various other animals, including doves, dogs, peacocks, parrots, deer, and cats) is one of the most frequently depicted images in the Middle Ages and the Renaissance. The only unconventional element involves the fact that an anonymous monk removes the thorn; in virtually every other painting on this topic, Jerome himself does the honors.

The story behind this odd mixture of piety and fairy tale goes like this. One day a lion wandered into St. Jerome's study in Palestine (given the date, approximately 400 A.D., it might have been the last wild lion to walk the Holy Land before the population went extinct). The monks scattered in terror; St. Jerome, however, kept his calm. He noticed the lion was limping from a thorn in its paw, and instructed the clerics to remove it. The lion was attended to, and afterward it became Jerome's faithful companion and a servant of the monks. This legend traces back to an earlier story about St. Gerasimus, and ultimately perhaps to Aesop's well-known fable about a slave who removes a thorn from the paw of a lion, who repays the kind deed by later sparing his life.

A rich religious symbolism surrounds this narrative. In medieval Christian iconography, the lion symbolized those who retire from the world to a life of religious contemplation, and hence secondarily Christ, as well as those who are spiritually vigilant—from the ancient yarn that lions sleep with their eyes open. In addition, the crippled lion typifies the human race, marred by original sin and redeemed spiritually by the church, just as the church father St. Jerome heals the king of the beasts physically. Finally, the lion's submission to the holy man points to the victory of the faithful over this carnal world of ours, and on a more visceral level, given the bloody history of lions and Christians, victory over pagan Rome.

So much for official symbolism. Very often, however, a society's core beliefs express themselves not in its great public monuments and declarations, but rather in quiet asides. Marginalia—the comments, observations, questions, even misunderstandings, found in the margins of texts and works of art—might say in a whisper what many people feel privately, but for whatever reason do not express publicly. This is true of Francés' painting.

While the work is more or less conventional, the catalogue description of the painting observes that the piece shows a monk about to collect blood from the lion for use as ink by Jerome and his scribes. Although the catalogue claims this remarkable interpretation is "according to legend," in fact no such legend exists. Nonetheless, the offhand, almost whimsical comment about using lion's blood as ink stumbles onto a deeper interpretation of the artwork and the fable of Jerome's lion. It prompts us to look at the painting with new eyes and see the image of the West's central sacred text translated and written out not with scholarly ink, but with the very lifeblood of a wild beast. Suddenly, the stodgy theme of St. Jerome laboring in his study bleary-eyed and smelling of lamp oil bursts into a profound metaphor about the way religious meaning depends upon the animal world, and we are invited to contemplate how and why this transubstantiation from wildlife to sacred text should take place.

To find that out, we have to visit another study, probably very much like Jerome's, but never depicted in any work of art or memorialized as the site of saintly tales. Conceivably this other study was situated just down the street from Jerome's, though more than likely it was somewhere in Egypt, probably Alexandria. There, a monk, as anonymous as the one that plucked the thorn from the lion's paw, puts pen to paper—perhaps at the very moment Jerome begins his translation of Genesis, though probably a century or so earlier—and writes: "We begin first of all by speaking of the Lion, the king of all the beasts . . ."

These words come from the *Physiologus*, a work that parallels Jerome's Bible in influencing our language about spiritual matters. In fact, the creator of the Jerome-lion legend that inspired Francés' work may have in turn been moved by the symbolism implicit in this very passage of the *Physiologus*: "The second nature of the lion is that, although he has fallen asleep, his eyes keep watch for him, for they remain open." Over the next millennium, this little book generated dozens of imitations, in virtually every European language (as well as Arabic, Syrian, Armenian, and Ethiopian), generally known as "bestiaries," which catalogued and commented upon the animal world. The *Physiologus* and its progeny quietly worked their way into every aspect of Western civilization, including the writings of Chaucer, Shakespeare, Milton, as well as the symbolism of virtually all Renaissance artists (Da Vinci, for instance, compiled his own bestiary, based on his readings and observations, which trace back to the *Physiologus*). Even today, in our thoroughly technological culture, when we discuss moral or religious matters, we often still follow the kind of thinking, if not the very wording, first explored in the *Physiologus*. It is one of the great ironies of history that during the last thousand years only a handful of scholars and graduate students have read this remarkable work, and most of them probably cannot remember what the title means (I'll get to that).

This excerpt, discussing the hedgehog, gives some sense of the approach the *Physiologus* takes toward animals:

The hedgehog does not quite have the appearance of a ball as he is full of quills. Physiologus said of the hedgehog that he climbs up to the grape on the vines and then throws down the berries (that is, the grapes) onto the ground. Then he rolls himself over on them, fastening the fruit of the vine to his quills, and carries it off to his young and discards the plucked stalk.

And you, O Christian, refrain from busying yourself about everything and stand watch over your spiritual vineyard from which you stock your spiritual cellar. Make a cache in the halls of God the King, in the holy tribunal of Christ, and you will receive eternal life. Do not let concern for this world and the pleasure of temporal goods preoccupy you, for then the prickly devil, scattering all your spiritual fruits, will pierce them with his quills and make you food for the beasts. Your soul will become bare, empty and barren like a tendril without fruit. After this you will cry out, "My own vineyard I have not kept," as the scripture of the Song of Songs bears witness.

In such a way have you allowed the most wicked spirit to climb up to your place, and he has scattered your abstinence. Thus he has deceived you with barbs of death in order to divide your plunder among hostile powers. Rightly, therefore, did Physiologus compare the ways of animals to spiritual matters.

At first blush, this kind of writing strikes modern readers as quaint, if not archaic. It appears to fall within the medieval *contemptus mundi* tradition with its harsh denunciation of this world in favor of a happier future in the next. The description of the hedgehog is fanciful, apparently based not on observation but on some folk belief or the misguided written accounts of Pliny, the Roman "naturalist." In reality, hedgehogs are insectivores that do not eat grapes, much less spear them on their quills. Elsewhere in the work, the author strikes unpleasantly dogmatic notes with attacks on "heresies" and Judaism. But granting all this, the important thing about the work is its *way* of understanding animals, not the particular conclusion it reaches.

In comparing "the ways of animals to spiritual matters," the author of the *Physiologus* is doing nothing less than discovering that animals have meaning, and in particular spiritual meaning. We rarely think about this issue nowadays, since animals have become so marginalized in our culture, reduced for the most part to resources or ornaments of one type or another. But the discovery of spiritual truths in the qualities and behaviors of animals must have struck a medieval scholar as a great adventure, a Holy Grail found in every leap of a deer or flight of a swallow. In discussing the hedgehog, and all the other animals that appear in the book, the author first gives a (generally inaccurate) description of an animal and its behavior, and then weaves from these qualities a spiritual interpretation. For him every animal is twofold. There is the actual physical animal that we can see and touch and hear. But through the use of our spiritual imagination, the animal is also "intelligible" (*intelligibilis* is the Latin word in the text); it has meanings important to us as moral beings, which go beyond what we can descry with our five senses.

Christian philosophers, such as St. Augustine (who conceivably may have had the *Physiologus* in mind), eventually worked out elaborate theories for this kind of allegorical interpretation, called exegeses. An exegesis of the hedgehog would designate the physical hedgehog as the *littera* (or literal meaning); the moral lesson it embodies about the care of the soul as the *moralis* (or moral meaning); the connection between the hedgehog and the devil the *typos* (or allegorical meaning); and the animal's mystical meaning, which God only knows unless he obliges to reveal it, as the *anagogue*. This way of understanding the world has its roots in Platonism and St. Paul's statement that the invisible things of God may be known through the visible things of this earth (*invisibilia Dei ex visibilibus intelligantur*, as Jerome translated it). Dionysius Areopagiticus, one of the earliest Christian scholars, expressed this sentiment in the phrase *Spiritualia sub metaphoris realium*, "Spiritual things under the metaphor of real things." Thus, the tenth-century Anglo-Saxon work *The Prose Solomon and Saturn* can demand, "Tell me which bird is best"—a request that makes no sense at all in our way of categorizing nature—and confidently reply: "I tell you, the dove is best; it signifies the Holy Ghost."

The author of the *Physiologus* is less interested in the terminology of exegesis than he is in the happy task of interpreting animals. Hedgehogs, he discovers, those "prickly devils," give us insights into the character of worldly temptations. So do partridges, foxes, monkeys, wild asses, dragons, whales, all of which represent the devil (though surprisingly snakes do not). Aspects of Christ's character can be found in an unlikely menagerie of panthers, lions, pelicans, phoenixes, snakes, elephants, oysters, and unicorns. Lessons for righteous living appear in the observations of antelopes, swordfish, eagles, and lizards.

It is difficult to capture the intellectual excitement the author must have felt as he began to perceive this world of meaning in the animals around him. Classical civilization, especially under Aristotle's influence, had taken the first tentative steps toward an accurate zoological classification of animal life. In contrast, the author of the *Physiologus* set out in a different direction: to give a *moral* taxonomy of animals. He was, in some sense, the medieval Christian equivalent of shaman, invoking animals to explore the world of the divine as eagerly as we send out spacecraft to explore other planets. Significantly, he rarely refers to the animals he interprets as "it," but rather "he" or "she," treating them as persons, not just zoological data.

The result was a rich, textured view of the animal world, one we can hardly imagine today. Children in the city where I live enjoy chasing lizards probably with the same zeal as juveniles did along the whitewashed walls of second-century Alexandria. But when the author of the *Physiologus* left his study to attend morning prayers and saw a lizard basking on a sun-drenched wall, a whole landscape of sacred meanings opened up to him, a landscape no longer visible to us:

There is a beast called the sun-lizard, that is, the sun-eel. When this animal grows old, he is hampered by [weakening of] his two eyes. No longer being able to perceive the sunlight, he goes blind. What does he do? Moved by his good nature, he finds a wall facing east, enters a crack in the wall, and gazes eastward. His eyes are then opened by the eastern sun and made new again.

And you, O man, if you have the clothing of the old man, see that, when the eyes of your heart are clouded, you seek out the intelligible eastern sun who is Jesus Christ and whose name is "the east" in Jeremiah. As the Apostle says, "He is the sun of justice." He will open for you the intelligible eyes of your heart, and for you the old clothing will become new.

Redemption, divinity, spiritual understanding—all this from a small reptile creeping over a garden wall. It is one of many examples of the author's ability to elicit the profound from the simple, an ability that lies near the heart of all religious thinking.

He must have felt an affinity and respect toward the creature that defies modern scientific attitudes toward animals, for the lizard represented the monk himself in an allegorical drama taking place around him at any given moment. At one point, apparently sensing resistance from a skeptical reader, he even says as much: "These things have been spoken about irrational animals and weak reptiles since they behave so prudently that none of them is foolish but all are found to be clever and wise." For all his lack of accurate zoological knowledge, the author had nothing but goodwill toward even the most unpleasant and seemingly insignificant fauna.

The author's zoological blunders are legendary. They became the butt of jokes by commentators of a more scientific, empirical age, and even some of the author's contemporaries questioned his more dubious assertions, such as the story that dead pelican chicks are resurrected by their parents, who pierce their own sides and drench the fledglings with life-giving blood. The author clearly spent little time observing real animals (except doves, which have three separate detailed entries in the work), but rather he patched together legends and folk tales to support his spiritual lessons. Nonetheless, what the author's menagerie lacks in zoological accuracy, it makes up for in spiritual complexity and depth. His discussion of elephants—a mammal he evidently never saw in person—proceeds without ever deviating into anything factual about the pachyderm (except the loyalty elephants often show to sick or injured comrades). Nonetheless, it is a tour de force of Christian exegesis, taking us through the

drama of original sin, the Good Samaritan, the mystery of divine incarnation, and the fulfillment of the Old Testament in the New, all
compressed into a single anecdote about elephants and a tricky
hunter:

This is the nature of the elephant: if he should fall, he is unable
to get up again. But how can he fall since he rests against a tree?
The elephant has no knee joints enabling him to sleep lying
down if he wanted to. Shortly before the beast arrives at the tree
against which he is accustomed to rest, the hunter who wishes to
capture the animal cuts partly through the tree. When the
elephant comes and rests against the tree, both tree and beast fall
at the same time. The elephant then cries out and immediately
there comes a great elephant who is unable to lift the first. Then
they both cry out, and twelve other elephants arrive, and not
even they can lift the one who is fallen. Then again, they all cry
out, and suddenly a tiny elephant appears who puts his trunk
under the great one and lifts him up . . .

The great elephant and his wife represent the persons of
Adam and Eve . . . Immediately, the dragon overthrows them
and makes them strangers to virtue (that is, by not pleasing
God). And they cry out, calling on God and a great elephant
comes (that is, the Law) and does not lift them. Indeed, even as
the priest did not lift up the one fallen among thieves. Nor did
the twelve elephants (that is, the chorus of prophets) raise him
up, even as the Levite failed to raise up the one wounded by
thieves. But the holy, intelligible elephant (that is, the Lord Jesus
Christ) did so. Although he is greater than all the rest, he was
made small in comparison. "For he humbled himself and
became obedient to death," in order to raise up man. He is the
intelligible Samaritan who raises us up onto his breast . . .
Physiologus spoke wisely, therefore, of the elephant.

Modern Christians might find the comparison of Jesus with a small elephant somewhat uncouth, if not downright sacrilegious. More than a few medieval religious authorities felt the same: the first confirmed mention of the book in the historical records is its condemnation as a heretical book by a decree of Pope Gelasius in 496 A.D. This reaction reveals more about our impoverished view of animals than it does about the author's religiosity. We make a sharp distinction between the spiritual and bestial, while the author of the *Physiologus* specifically intended to show that divinity can be found everywhere, even in a lumbering pachyderm. Our vision stops at the zoological fact of *Elephas*; the *Physiologus* scrutinizes a deeper reality, transforming the physical animal into a "holy, intelligible elephant." This is the emblematic elephant that appears in numerous medieval manuscripts and Renaissance church carvings, signaled by its frequent association with a hostile dragon.

It is no coincidence that the work was written in the early first millennium, before Christianity had become thoroughly institutionalized, even before the various writings that would become the modern Bible had been canonized. The author was exploring unknown terrain, trying to discover Christian principles in a world that had up till then been interpreted solely through the classical cultures of Greece and Rome. The ideals of faith, of loving one's neighbor, of humility, personal restraint, and peacemaking were just being discovered in the West. Similar values may have appeared in Hellenic and Roman form, but they were seen only in terms of civic virtue and social good unrelated to spiritual truths. Christianity had to "discover" a language of spirituality as yet unknown to the West. It did so through animals.

This reinterpretation of the animals began in the subterranean cradle of Western Christianity—the catacombs of Rome, where paintings depict Juno's peacock as a symbol of resurrection; the dove as the soul; water creatures as the soul's spiritual refreshment; and fish as an acrostic for Christ. It remains a concern in Byzantine art, less so during the Renaissance, where animal motifs become secondary to human forms, and it then sputters out during modern times, when representational art wanders into a zoological desert, the art of animal absence in the face of an all-consuming human narcissism.

The *Physiologus* must be read in this context. The author turned toward animals, not as examples for a fully formed religious system, but rather as a way to *discover* for the first time what his faith meant. Behind every beast he catalogues, there is a tacit question painfully relevant to a second- or third-century Christian: What constitutes a moral life? What is the nature of God? How do we interpret the Old Testament in light of the New? His answer in part is to direct our attention to an ant, an elephant, or a lion.

And so, Jerome's Bible was indeed written in the blood of a lion, the intelligible lion of the *Physiologus*.

In one sense, this view of animals is radically new. In another, it is older than history itself. The *Physiologus* harks back to a sacred view of animals, an aboriginal belief in a primeval kinship with all creatures and the essential continuity among them all. This belief has its roots in the Paleolithic period, when people "likely envisaged nature as alive and responsive, nurturing humankind much as a mother nourishes her baby at her breast," as Max Oelschlaeger puts it. Today we can scarcely imagine the vast dimension of connotations a Pleistocene hunter must have sensed overlooking the same Egyptian plain of our nameless monk, filled with the crescendos and diminuendos of giant Ice Age beasts.

This sacred view of animals worked its way down the millennia into the paganism of Greece and Rome. The author of the *Physiologus*, however, did not find himself writing in a world where sacred pagan animals walked the landscape with respect and impunity. In late Roman culture, paganism as a spiritual force was moribund, and animals had become mere objects of sport, slaughtered by the tens of thousands each year in the gladiatorial games. The *Physiologus* became a shepherd of animal meanings not against a "devil-worshiping" paganism, but against the triumph of Greek rationalism, represented especially in the person of Aristotle.

Aristotle wrote his own *Physiologus* of sorts, a masterpiece in its own right: his *History of Animals* (and related texts). The *History* is a remarkable achievement of zoology, giving detailed, generally accurate descriptions of the anatomy and habits of several hundred animals, from wasps to elephants to whales. Although he obtained some of his information secondhand and made some notable blunders, the Greek philosopher made close observations of most of the animals he wrote about, both alive and dead, and even performed dissections to increase his anatomical knowledge. His pupil, Alexander the Great, reportedly sent back specimens of exotic fauna from conquered lands, which must have made Aristotle the curator of the greatest zoological collection in the known world. Although it was written in the fourth century B.C., much of the work stands up to scientific scrutiny even today. In short, Aristotle's *History* is everything the *Physiologus* is not: empirical, objective, systematic, rational, "modern." A milestone of reason and observation, it differs from contemporary zoological textbooks only in quality, not in kind.

Here is what Aristotle says about elephants, almost as if surveying the centuries to come from the height of his great intellect to personally rebuke his future Christian counterpart for his lack of anatomical knowledge:

The elephant is not as some used to assert, but it bends its legs and settles down; only that in consequence of its weight it cannot bend its legs on both sides simultaneously, but falls into a recumbent position on one side or the other, and in this position it goes to sleep. And it bends its hind legs just as a man bends his legs.

History has sided with Aristotle and his empiricism about the elephant and the rest of the animal kingdom. As implied by the name, the Middle Ages appears to us today as a dark interregnum, an unfortunate trough between the crests of classical rationalism and the Renaissance with its stirrings of modern scientific inquiry. The justification for this view finds its paradigm in the fortunes of the Greek scholar Aristarchus, whose brilliant insight allowed him to calculate the circumference of the globe in the second century B.C., missing the mark by only six percent, by making some simple measurements of the angle of the sun at midsummer. His discovery that the earth was round was lost in the dogmatism of medieval scholars who argued for a flat earth based on their literalist reading of the Bible, threatening anyone who thought otherwise with accusations of heresy. A thousand years passed before Aristarchus was vindicated. Similarly, today, the *Physiologus* and the mystical world it represented look at best like a quaint diversion from the real business of culture, as colorful and useless as heraldic animals on a coat of arms. At worst, it seems to mark a descent into blindness about the zoological reality Aristotle so painstakingly accumulated.

Aristotle even won the war of definitions. The Greek equivalent of the noun *physiologus* appears in his text, basically meaning what the word now conveys to us: one who studies the physiology of animals, i.e. a zoologist or naturalist. The meaning of the word used by our anonymous monk—"an interpreter of the metaphysical, moral, and mystical significance of animals and the natural world"—has been lost from our vocabulary, and even from our logic.

And yet, and yet . . .

We say a shrewd person is "sly as a fox," without even thinking about the zoological veracity of the statement. In fact, foxes possess no more cunning than most mammalian predators, and other, non-Western cultures do not see the fox as particularly clever. This should come as no surprise; the phrase has nothing to do with observable foxes in actual landscapes. It has nothing to do with Aristotle's *His-*

tory or vulpine behavior. Rather it derives from the *Physiologus*, probably indirectly through one of the many bestiaries it engendered: "The fox is an entirely deceitful animal who plays tricks."

We watch a performance of Shakespeare's *Midsummer Night's Dream*, and when the fairies magically give the countrified Bottom the head of an ass, we know the transformation symbolizes the poor rustic's utter foolishness. But why? Donkeys are no less intelligent than horses or antelopes or ibexes. Again, the bestiary tradition that begins with the *Physiologus* is at work in our very Aristotelian heads, even among those who never heard of a bestiary, much less an "intelligible ass."

Our oblique devotions to the *Physiologus* reach monumental heights in the cinema, especially the monster movie—modern society's own version of aboriginal dreamtime. Seemingly under the influence of an ancient religious legacy, the writers of *King Kong* thought that the obvious thing for the natives to do with their constantly screaming captive, Fay Wray, was to sacrifice her to their simian deity. The eventual result was the great ape's death and the birth of the monster movie genre, with its moralization about unnatural beasts and the havoc they cause. Twenty years later, the threat to civilization took the form of the giant, mutant ants in *Them*, the first in a long line of films featuring benign creatures grown large and homicidal through exposure to radiation. By convention, a scientist spells out (in excruciating detail) the moral of the story in an epilogue: the ants represent the unknown threats we have let loose upon the world when we split the atom. Even *The Wizard of Oz* makes philosophical points in animal guise. When the Wicked Witch of the West finally captures Dorothy and her companions (including the Cowardly Lion), her henchmen are the unforgettable winged monkeys, whose evil essence is signaled by their unnatural and disturbing genetics.

Old B movies like *Godzilla* and remarkable thrillers like *Alien* or *Jurassic Park* all tend to follow the genre in having a singular moral:

people (usually scientists) who tamper with powers they do not have the wisdom to understand invariably let loose monsters that punish the reckless and the arrogant. At the end of Ed Wood's inept *Bride of the Monster*, the police chief blathers that the mad, monster-making scientist had "tampered in God's domain," obtusely summing up the essence of the genre—at its best and worst. The avenging monster almost always takes the form of an unnatural animal, often a dragon of one kind or another. This structure, if not the actual imagery, comes not from Aristotle's orderly collection of dissected specimens, but from the mystically charged wilderness of the *Physiologus*.

Even with just these few examples, we are entitled to entertain the fancy that Kong, Godzilla, the Alien, and a hundred other monstrous zoological shapes crawled out of the *Physiologus*, and dragging their moral lessons behind them, flung themselves onto the celluloid of the modern creature feature.

If he were alive today, the author of the *Physiologus* might have written of *Jurassic Park*:

Velociraptor is a type of dragon that died out long ago. But foolish men, not understanding God's plan, devised a means to bring the creature back to life, and its strength and cunning, once held in check by nature, became a threat to children and a battleground of men's greed. O man, do not be like those reckless men who use their knowledge to release the power of the intelligible velociraptor, which is the devil himself, tempting us to put reason and pride above spiritual things. Therefore, Physiologus spoke well of the velociraptor.

We "read" animals in works of fiction and art not as Aristotelians, but along the lines the *Physiologus* taught. We only have to go a short way into Faulkner's story "The Bear" to know that the bear is more than just a zoological fact in the text, but rather is an "intelligible" ursine, one the author invites us to interpret. Even before the sappy promoter in *King Kong* tells us the moral of the film that "T'was beauty killed the beast," we see the screenwriter's allegory at work, and probably nowadays some additional unintended meanings about the destructive nature of civilization. Without realizing it, we are all in our own right modern physiologuses.

We denigrate the medieval period as a time of ignorance and intolerance. But it was also a time of deep religious devotion and the cultivation of values such as altruism, suspicion of materialism, and respect for creation that resonate with our culture today. Aristotle and the modern scientific age he foreshadowed have in a profound sense lost out to our Physiologus. The herds of meaningful animals found in the *Physiologus* never died out, even under the assault of modern science and its single-minded description of animal life. Instead, they went underground, into the very fabric of our culture. For us, despite the official language of science, animals *always* have meaning, though the content may have become faded and vague, and the distractions of mechanical culture have diminished their day-to-day importance.

Put more accurately, our culture suffers from a kind of schizophrenia about animals. In the operations of industry and science, Aristotle's one-dimensional view of animals reigns. Animals are machines, to use the Cartesian metaphor, clockwork creatures with structure but no souls or meaning beyond the practical purposes to which we put them. At the same time, we immediately read the spiritual significance of the white whale in *Moby Dick*, even if we cannot agree what that meaning is. We create fictional menageries in cartoons, movies, and literature, all embodying a moral and often religious import. And at times, this safe fictional world of animals breaks into our personal reality, much as it did for the *Physiologus*, sometimes during moments of solitude and reflection about the natural world, and sometimes suddenly and without warning.

In 1995 a white buffalo was born in Wisconsin to a rancher. This was a rare genetic event, but nothing miraculous from a zoological perspective. Within a week, however, hundreds of visitors, many of them Lakota Sioux, were flocking to the corral to see the prodigy. According to Lakota tradition, six hundred years ago a white buffalo also appeared to their people. The animal was a form of a spirit called White Buffalo Calf Woman, who brought the people a sacred pipe and a code of laws to live by. White Buffalo Calf Woman departed, but she promised to return, signaling a time of great upheaval to be followed by a period of universal peace and harmony. The Wisconsin white buffalo attracted not only Native Americans, but people of all backgrounds, who sometimes brought their children to have them touch the creature and receive a blessing. At one point over two thousand visitors a day came to see the rare calf.

Leave aside the imponderable issue of whether White Buffalo Calf Woman has returned to fulfill her prophecy in the shape of this particular Wisconsin ruminant (only time will tell). The point is, the physical animal has a spiritual resonance for many people, demonstrating a deep connection between animals and religion even in our machine-driven, abstracted culture. In fact, the reaction to the white buffalo suggests a keen thirst for a revival of the organic spirituality of the *Physiologus*. It indicates that abstract religious ideals have difficulty existing apart from the bestiary in which they took shape. The God of Michelangelo's Sistine Chapel is noble and awesome, but even in our culture it is a late development: prior to the eighth century the church prohibited all images of God or angels (a taboo sustained to this day in orthodox Judaism and Islam), so that early Christian art is to a great degree the art of symbolic fauna. But the intimation of divinity in animal form is as old as religion itself, as primal as the Paleolithic cave paintings, as favored as Luke 3:22: "And the Holy Ghost descended in a bodily shape like a dove."

One person I interviewed for this book told the following story about her own religious encounter with an animal:

"I moved to Texas about seven years ago and it was like the whole world changed. After finishing my high school years, I immediately started working at the local animal shelter. It was both a sorrow and a joy to work there. Most of the animals there liked me (even the nasty ones in rabies observation). I had a special understanding that went beyond the basics of them. I suppose I just knew how to read their body language without ever knowing it. I was frequently called on to settle new, frightened animals in their kennels. Even though we had many adoptions, we had to euthanize many animals a day, sometimes over a hundred.

"One day after I had worked there for a while we had a call that a fox was stuck in one of our humane dog traps. I didn't think anything of it, I was like 'Okay, that happens.' They brought the fox into the EU room (where we euthanized animals) to stay until they could contact a release program to pick him up. When no one was there, I would go and watch him. I can't adequately describe how I felt the first time I saw him up close, but I'll try. He was afraid, I could smell his fear, even as he could smell the death of the EU room. He was huddled in the back of the cage staring at me . . . he did not fear me. I put my face close to the cage so I could see him, I could feel his fear of his surroundings, but he didn't fear me, nor I him. I had a rush of adrenaline which made me slightly dizzy so I left the room. For some reason I knew the fox was hungry, so I gave him the chunks of roast beef out of my sandwich I had brought. The first piece I slid through the cage, then backed off so he could investigate. The other he took from my hand. It felt good.

"I had quit working at the shelter for a few years now. The image of the fox was always a close memory. One day while driving home from my current job I was once again thinking of the fox in the cage. I looked to the side of the road and there was a sable fox at the edge of the road. I had a quick feeling of oneness, like an adrenaline rush, with the fox."

This woman's experience with a fox had an important spiritual significance for her, important enough to be remembered and repeated, even if the exact meaning remains unclear. Her reaction is probably not uncommon, and it fits in perfectly with the allegorical world of the *Physiologus*. The interpretation of animals would not be necessary if their meanings were transparently evident.

If this story still seems too exotic to be an example of mainstream religious sentiment, then turn to the April 1995 issue of *Christianity Today*. It contains an article by Lynn N. Austin entitled "What Two Ducks Taught Me About Prayer: Their antics made me take a closer look at my relationship with God." The article describes how the author adopted a couple abandoned ducklings, and learned through the experience certain spiritual lessons about faith and personal action. The art of the *Physiologus* lingers on, even if frowned upon by the Aristotles of our culture.

And what if it had not? What if the *Physiologus* had never been written, and the bestiaries never compiled? Our anonymous monk lived in unstable times, when traditional religion had lost its grip on people's imaginations, and new sects and cults rose and fell seemingly overnight. Human knowledge had reached a level unimagined in earlier ages, measuring the earth, mapping the procession of the stars, classifying the natural world in all its diversity, and creating orderly disciplines out of math, economics, and rhetoric. Political and economic power lay in the hands of a privileged elite. Political leaders commonly declared themselves gods, and whole populations were wiped out by the whim of some autocrat or mentally unbalanced zealot.

In short, it was a time not unlike our own.

Into this world the Physiologus brought his simple interpretations of animals, declaring that perhaps scientific knowledge and the power it brings were not as important as wisdom and balance and humility in the face of the teachings hidden in the world of nature. The Physiologus won the day over Aristotle, at least for a little while. But if he had not, Western civilization would surely have faced a crisis analogous to the detonation of the first atomic bomb. The explosion of scientific knowledge during the classical period, without any political or moral restraints, presaged the same kind of threatened apocalypse. Imagine the petty and cruel emperors of the Middle Ages with cannons and grenades. Imagine the Visigoths with firearms, the Huns with steam engines. Obscurantism is never a virtue, but as a historical fact the spiritual emphasis of the medieval period tempered the progress of science at a time when no political institutions existed to help insure that scientific discoveries would be used wisely. The Physiologus played his part in keeping a balance between the physical and spiritual understanding of the natural world, and through this accomplishment perhaps helped preserve civilization itself.

We need that balance today more than ever. As E. O. Wilson points out, "When very little is known about an important subject, the questions people raise are almost invariably ethical. Then as knowledge grows, they become more concerned with information and amoral, in other words more narrowly intellectual. Finally as understanding becomes sufficiently complete, the questions turn ethical again." Something like this has happened in our understanding of animals, except we are challenged not merely with ethical questions about their treatment, but by a deeper issue concerning what animals mean to our inner, creative lives. Since the scientific revolution we have compiled endless volumes of facts about animals. But as a culture, we have relegated the interpretation of those facts to marginal activities such as art appreciation and nature writing, while we neglect the stories animals have to tell us, that "animals are good for thinking."

All of us are within walking distance of some remarkable species going about its business totally unnoticed by us; an orb spider weaving a web on the backyard fence, a crow nesting in a juniper tree, a snail searching for a mate among the dead leaves of last year's garden. The accumulation of sheer zoological data cannot substitute for the cultivation of the Physiologus' art: the search for the significance of the creatures we already know.

Every year in spring I hike to some of the palm oases scattered about the Sonoran Desert where I live. These are magical places, rare and remote fragments of paradise, where the silver green fronds of California's only native palm, the elegant *Washingtonia filifera*, shade secret pools of water and preside over a silence that seems as vast as the desert itself. The oases attract a host of desert animals: bobcats, yellow-winged bats, tree frogs, owls. Sometimes I come across a coyote, and if I'm very lucky, a mother coyote with pups. The animal helps sustain the oases by digging "coyote holes" that bring water to the surface, and it's easy to see them as local guardians, loping from one oasis to the next, patrolling their disjunct Eden. God's Dog, the palindrome by which the animal is sometimes called by Native Americans, holds a special place in the mythology of the Southwest. Coyote is not just a species, but a spiritual force, a cosmic personality, a cultural hero from dreamtime, who often benefits those around him by sheer bumbling. He is the comic relief to the seriousness of the Great Spirit, an antishaman trickster who more often than not tricks himself.

I watch the coyote and her pups playing in some bunchgrass. I cannot say that I perceive the Coyote of native myth, the intelligible coyote. But I know I experience more than just a specimen of *Canis*, because I keep coming back to see the coyotes again, just as I return to the Beatitudes or to the Tao without ever fully grasping their meaning.

Rightly, therefore, did Physiologus compare the ways of animals to spiritual matters.

CHAPTER THREE

Signifying Animals

The knowing animals are aware
that we are not really at home in our interpreted world.
—RAINER MARIA RILKE

A is for Apple. B is for Boy. C is for Cat.

Like an aimless incantation, these simple, childish sentences, and the ones we know that follow, have reverberated from one generation down to the next since almost the very beginning of literacy in our culture. Virtually every person reading this sentence began the trek to literacy with these or similar pithy associations between letters and things in the world, mostly living things. So basic is the formula for learning the ABC's that we never imagine it might tell us anything about the boys and girls, cats and dogs that bring the letters to life, much less about the sublime matters of the soul.

But the obvious things, the things we hold in common, often repay closer examination. The ABC's of childhood—and the whole mysterious history of literacy—tell us a great deal not only about the meanings animals hold for us, but also how religious meaning happens at all. For the moment, let's revisit the zero point of our literacy, and look at the alphabet primers (once known as abecedaria) not as mere teaching tools, but as windows onto a sensibility that sees both letters and animals as magical.

Once we look past the instructional purpose of alphabet primers, we can't help but notice the fact that they refer again and again to animal life. C is for Cat (or Cow); D is for Dog (or Duck); E is for Elephant; G is for Goat; and so on. Not all the same animals appear in every primer: sometimes there are snakes but no dogs, rabbits with no cats, and every other combination possible. But on average, animals make up roughly a third of the nouns employed in the modern primers I have examined. Not surprisingly, the figure increases the further back in time we go, so that nineteenth-century abecedaria generally mention more fauna, especially livestock. Until the 1920s, more Americans lived in the country than in cities, which meant most children had regular contacts with farm animals and wildlife. Today, with the vast majority of Americans growing up in urban areas, many children never see, much less observe at close quarters, any animal larger than a lapdog.

Pointing to the fact that children's primers teem with fauna offers more than just an illumination of the banal. Granted, children tend to like animals, and it follows that books instructing children to read would include references to things they find familiar and attractive. E. O. Wilson's "biophilia" thesis—that humans, especially children, have an inherent, genetic attraction to animal life—is probably at work in primers, just as it explains the popularity of animal acts on nighttime talk shows. But we should not stop there.

The relationship between animals and the alphabet goes much deeper than the need to accommodate a juvenile attention span. The letters themselves, the marks on the page, point silently beyond civilization to a forgotten natural history of the alphabet, and of our religious understanding. The etymologies of the Roman letters we use have for the most part been erased by time, but among those we can identify, many refer to animals. Our letter A derives from the Hebrew *aleph*, meaning "ox." G comes from the Hebrew *gimmel*, "camel." N is *nun*, "fish." K is *koph*, "monkey." One scholar traces the origin of F to an Egyptian hieroglyph of a horned serpent. Every time a child recites the alphabet, she may be enduring the rote memorization of a basic skill, but at the same time she is also unknowingly reiterating the ancient names of animals that became associated with writing at the very beginning of literate civilization.

That primal association between animals and letters was anything but child's play. The Hebrew literary tradition from which we derive our alphabet embraced a powerful sense of the magical, even divine, nature of letters. "Much of the Kabbalah," writes one scholar, "the esoteric body of Jewish mysticism, is centered around the conviction that each of the twenty-two letters of the Hebrew *aleph-beth* is a magic gateway or guide into an entire sphere of existence." Some Orthodox Jews to this day will not write the name of God, either in Hebrew or any other language, manifesting an ancient anxiety that the letters themselves have a potency beyond the spoken words they spell out. The same respect toward written characters flowed into Christianity, embodied in the remarkable comparison Jesus makes between his divinity and the first and last letters of the Greek alphabet: "I am Alpha and Omega," it says in Revelation, as if God were hidden in the vowels and consonants of a child's primer. Unlike his pagan counterparts, the God of the Bible is just that, a *textual* divinity, more aptly depicted as holding a pen than brandishing a thunderbolt or sword. From Genesis, where Yahweh speaks the universe into existence, to Exodus, where the Law is carved in stone, to Revelation, where salvation is recorded in a Book of Life, the biblical God operates more through language and writing than in physical action of the type found, for instance, in Greek mythology. Indeed, one of the most interesting differences between Yahweh and pagan deities is the fact that God is literate, while the gods of Greece and Rome seem unschooled or uninterested in letters altogether. The naming of letters after animals, therefore, meant something important to the early Hebrew scribes who first began to piece together the written symbols that would declare our civilization.

Nor is Judaism alone in connecting writing with sacred, or at least supernatural, forces. Most Western cultures once ascribed magical power to writing when first introduced to literacy. The Egyptians considered their writing system so holy that when they washed the text off old papyruses for reuse, they used beer and drank it, literally making their hieroglyphs part of their bodies. In Northern Europe, Germanic tribes developed a runic alphabet for the most part distinct from classical letters, whose purpose was almost entirely magical. In all Germanic languages, the word "rune" originally meant "mystery," "secret," or "wisdom." (Wulfias, in his fourth-century Gothic translation of the Bible, uses this term to translate the Greek μυστηριον in the phrase "the mysteries of the Kingdom of God.") In Norse myth, runes were a gift of Oðin, the chief Germanic god, who was associated with shamanistic practices such as shape-shifting, sojourns to the underworld, and spiritual ecstasies (the name "Oðin," English "Woden," is itself related to the archaic adjective "wood," meaning "berserk," "insane"). To obtain these esoteric symbols of writing, the shaman god had to suffer by plucking out his own eye and hanging Christ-like nine days on the World Tree.

In keeping with this sacred background, runes were never really used to produce secular texts, but rather were carved into wood, stone, or metal to memorialize great acts, to bless, or to curse (this explains the runes' angular forms and absence of hard-to-cut curves). If the Icelandic sagas are to be believed, apparently the preferred way for a Viking to bring bad luck to an enemy was to place a severed horse head on a pole facing the direction of the victim's house, and to attach an appropriate runic imprecation cut onto a wooden plaque.

As with the Hebrew alphabet, animals appear prominently in the names of runes: the runic F is Old English *feoh*, cattle (or word "fee," since cattle once served as money); U is *úr*, ox or aurochs, the extinct European bison that provided the famed Norse drinking horns; Z is *eolh*, elk; E is *eh*, war stallion.

I lived several years in Iceland, where rune magic is still practiced by a few people, some seriously, some merely in an eccentric expression of nationalist feelings. The chief practitioner of this ancient form of magic was Thorbjorn Beinteinsson, an elderly man with a long grizzled beard who lived on a remote farm. I asked Thorbjorn if rune magic worked, and he replied he had seen runes do things that he could not even begin to describe. His attitude toward runes was almost exactly that of Jewish mysticism toward the Hebrew letters: the signs themselves are seen as animate, if not conscious.

But we don't have to go to the distant past or strange traditions to show the magic of letters. Every time a fan gets the autograph of a baseball player or movie star, he tacitly admits that these particular letters have a secret virtue beyond the names they spell. The mania for celebrity autographs itself seems almost devotional in nature. What makes the original copy of the Declaration of Independence priceless while a transcript of it in newsprint has no monetary value at all? It's the letters themselves.

The rise of modern printing let loose a black-and-white blizzard of texts that constantly swirls before our eyes, distracting us from seeing how precious, how *physical* the presence of written words once appeared. To get a sense of this experience, imagine a scriptorium in a twelfth-century monastery where monks congregated to read the twenty or thirty manuscripts that constituted their library, each volume painstakingly hand-copied at a cost of tens of thousands of dollars in today's currency. The monks would mouth each word they read softly, but audibly, since until the end of the Middle Ages, people did not know how to read silently. The light illuminating the pages would likely stream through a small window, not of glass, which was enormously expensive, but translucent parchment, the same material as the pages being read. The room would have seemed almost to pulse with the murmur of voices and the rustle of parchment, all held in a diffuse natural light, investing the practice of reading with a tangible, sensuous quality we no longer experience. And with the rise of computers, letters have become even more ghostly and insubstantial, mere pixels on a computer screen.

This sensuous quality of letters would have made the thirteenth-century poem "An ABC," guardedly ascribed to Chaucer, more than just a clever, courtly primer. We read the poem and see only an artifice whereby the initial letters of the first words of twenty-three stanzas about the Virgin Mary spell out the alphabet (only twenty-three because J did not become part of our alphabet until the seventeenth century):

> *Almighty and al merciable queen . . .*
> *Bountee so fix hath in thin herte his tente . . .*
> *Comfort is noon but in yow, ladi deere . . .*

For the medieval reader, in contrast, each audible consonant and vowel would have been as palpable and wondrous as an amber bead on a rosary.

Even in modern English, buried amid our literary vocabulary lie fossils of an ancient belief in the sorcery of letters. The verb "to write" itself originally meant "to carve," and referred, not to the Roman alphabet brought to England by Christian missionaries, but to the cutting of mystical runes. Our word "read" has the same root as *Rædend*, the Anglo-Saxon poetic word for God, glossed as "Ruler," but literally meaning "Reader," in the sense of one who interprets, understands, and hence can counsel. We "spell" words, but sorcerers and witches can cast a "spell": the two meanings, which superficially appear worlds apart to us now, derive from the same root, converging sometime in the medieval past when the ability to properly arrange letters suggested mastery over the physical things named, and hence magic.

Animals, alphabets, and divinity form an unlikely troika. Unlikely at least to our minds. To societies closer both to animals and the passions of religious faith, the three go together naturally. So deep-seated was this association that in the medieval imagination the depiction of animals began actually to assume the shapes of letters.

For a thousand years, manuscript illuminators from Armenia to Ireland wove into the text of the Bible images of snakes, birds, dragons, and wildcats. The design, generally called "lacertine" or "interlace," could be as simple as using the neck of a bird to represent the initial capital I in the first words of a Greco-Latin version of Genesis: *In principio*, "In the beginning . . ." Or, as in the Irish Book of Kells and various Anglo-Saxon Gospels, the interlace design could reach dizzying complexity, involving dozens of highly stylized beasts intertwining with each other and with abstract patterns to make up the very body of an illuminated letter. Each time a medieval reader picked up one of these illuminated manuscripts, he would have undergone a multilayered experience, seeing the animal figures, hearing the initial letter the animals formed as he whispered the word, understanding the sacred meanings the letters spelled out. "In the beginning," this literary sensibility seemed to express graphically, "was a bird, a snake, nature."

The spontaneous association illuminators made among letters, animals, and religious themes eventually faded out, and the lacertine animals that populated most illuminated Bibles gave way to human forms, especially after the eleventh century, just as the *Physiologus'* interpretation of fauna languished with the rise of science and systematic zoology. Animal motifs disappeared completely from typography when the stupefying efficiency of the printing press cheapened the written word and made manuscript illumination an empty artistic gesture. The first recorded mass extinction of animals by Europeans did not occur in the physical landscape, but in the calligraphy of religious texts.

It is no coincidence that Western civilization's interpretation of sacred texts and animals reached its zenith in the Middle Ages. During this time, the great commentaries on the Torah, the Bible, and the Koran took shape. Judaism produced the Talmud, Christianity the writing of the church fathers, Islam the Sunna. Never before has our culture shown such a commitment to the close reading of spiritual texts, with an intellectual rigor and respect for each word we hardly fathom today. And at this very time, the *Physiologus* and the bestiaries appear, filled with a similar passion for reaching the hidden meanings of animals. The turn from the *Physiologus* to Aristotle, from St. Francis to zoology was accompanied by growing disinterest in the commentaries, so that the bestiary tradition wandered into cultural limbo, just as the exegeses of Origen and Augustine ceased to inform the daily faith of most Christians. The reading of sacred texts and the reading of animals shared a common fate because at heart they expressed the same impulse to find spiritual coherence in a world of whirling, often distressing, physical diversity.

Perhaps the strangest thing about the interplay of animals and sacred letters is how thoroughly we have forgotten it. Like the linked rings of a magician, they mysteriously come together in the distant past, and just as mysteriously fly apart in more modern times, seemingly with the wave of a hand. Yet, even today, curious and unexpected alignments occur, in childhood primers, in our literary and religious vocabulary, that pose the question: what invisible force pulls animals and sacred texts together?

To answer that question we have to explore the *literary* nature of our religious beliefs. Judaism, Christianity, Islam, Hinduism, Taoism, Buddhism, and all the other major world religions are "religions of the book," in the sense that they all have sacred or otherwise authoritative texts that define what it means to follow a particular faith. Judaism and Christianity have the Bible; Islam, the Koran; Hinduism, the Vedas; and so on. Even nontraditional beliefs, such as New Age philosophy, find an audience not through prophets crying out in the wilderness, but through books, tracts, pamphlets, articles. Being members of a literate culture, we take it for granted that religious doctrines exist as something written down.

But we are the anomaly. Most religions for most of history were oral in nature, and millions of indigenous people today still practice their spiritual beliefs without the use of pen and paper. The contrast between literate and nonliterate religion puts into focus the role animals play in spirituality.

Nonliterate religions are almost by definition animistic in nature. They exist only through oral histories, myths, and sacred narratives handed down from one generation to the next. As discussed earlier, animism perceives animals as inspirited, as personalities and subjects in their own right, often in touch with the spirit realm, often divine beings themselves. Lévi-Strauss has shown that the myths of nonliterate cultures flow and alter course quite easily over time, when migration or other changed circumstances bring new challenges to the forefront. While the jaguar spirit may play a prominent role in the myth and ritual of Bororo that dwell in the interior of Brazil and live predominantly by hunting, coastal Bororo just a few hundred miles away may emphasize mythic cycles involving marine creatures. There is no Bororo bible, no tribal inquisition to validate one sacred narrative over the other, and it would never occur to any Bororo that such authority would be desirable or even possible.

Perhaps for this reason, nonliterate religions tend to be more personal in nature than religions of the book. They often involve private visions, individual spirit guides, self-styled quests for enlightenment. As if harking back to this sensibility, the stories I collected from people who have had spiritual experiences involving animals almost always involved personal insights, often occurring in the most private realm of dreams, and often so personal the storyteller could not even say what the experience meant, only that it was meaningful. Here is one such story, which, like St. Paul's vision on the road to Damascus, altered the narrator's life:

"When I was about seventeen, a friend and I were driving along through a far country road, miles from anywhere. Night had just descended, and it was midsummer. At this time I was rather 'screwed up . . .' I was looking for something other than Aristotelian logic in my life. This particular night, my friend and I, avid herpetologists that we were, were searching for snakes on the road. We used to collect them, take them home for a few days, then return them to where we found them.

"As we rounded a bend, I suddenly felt an incredible upsurge of awe, something about the night, this road, this area . . . And then, standing in the middle of the road, we saw the most gigantic eagle I could ever imagine. I had always imagined an eagle to be the size of a cockatoo, perhaps, but this magnificent being stood full three feet high. It peered at us, its gaze unflinching, its feathers unruffled. At its feet was a dead rabbit. It stared directly at me, and I was transfixed, absolutely unable to move even if I had wanted to. I had never in my life experienced such emotions, such kindred.

"Suddenly a voice as pure and rich as you can imagine spoke to me, and said, 'Quiet Eagle.' I was stunned, awestruck. My friend reached over and switched off the headlights, and in the radiance of an almost full moon, we continued to stare at this impossibly beautiful Eagle. I could feel its heartbeat, even the adrenaline coursing through its body as a result of its kill, on top of my own adrenaline. Then it hopped forward and leaped onto the body of its victim, and rose into the air, and as it left I could feel the wind on my face, the sight of the earth dropping away beneath me, even the tight grip of my talons clenching the rabbit. I had effectively become the Eagle. After a while, I got out of the car (my friend was worrying about me at this point!) and walked over to the spot where the Eagle had stood. There was a feather lying there. Not a very big feather, but a feather. So of course I took it with me. Thus I began to walk the path of the shaman, and began to discover totem animals. This seemed to me to be the most perfect way of life, but often I would become very sad that so many people miss out because of their incessant urge to make money and lots of it. Totems come, and totems go, leaving behind priceless gifts of understanding, as you dance with the animals and learn from their natures. But Eagle has never left, and continues to guide me as I dream."

While similar to St. Paul's vision in the religious transformation it brings about, this experience does not relate to a text, as did Paul's, that could explain and situate the vision in a larger narrative. The meaning of the enigmatic declaration "Quiet Eagle," which may be either a name or an imperative, sends the narrator not to a book for clarification, but to deeper introspection and further personal visions (though being a member of a literate culture, the narrator did go on to read books on shamanism to understand his experience, the books themselves were not "sacred texts").

Religions of the book lack the fluidity of nonliterate mythologies, and do not encourage the kind of spiritual individualism common in oral cultures. Once a sacred text is written down and becomes authoritative, it usually persists unchanged, and later texts must conform themselves to it or explain the divergence. Christianity, for example, was tethered to the Old Testament, and did not have the option Bororo mythmakers have of initiating new and totally unrelated sacred narratives to suit their new insights and changing circumstances. Literate religions, to the extent they accept a sacred text, always face novel situations with an eye to their literary past, since every time new written material enters a religion, the threat of contradiction, and hence rejection, arises. The Old Testament says "an eye for an eye"; the New Testament says "turn the other cheek." Generation after generation of Christians have confronted the questions, Which one of these two statements is right? and How do they relate to each other?

Nonliterate religions rarely face problems like this. Not that contradictions do not occur in oral mythologies, but the differences never become glaring or important, since cultures without letters cannot place one narrative alongside another and cross-reference them the way literate societies can. Close readings require a text, not just a story. Nonliterate religion exists as a series of evanescent utterances and cyclical rituals, capable of being repeated but not necessarily minutely compared. The religious truth of myths rests in the narrative itself, not the particular words used to express the story. In contrast, written contradictions leap off the page, and literate religions have to explain them or appear incoherent. In discussing the role of literacy and doctrine, Jack Goody argues that alphabetic writing "changes the nature of the representations of the world," because it allows humans to lay out discourse and "examine it in a more abstract, generalised and 'rational' way," leading both to "criticism and commentary on the one hand and the orthodoxy of the book on the other."

This is what happened to the religions of the book. Christianity in particular faced the contradictions and differences between the Old and New Testaments through commentary, glosses, interpretations, cross-references. In this way, the theology of "an eye for an eye," for instance, developed a gloss, stating that it referred to the unregenerate condition of humanity, in opposition to the redeemed nature wrought by Christ, where people were to pursue universal love and peace, even in a world of retribution and violence. A contradiction becomes, through commentary, a fulfillment.

Indeed, much of medieval theology can be seen as an ambitious attempt to cross-reference every line of the Old Testament with the New, to explain every word of the prophets and the law in light of the new texts surrounding Jesus. The task was not so much an invention of the Middle Ages as an elaboration of biblical logic. When asked for a sign of his divinity, Jesus states: "An evil and adulterous generation seeketh after a sign; and there shall be no sign given to it, but the sign of prophet Jonas." Jonah's "sign," Jesus then explains to the disciples, is the fact that he spent three days in the belly of a whale, just as the Messiah must remain three days in his tomb before resurrection. In medieval parlance, Jonah was a "type" or "figure" of the Messiah, whose astounding symbolic meaning—hidden in the Old Testament—suddenly reveals itself in the New Testament like a bolt of lightning.

Commentary, cross-referencing, and the discovery of types resulted in the symbolic exegesis of the Bible. Ultimately, exegesis overflowed the pages of the Bible onto the "text" of nature, so that by the twelfth century, Hugh of St. Victor, the German philosopher, could talk about "the Book of nature" *(lex naturalis)* and actually be understood—as he probably would not have been by an eleventh-century European outside of a monastery.

Like the sparrows and lambs in Jesus' parables, the things in nature could also be seen as mere *littera*, literal obvious signs that served as an occasion for discovering deeper realms of meaning that determined the forms of nature. Thus, according to the *Physiologus*, because eagles were put on earth to symbolize people who hear the gospel and are spiritually renewed, an eagle soars high up toward the sun when it grows old, where the bird's tattered coat of feathers is burned off and rejuvenated as it plunges into a clear pool of water. Of course, the behavior of eagles could have additional meanings. It could symbolize St. John and his apocalyptic vision; or the spirit of philosophy. But the result in any case stems from a vision of the world as a legible text. "From the simplest reading of animals as sentences in medieval bestiaries," writes Jesse Gellrich of exegesis, "to the vast panorama of Vincent of Beauvais's *Natural History*, medieval intellectuals read nature as the validation of history, saw in natural phenomena the glowing proof of their ideas."

The metaphor of nature as book has implications for us today. Animals were transformed from spiritual entities into intelligible texts, filled with meaning, but bereft of souls. The Shakespearean sermons in stones and books in running brooks seem familiar to us in ways shamanism's realm of inspirited animals does not. And yet the participatory spirituality of animism did not simply vanish into oblivion. Written texts themselves have become the locus of animism's inspirited universe:

As a Zuñi elder focuses her eyes upon a cactus and hears the cactus begin to speak, so we focus our eyes upon these printed marks and immediately hear voices. We hear spoken words, witness strange scenes or visions, even experience other lives. As nonhuman animals, plants, and even "inanimate" rivers once spoke to our tribal ancestors, so the "inert" letters on the page now speak to us!

The transmigration of spirit from animals to texts may seem strange, yet it was probably all but inevitable. From the time of our earliest ancestors, humans have been "reading" the world. The earliest writings were not the hieroglyph or cuneiform made by human hands, but the tracks of animals we hunted, the alterations in cloud patterns presaging a storm, the ripples of sand marking the variations of the tide. Nature, and animal life in particular, provided a "universaal and publick Manuscript," to use Thomas Browne's phrase, that for thousands of years we had to properly interpret in order to survive. Only by constantly refining the ability to decipher the world, to construe the intentions of distant and elusive creatures from the slightest presence of paw prints in the mud, broken twigs along a forest path, or far-off distinct calls, did we acquire the capacity to make and read our own symbolic marks and sense in them spiritual meanings not completely apparent in the physical world. As any modern naturalist or hunter can attest, the signs left by animals on a landscape tell a story, relate a narrative, for those who know how to read them. Literacy is in many ways just a special form of hunter-gathering that substitutes ideas for elk, tapir, or woolly mammoths.

Every time we pick up the Bible, the Koran, or any other sacred text, we step back into an ancestral landscape teeming with the typography of animals. Reading the words, we are again scanning the horizon for signs of some long extinct antelope; following the logic of an argument, we stalk some vanished Ice Age beast. Delighted at the poetry of a phrase, we see gazelles leap before our eyes and take flight as they did at the dawn of humankind.

Animals, alphabets, and the sense of the sacred, therefore, are bound together in a profound manner. The "reading" of animals made the religion of the book possible; literate religion led to a new, spiritualized interpretation of animals, and the ability to comment and gloss those readings, as seen in the words on this page. The correlation teases our understanding like a hall of mirrors, reflecting reflections of each other, at once mundane as a newspaper and esoteric as ancient sorcery or an inexplicable vision of an eagle on a country road. But perhaps by entering this hall of mirrors, we can catch a glimmer of our true spiritual selves, the shamans and exegetes, the magicians and pilgrims, the believers and skeptics that make up what it means to be an enlightened, searching person.

PART TWO

Animal Parts

CHAPTER FOUR

Healing

Thurson of Hermione, a blind boy, had his eyes licked
in the daytime by one of the dogs about the temple,
and departed cured.
—INSCRIPTION ON A TABLET FOUND AT EPIDAURUS,
THE SITE OF THE TEMPLE OF ASKLEPIOS,
GREEK GOD OF MEDICINE

In the early 1970s, Dr. James P. Lynch of the University of Maryland Medical School began research on dogs to investigate how social interaction influenced health. He discovered the seemingly innocuous fact that when the animals were petted, their heart rates decreased. During the study, however, he also noticed that the research workers doing the petting also seemed generally calmer and more cheerful. He investigated the matter and corroborated his intuition: petting dogs not only lowered the canines' heart rate, it did the same for the people involved.

Later research has repeatedly demonstrated the healing power of pets. A 1980 study of people hospitalized for heart disease found a higher survival rate among pet owners one year after their release. In 1990, psychologist Judith Siegel of UCLA tracked the medical treatment of about one thousand elderly persons for one year and discovered that those who owned pets went to physicians less often than those without pets. Interestingly enough, dog owners did better than people with cats or other pets, presumably due to the unique, good-natured companionship canines provide. At least that was Dr. Siegel's surmise.

One study even found that the mere presence of dogs has a soothing effect on human physiology. A test group of women—all dog owners—

was given a series of stressful mental tasks, such as counting rapidly backward from a four-digit number. When the women did the assignment in the company of the researcher, or in the presence of a friend, they exhibited relatively high levels of stress. But when their dogs were present during the tests, they exhibited hardly any anxiety at all.

Other research shows that pets bestow health benefits on cancer patients, autistic children, even on the morale of health care workers.

No one knows for sure just how pets bring about this effect on people's health. One theory suggests that pets provide people with emotional bonds and an increased sense of social belonging (without much of the conflict that comes with human contacts), which in some way acts as a tonic to human physiology. We are above all else social animals; the lack of companionship and social ties can be as lethal as a disease. But whatever the explanation, these results are important in that they highlight the mysterious relationship between the mind and body only recently and begrudgingly recognized by modern medicine. The relationship should seem all the more mystifying in that it took a dog to help prove its existence to the satisfaction of medical science, as if animals were somehow the bridge between the human body and psyche.

The scientific study of how animals affect our health, no matter how puzzling the results, remains a purely secular concern in the medical profession. Where practical treatment is involved, we probably would not want it any other way. Starting with Hippocrates, Western medicine has consciously tried to insulate itself from political, religious, and economic forces, though not always with complete success, as the French philosopher Michel Foucault has shown. If medical questions existed only on a true/false exam, if the effectiveness of treatment were the only interest we had about our health, no one could dispute this approach. But the concept of human health always transcends the practical therapies science devises, raising essentially religious questions, about the nature of the human body, about the existence of the soul, about mortality. A full, healthy life embraces a variety of experiences broader than anything the scientific method can describe, and the penury of modern spirituality begins with our unwillingness to go beyond what William Blake called "single vision," a one-dimensional view of our existence uninformed by history, inspiration, and wonder. Blake's admonition applies to our biomedical theory of health. Medical findings about the beneficial effect of pets restate in narrow terms a rich allegory of healing animals going back to the origins of religion, an allegory that weaves together body and spirit, informing us about both.

A friend of mine, David Abram, has the unusual distinction of being both a doctor of philosophy and a professional magician. He tells the story of a visit he made to rural Indonesia to study the relationship between magic and medicine for his dissertation. He found that when he performed sleight-of-hand magic on the street, he could always attract a large crowd of local people. But it wasn't so much his sleight-of-hand expertise that caught their attention as the fact that a Westerner seemingly knew the therapeutic procedures of their native healers. Sometimes he was even asked to cure a sick person based on his skill at legerdemain. He found that his knowledge of magic was an entrée to meeting medicine men, who often wanted to share magic techniques and sometimes asked him to participate in their ceremonies. All because he could perform tricks we generally associate with parlor games and gaudy Las Vegas stage shows.

The anecdote reminds us of the deep connection between healing and religious belief, a connection that in modern times has mostly degenerated into the dubious spectacle of televangelists exhorting paraplegics to rise up out of their wheelchairs and walk. Among the basically animistic cultures Abram visited, medical therapy involves more than just treating a patient's body; a healer has to alter a patient's perception, draw on powers beyond the limits of human anatomy, and ultimately identify and remedy the spiritual causes of an illness. Human health is in this context always more than human.

Our society, too, once understood health in broader, more religious terms. The words "healthy" and "holy" are etymologically related, and were often indistinguishable in Anglo-Saxon times. Grendel, the ghastly monster in the Old English epic poem *Beowulf*, is called a *wiht unhælo*, which means both a "creature of evil" ("unholiness") and a "creature of destruction" ("unhealth"). The two meanings would have struck a pre-Conquest Englishman as more or less synonymous. The first medical institutions in the West were religious in nature, whether the pagan temple to Asklepios, the Greek god of health, in Epidaurus, or Christian shrines, such as Canterbury, where according to Chaucer, pilgrims visited to ask for the martyred St. Thomas à Becket for help "whan that they were seke."

The very core narratives of Christianity, the Gospels, unfold through account after account of miraculous healings performed by Jesus, who several times used the metaphor of a physician to describe his role as spiritual teacher. In fact, according to John's Gospel, one particular miracle, the raising of Lazarus from the dead, was the straw that broke the camel's back for the religious authorities opposing Jesus, provoking them into plotting his death. The important thing to note is that Jesus' miracles, far from being seen as outré, fit more or less comfortably into the spiritually oriented theory of health at the time. There were apparently more than a few itinerant faith healers roaming the Mediterranean during the first century A.D. (as by the way there still are throughout the world, including this country). Medical treatment may have been at least one of the functions of the religious complex at Qumran, the apparent stronghold of the Essenes, an ascetic Jewish sect associated with John the Baptist, according to some scholars. The sect studied medicinal roots and stones, and the name "Essene" seems to mean both "pious" and "healer."

The tumult raised by Jesus' miracles had very little to do with the fact that they were "magical"—such was expected from a physician/magus/medicine man of the time—but rather that, unlike his contemporaries, he identified his thaumaturgy with a unique teaching about universal brotherhood and the mercy of God, a teaching that threatened the established religious and secular authorities.

This is made plain in Luke, when a religious functionary carps about the healing of a woman, not because it involved the supernatural, but because it took place on a Saturday: "There are six days in which men are to work: in them therefore come and be healed, and not on the sabbath day" (Luke 13:14). Other opponents of Jesus also took doctrinal concerns to the extreme, questioning whether his healing powers came from God or Satan. To use the argot of anthropology, they accused him of practicing black rather than white shamanism.

Shamans, medicine men, witch doctors, and native healers of all kinds prior to the rise of medical science perceived human health as rooted in a larger natural and spiritual world. Nonindustrial societies often regard illness "as a misfortune involving the entire person, directly affecting his relationships with the spirit world and with other members of his group." And we might add, noting the pets in Dr. Siegel's research, with animals. Animals and animal parts play an almost inevitable role in native healing, appearing as guiding spirits, visible symbols of disease, or intermediaries between the human body and the supermundane.

An Anglo-Saxon "metrical charm," the medieval equivalent of a modern prescription from a doctor, demonstrates how this magic was deemed to work:

A woman who cannot nurse her child should take up in her hand
the milk from a cow of one pure hue and sip it into her mouth
and go to a place of running water and spit the milk into the
water and then with the selfsame hand take up a mouthful of the
water and swallow.

The charm was probably written down sometime in the tenth century, but the way of thinking goes back hundreds, even thousands of years into the misty realm of folk beliefs and sympathetic magic. The symbolic syntax of this cure is not difficult to decipher. Cow's milk is like mother's milk, and running water corresponds to a mother nursing her child. By intermingling the cow's milk with the running water, the patient symbolically calls on the power in both to restore in her body the power to lactate. The magico-religious principle at work here appears in folk beliefs throughout the world: like affects like. It is at work in our society when people with hangovers take a sip of liquor as a "cure" known as the hair of the dog that bit you. It is why people burn effigies of hated public figures.

The things in the world we most resemble are other animals. In fact, we not only resemble animals, we indisputably *are* animals. A recent comparison of the DNA of humans and chimpanzees found that ninety-eight percent of their genetic codes overlap. Birth, growth, mortality, bodies of flesh, minds that think and nerves that respond—animal existence in all its deep structures runs parallel to our own. But just like parallel lines, the lives of humans and animals, while often infinitely close, never quite intersect. The similarities between the two draw our attention to the differences, the space that distances us from other living creatures and allows us to see animals both as physical entities and as an inexhaustible source of metaphor.

In the animistic theory of health, the animal kingdom acts like a vast transmission system, whose differences and similarities connect us to powers that sustain human existence, whatever those powers may be: local spirits, ancestors, the harmonies of nature, God. During a native healing, a medicine man often produces an insect, worm, or lizard, supposedly extracted from the patient as the embodiment of the illness. Baganda medicine men, for instance, pass herbs over the sick person, tie the herbs to an animal, and drive the creature away. It is as if the mysteries of wholeness and sickness require a tangible artifact, a flesh and blood shape to our fears and desires about the continued existence of our bodies and minds.

This primal concern now and again crossed into Christian lore. One of the stories related about St. Francis of Paula involves a vicious

and violent young nobleman named Jean de la Roque. Sensing that
the young man was possessed, St. Francis had him arrested and held
in a monastery. On visiting his cell, the saint ordered Jean to pull
from his ears the demons possessing him, whereupon the sinner drew
forth two hideous worms. The worms that represented his evil nature
having been extracted, the man became a monk.

Even the Bible, which for the most part shuns an animistic view
of nature, gives disease an animal shape on at least one occasion, perhaps the most curious example of Jesus' miracles, the curing of the
Garasene demoniac. Over half of Jesus' individual miracles appear in
only one or two of the Gospels. The Garasene healing earns a mention in three books, Matthew, Mark, and Luke; and it occupies more
verses than any other healing miracle; all of which suggests the story
held some special fascination to the early Christian audience. The
incident is unique also in that it takes place in pagan territory, near a
Greek city, with a cast of characters almost entirely non-Jewish.

The story begins with Jesus coming to shore after crossing the
Sea of Galilee (or some other body of water). Immediately upon dis-
embarking from his ship, he is confronted by a man bereft of reason,
homeless, naked, covered with self-inflicted wounds, and filled with
such violent rage that no chains can bind him and no amount of force
can drag him away from his favorite haunts—a cemetery and a mountain wilderness. According to the text, unclean spirits have caused the
man's degraded state. As Jesus goes about restoring the man to his
senses, he questions these demons, who identify themselves collec-
tively as "Legion." Frightened at the prospect of being exorcised, Legion makes the mysterious request that they be allowed to stay in
the country and not "go into the deep," perhaps an allusion to the
underworld. More specifically, they ask to be allowed to possess a
herd of pigs feeding nearby, two thousand strong according to Mark.
Strangely enough, Jesus grants the request, allowing the evil spirits to
enter the swine, which immediately plunge wildly down a cliff into
the sea, where they drown.

The details of this narrative have perplexed Christian commentators for two millennia, especially when it came to the significance of the unlucky pigs. Even the early church fathers, renowned for their skill at exegesis, had trouble making sense out of the swines' doomed cameo appearance in the drama. Some commentators have suggested that the pigs represent the Gentile nations in their spiritual benightedness before the revelation of Christ. Others have sought rational explanations for the stampede. Still others have simply thrown up their hands, cited evidence that the narrative strand about the pigs may be a later addition, and called the story "confused," "rambling," and "bizarre." Setting all this commentary aside for the moment, the fact is, the healing of the Garasene demoniac represents one of the most structured and thoughtful miracles in the New Testament, and its sense becomes clearer once we view it through the template of animal spirituality and healing.

In contrast to most of Jesus' other miracles, which occur merely at a touch of his hand or a spoken word, this therapy involves a drama where Jesus commands and questions the afflicting demons, identifies them, responds to their pleadings, and ultimately uses animals to ferry them away from their victim toward apparent destruction. Superficially at least, the performance appears similar to the therapy of native healers throughout the world, with the swine playing the role of the "disease animal" that symbolizes the expulsion of the illness from the sick person's body. The pigs' rush to destruction manifests the magical cure.

But, as John Meier points out, Jesus is specifically not a medicine man, magical healer, or shaman. Jesus himself tells the disciples that he performs miracles as a way to testify to God's power and mercy, and to lead people to faith. He constantly reminds the healed that their faith in God, not any wizardry on his part, has cured them. Shamans simply do not fulfill this evangelical and self-effacing function. Like modern physicians, their sole aim is to cure their paying client, at supposedly great personal risk: the practicing shaman risks a confrontation with so-called "soul-death," a demise brought about when the phantasms of disease defeat the disembodied shaman in spiritual battle and prevent him from returning to his comatose, soul-less body. As a result of these professional perils, native healers readily attribute their medical successes to their own efforts, rather than to their patients or the gods. Shamanistic healing is not for amateurs, or as far as that goes for a Nazarene carpenter.

If Jesus was so self-consciously not a magician, then the similarities between native therapy and the healing of the Garasene demoniac must derive from some other source, a common ground that has escaped students of both shamanism and Christology. That point of intersection is the role animals play in human self-identity. All cultures, from animistic hunter-gatherers to the urban industrialists who put a man on the moon, categorize humans as animals. "I said in my heart concerning the estates of the sons of men," Ecclesiastes states, "that God might manifest them, and that they might see that they themselves are beasts." And yet, animals are at the same time strikingly different from us, in shape, size, temperament, texture. Our emergence into self-awareness about our bodies and souls took place in the context of an ongoing dialogue with the animal world, which gave us points of comparison and contrast. Living creatures beyond our own species provided "the most readily available point of reference for the continuous process of self-definition."

Sometimes this process was very concrete: our first steps toward an understanding of human anatomy sprang from the hunting and butchering of animals, and in historical times from dissections. Sometimes the process was metaphoric: for almost all of our emotional states we have found a corresponding zoological metaphor. A person can be a chicken or a lovebird or a snake in the grass, angry as a hornet, crazy as a loon, hungry as a wolf.

And sometimes the process was philosophical. One of the major motifs in Western thought has been the definition of humanity in terms of our similarities to and (mostly) differences from animal creation. Plato started off this philosophical pin-the-tail-on-the-donkey by defining man as a two-legged animal without feathers. Other thinkers have sought the uniqueness of *Homo sapiens* in reason, language, toolmaking, or more whimsically, as Twain put it, in the fact that we are the only animals that blush, or need to. Although all these distinctions have, interestingly enough, failed the scrutiny of science (octopi use logic, chimpanzees learn sign language, finches make tools, and cuttlefish blush), the point remains that for aeons animals have served as the mirrors by which we visualize our own bodies and souls.

This is why shamanist therapy and the healing of the Garasene demoniac seem strangely similar. For all their emphasis on physical disease, both native healing and Jesus' miracles ultimately pose the same philosophical question to the sick person, which never arises for modern medicine: Who are you? How do you relate to your neighbors, to the past, to the natural world around you, to evil and to the divine? Magical healers may cast this question in terms of a disharmony or hostility in a person's relationship to the spirit realm. Jesus made the issue a matter of faith in the power and mercy of God. But the implied question is always about identity.

Returning to the Garasene narrative, it carries out a tour de force in raising and resolving the issue of human identity. Whatever other diagnosis one wants to make about the wild man, whether religious or psychological, the important fact is that he has lost the sense of who he is and how he fits into a broader community. He lives in isolation, his only interactions with people involve violence, and his loss of the capacity to reason makes him appear more like a beast than a human. The name of the demons afflicting him, Legion, suggests the fragmentation of his personality, as if his existence lacked a core. In short, he is out of sync with his surroundings and his own human nature.

Jesus' arrival is the catalyst for restoring the demoniac's proper relations with himself, with others, and with God. The narrative proceeds with a series of distinctions: Jesus the divine presence and Legion the Satanic; the Jewish apostles with their revealed religion and the Greek population with their pagan humanism; the lone demoniac dwelling among the dead and the swineherds with their animals as members of a living community. The restoration of the demoniac's place in this tableu liberates his humanity and constitutes his healing. This is why Jesus identifies the demon by name, something he does in no other miracle. And this is why the herd of swine appears. The demoniac's loss of humanity derives from his loss of place in the more than human world of nature and the divine. Without the pigs, this story of physical and spiritual ascension would be like a ladder with a missing rung. They literally and symbolically bear away the disease spirits, just as in a shamanistic ceremony, because part of knowing who we are means living in relationship with the animals that constantly define us.

As a poignant epilogue to the healing, the nearby townsfolk hear about the suicidal pigs and rush out to see what has happened. They find their countryman in his right mind, clothed, seated at the feet of Jesus—an emblem of his renewed integration into the human and spiritual community. This joyous fact, however, is lost on the Garasenes, who find the whole episode disturbing, not to mention costly in terms of livestock, and ask Jesus to leave their country. Pearls before swine, Jesus may have muttered to his disciples. For his part, the former madman, at Jesus' behest, returns to his city and proclaims the greatness of the man who healed him, apparently the first non-Jew to proselytize on Jesus' behalf.

It is not difficult to imagine the man years later, back in his hometown in the Hellenized region of Decapolis, repeating like the Ancient Mariner his strange tale about the swine and the Jewish healer, to his family and friends, to Greek traders and Roman soldiers, to anyone who will listen. One of his listeners may have made a connection in his mind with another place, across the Aegean at the foot of Mt. Parnassus in Greece, also famous for the gift of self-knowledge and for fauna with strange healing powers: the shrine at Delphi. He may have consulted the Delphic Oracle before traveling abroad to Decapolis, and read the famous words inscribed on the temple: *gnothi seauton*, "know thyself." He would have called the Oracle "Pythia" or "pythoness," the Greek and Roman words for seer, since the Oracle at Delphi received her mantic gifts from the god Apollo, who had wrested them from the spirit of the Python, a gigantic serpent slain by the sun god at Parnassus. From the Python, Apollo also obtained knowledge of the medical arts, which (through the tutoring of a half-man, half-horse centaur called Chiron) he passed on to his son, Asklepios (better known by his Latin name, Aesculapius), who sometimes took the form of a golden snake to those seeking a cure to their ills at his many shrines. Asklepios' symbol was a winged staff entwined with one or two snakes, which his father Apollo had given to Hermes in exchange for a lyre. Like Jesus, Asklepios' healing powers eventually led to his demise, and deification. When his healing skills grew so great that he was able to restore a dead man to life, the gods took alarm and killed him, whereupon he was transformed into the god of medicine.

Perhaps these stories swam through the listener's mind and the tale of the Garasene demoniac made perfect sense to him. Now, two thousand years later, whenever we go to the doctor's office and get a prescription, we might notice an emblem on an American Medical Association pamphlet, or on a bottle of medicine. It is the caduceus, Asklepios' serpent-entwined staff, the symbol of the medical profession, passed down to modern physicians from wandering faith healers and ancient demigods and miracle-working serpents.

Like the caduceus itself, beasts of holiness and of health have remained entwined together through the passage of centuries. During the Middle Ages, animals acted as a focus of physical and spiritual healing in folk medicine and religious discourse. The *Physiologus* mentions a bird called the charadrius (perhaps the white wagtail), which has unusual curative and diagnostic powers:

His excrement is a cure for those whose eyes are growing dim
. . . If someone is ill, whether he will live or die can be known
from the charadrius. The bird turns his face away from the man
whose illness will bring death and thus everyone knows that he
is going to die. On the other hand, if the disease is not fatal, the
charadrius stares the sick man in the face and the sick man stares
back at the charadrius, who releases him from his illness. Then,
flying up to the atmosphere of the sun, the charadrius burns
away the sick man's illness and scatters it abroad.

In the next paragraph, the author identifies the bird as a symbol
of Christ, "taking away our infirmities and carrying off our sins."
This multilayered understanding of maladies physical and spiritual is
peeled back by the *Physiologus* to reveal creatures that bear away illness, while acting as a conduit to supernatural powers, in this case
through prophecies of life or death, and through the creature's emblematic function as a redeemer of sins.

Walk into the Cluny Museum in Paris, and the complex religious
role of healing animals in the Garasene incident and the *Physiologus*
takes on visible dimensions. In the museum's circular hall hang a
series of large tapestries from the early sixteenth century, under the
name *The Lady of the Unicorn*. Generally considered the finest of their
time, the weavings apparently allegorize the five senses using an ornate dramatis personæ: a noble lady and her servant, a unicorn, various dogs, apes, rabbits, sheep, birds, and plants. The tapestry
depicting Sight portrays a unicorn resting with its forefeet in the lap
of a seated lady holding a mirror. The lady looks at the unicorn, who
stares into the mirror, where we in our position as viewers of the scene
can see the creature's reflection. All this strange imagery speaks a
parable about the zoology of self-knowledge, focused on the legendary
unicorn.

At the time this tapestry was woven, the unicorn bore a weighty and conflicting burden of symbolic meanings on its back. It was an ideograph for Christ, but also for the devil; it stood for meekness as well as wildness, chastity and lust, fertility and destruction. Its horn supposedly held tremendous curative powers against epilepsy, fever, plague, leprosy, rabies, infections, worms, even poison. With this dense symbolism in mind, the tapestry of Sight becomes a contemplation on the quandaries of human identity. We look into the lady's mirror, but instead of seeing our own reflections, as we would expect if the tapestry were a three-dimensional world, we glimpse the placid face of the unicorn, who following the optics must in return see us. The best vision, suggests the work, comprises not just clarity of eyesight, but insight into how we relate to all the contradictory qualities and communities, both sacred and profane, embodied by the unicorn. Through a trick of optics, the artist forces us to see ourselves by seeing an animal instead, and moreover one that exists only in legend. Perhaps this emphasis on seeing ourselves in the animal also explains the intense stare between the sick person and the charadrius described in the *Physiologus*, a look integral to the bird's magical cure.

The animal look perplexes us still. According to John Berger, the gaze between humans and animals was central to our passage into self-awareness. The otherness of animals, inscribed in their deep similitude to us, made man "aware of himself returning the look . . . And so, when he is being seen by the animal, he is being seen as his surroundings are seen by him." This capacity to sympathize lies at the foundation of all spirituality, the recognition that the hawk I view hovering in the sky also views me, that I am not the epicenter of the world but only one life in relation to countless other biographies set in motion by the divine.

Of course, belonging to a larger community is a two-edged sword. If animals have the power of healing, then it follows they have the ability to harm. The threat may be as apparently arbitrary and legalistic as the "unclean" animals listed in Leviticus and Deuteronomy. Or it may reflect the dark underworld of black magic, summed up in the infamous witches' incantation in *Macbeth*:

> *Eye of newt and toe of frog,*
> *Wool of bat and tongue of dog.*
> *Adders fork and blind-worm's sting,*
> *Lizard's leg and howlet's wing,*
> *For a charm of powerful trouble,*
> *Like a hell-broth boil and bubble.*

"Eye of newt" has become for us a kind of shorthand for magical mumbo jumbo. We listen to the Shakespearean lines, and hear only a literary construct, one that probably strikes us as somewhat overwrought. But to Shakespeare's audience, the passage probably evoked considerable discomfort, even dread. Such "charms," if practiced outside the theater as serious magic, were prohibited by law. And at the very time the play was being performed at the Globe, fearful magistrates across Britain and Europe were standing in ecclesiastical and civil courts bringing criminal charges against dogs, weevils, pigs, and mares, for supposed murders, impieties, and depredations, often leading to the hanging of the felonious creatures on the gallows. The imaginary animal parts bubbling in the witches' cauldron existed at a time when animals were dangerous and beneficent, a time when animals supplied the symbolic images and physical elixirs of sickness and health, of murder and creation, a time when animals mattered.

Our medical arts have no room for animal intermediaries, existential self-reflection, or the symbolic representations of disease. Except as objects of research, animals have become invisible to the craft they once defined. With the recent development of interspecies transplants, using baboon and pig organs in humans, we may, however, be coming round full circle. What symbolic significance might reattach in the future to beasts whose living body parts become integrated into our flesh and blood? Will the therapeutic sense of asking who a patient is and where he belongs again take on meaning if people become composite beings, augmented by animal tissue? The power of animals to embody and define health persists. "Strong as an ox," "sick as a dog," "the constitution of a horse" are the common similes we use to describe medical conditions. These may be just fossils of dead beliefs, but they suggest that our culture associates true health with more than mere physiology, that we cannot help but search for the unicorn in the mirror.

As the hour of his death fast approached, Edward Abbey, the writer and champion of wilderness preservation, asked his friends and family to take him from the hospital and drive him out into the wild desert landscape that he loved. Slowly hemorrhaging to death, he and a few people close to him hiked out somewhere into the Sonoran Desert. They sat around a campfire as he waited, hoping to die surrounded by his companions and the natural world he had celebrated all his artistic life. But death would not come. "Sometimes the magic fails," he said, and they drove him back to town, where he died a few days later.

Abbey was wrong. The magic didn't fail. His last gesture showed how his belonging to his friends and to the natural community had shaped him into a fuller human being who knew himself: a much greater gift than choosing the hour and place of his demise. And as far as that goes, a gift greater than physical curatives. Medical science has replaced the rituals of the shaman in healing disease, but it cannot replace the subtle magic of animals that help us discover true health, the knowledge of our place in this world, and perhaps the next.

CHAPTER FIVE

Flesh

Unseen, unheard, and unsuspected.
—BUDDHIST DESCRIPTION OF MEAT FIT TO BE EATEN BY
MONKS, REQUIRING THEM NOT TO SEE THE ANIMAL
KILLED, HEAR THE SLAUGHTER, OR SUSPECT THE KILLING WAS
DONE FOR THEM.

I grew up in a family that was an ecumenical council in its own right. My immediate relatives included German Protestants, Roman Catholics, Greek Orthodox, evangelicals, and agnostics, with a great deal of overlap among them, especially with the last category. At least for us children, the most obvious benefit from our religious Tower of Babel was the fact that the pipeline of religious holidays seemed never to stop flowing, sometimes to the point of redundancy. We celebrated two Easters, one "American," the other Eastern Orthodox, usually a week or two later (it has to do with different calculations based on the full moon and Passover); after Christmas came a muted echo of Christmas in January; we had name days for those by chance christened after a saint with a day set aside in his or her honor.

Along with the different holidays came a mixture of dietary traditions. Our Easter eggs, in Greek fashion, were dyed blood-red and eaten only after a ritual contest in which one shell tip was tapped against another until only the winner's egg remained unbroken. The red represented Christ's blood, and the cracking of the eggs, the opening of the tomb after the resurrection. For a good part of my childhood, my family never ate meat on Friday, until the practice became optional. Lent, with its repetitive bowls of lentil soup, was a serious matter to my grandmother, which regrettably made it a serious matter for the rest of us since she did all the cooking.

I did not know then, but these traditional practices harbored one of the greatest mysteries of religious belief: Why do people all over the world and in every era, including our technological age, feel moved, even compelled, to express their spirituality through the eating or the avoidance of animal flesh? Taboos against eating certain types of meat at certain times by certain people are one of the few practices common to all religions, and ironically one of the major causes of strife among them.

More than a few religious revolts have taken place over the consumption of animal flesh. The Sepoy Rebellion of 1857 against British rule in India was sparked by the rumor, apparently accurate, that the Enfield rifle cartridges issued to the Indian soldiers serving in the British Army were greased with the fat of cows and pigs. To uncap the cartridges, the gunners would have to use their mouths, causing Hindus to ingest the animal they held sacred, and Moslems the animal they considered impure. The Mau Mau revolt in Kenya exploded into existence when a European farmer shot a wild cat suspected of killing his chickens, and presented the carcass to a local tribal leader for whom the cat was a totem animal, saying contemptuously, "Okay, how about eating that?" In the second century B.C., Jewish resistance to the Syrian rule of Antiochus Epiphanes, who ordered the Jews to sacrifice swine to his pagan gods, found its rallying point in a pious old scribe named Eleazar, who chose martyrdom by spitting out the piece of pork the Syrians forced into his mouth.

As is true in every society, the dietary restrictions of minority religions seem conspicuous to us, while for the most part we take our own for granted. Mention the topic of alimentary taboos, and the Hindu proscription against eating beef comes to mind, or the vegetarianism encouraged by Buddhism. Most Christians find the avoidance of pork practiced by Orthodox Judaism and Islam unfathomable, especially since it is not merely a cultural tradition (like our revulsion toward dog meat) but an edict found in the sacred texts of both religions. Yet without even thinking about it, the majority of religious people in our culture also follow restrictions on eating meat of some kind or another. Many Christians observe Lent, the ritual avoidance of meat prior to Easter. Until Pope Paul VI issued "On Christian Penance" in 1966, it was a sin for Catholics to eat any meat except fish on Fridays, and American Catholics fourteen years of age and older still are directed to abstain from meat on Ash Wednesday, Good Friday, and the Fridays of Lent. To this day, Chaldean Christians of the Middle East require that candidates for their patriarch must have never tasted meat, and even that their mothers avoided flesh during pregnancy and nursing. Less obviously, the aversion to eating horse-flesh found in America and most Anglo-Saxon countries probably has its origins in the struggle between paganism and Christianity: prior to the coming of Christianity, horse meat was commonly eaten throughout Europe, and still is in some countries where the first missionaries did not find pagan deities that held the horse sacred. And, of course, though we rarely look at it this way, the central sacrament of many Christian denominations, Communion, involves the symbolic partaking of human/divine flesh.

These few examples only begin to suggest the universality of religious rules concerning the consumption of animals. In various places in the world, chickens, camels, dogs, snakes, and every type of wild creature all fall under some dietary prohibition or encouragement sacramental in nature.

Anthropologists have had little success providing a general explanation of the ritual avoidance of meat. The religious uses of these restrictions seem as varied as the animals whose flesh is declared inedible. Nonetheless, in tune with our culture, many have tried to rationalize flesh taboos, especially regarding the dietary laws set down in Leviticus and Deuteronomy, parts of the Bible which strike most modern readers as particularly alien to their sensibilities. The most widely held notion about the injunction against pork in the Bible cites the "hygienic" concerns about pigs as carriers of trichinosis. But the fact is, it took medical science until the middle of the nineteenth century to discover the trichina parasite and its manner of transmission to humans. Since people rarely get sick immediately upon contracting trichinosis, the likelihood that the ancient Hebrews could have made the association between pork consumption and parasites seems minuscule.

Moreover, the biblical ban on pork takes place in the context of restrictions on eating more than thirty other kinds of animals, most of which simply do not raise hygienic risks (indeed, the Bible indicates that prior to the Flood, Yahweh banned the consumption of *any* animal). Swans, pelicans, and birds of prey are pronounced "unclean," even though such wild fowl is notably free from diseases affecting humans. Other forbidden flesh includes bats, ravens, and insects—creatures most people tend to avoid eating without the cudgel of divine sanctions (members of the genus *Corvus*, which includes ravens, while not poison, are virtually inedible). Also, the biblical restrictions apply only to meat: no mineral or vegetable prohibitions appear, even though a multitude of plants and elements are toxic to humans, and more likely to be ingested unless a person takes precautions. Finally, the Old Testament distinction between clean and unclean animals encompasses more than just dietary restrictions. Any physical contact with the carcass of unclean animals defiled the person or object touched, necessitating ritual purification.

Something deeper and more mysterious is going on in these dietary restrictions, something relating directly to the spiritual role animals play.

A friend of mine, who is an Orthodox Jew, once explained to me that the practice of kosher dietary laws may seem burdensome and irrational to non-Jews, and they very well may be right about that. But on the other hand, he knew exactly what to do to fulfill his religious duties because God has provided clear-cut rules. The spiritual importance, my friend insisted, is not the nature of the restrictions themselves, but his willingness to follow them.

The Talmud, the body of rabbinical commentaries on the Torah, expresses the same view. According to the Talmud, some of the commandments simply have no rational explanation. The ban on eating pork is one of these. Nonetheless, believers hallow their lives by obeying without requiring a rationale. The rejection of pork, in other words, is simply a mystery Orthodox Judaism is willing to embrace on faith.

In animistic cultures, prohibitions on eating certain kinds of animal flesh make a rough kind of sense. Animals in this perspective have souls that transcend death, requiring careful consideration on what and how people eat in order not to make a perpetual enemy in the spirit realm. Even Buddhism and Jainism can "rationally" mandate vegetarianism, based on the belief in reincarnation of humans as animals, and the general principle that humans should strive to cause no suffering.

The religious mainstream in the West does not have the option of justifying meat taboos based on explicable theological principles. Official Judaism, Christianity, and Islam generally gainsay the existence of animal souls, and in some instances not only allow, but mandate the consumption of meat. The priest who performed the Levitical *chatat*, or "sin offering," of a female sheep had to eat at least part of the sacrifice. Christianity and Islam do have a spiritual explanation for the avoidance of meat at Lent and Ramadan, namely the practice of self-denial and penance. But this rationale does not explain why animal flesh, as opposed to pomegranates or truffles, should be the object of this religious discipline. On the surface at least, these three great ethical religions distinguish between the spiritual nature of humanity and the soulless existence of plants, animals, and minerals. The distinction informs the radical dietary pronouncement made by Jesus that nothing eaten can have any effect on the condition of a person's soul: "Not that which goeth into the mouth defileth a man; but that which cometh out of the mouth, this defileth a man" (Matthew 15:11). It is unclear whether Jesus is referring to actual food or the "taint" removed by ritual cleansing of the hands (which is the context of his statement), but in either case the line he draws between the physical world and the human spirit accords with a tradition that traces back to Genesis.

The key, if there is one, regarding meat avoidance seems to involve the way we use animals to define ourselves, with dietary restrictions playing the role of distinguishing the group we belong to from other groups. Anthropologist Frederick Simoons notes that the food prohibitions of the major religions seem to have arisen in the wake of sharpened conflict between one religion or nation and another. It is fairly common for people to define rival groups negatively by their food, especially foods considered unfamiliar. In American English, the words "Krauts," "Frogs," and "Limeys" were once used disparagingly to refer to Germans, Frenchmen, and Englishmen. The association between food and group identity might easily lead to the rejection of foods associated with antagonistic groups. Some readers might recall that the word "frankfurter" was virtually banned during World War I due to its associations with Germany. And although Americans of the time could not bring themselves to give up that particular food, they did the next best thing by giving it a new name free of Kaiser Wilhelm's blot.

Something like this may have happened in earlier times. The ancient Hebrews were a pastoral people whose highly mobile way of life did not accommodate the raising of pigs. Swine belonged to the settled pagan peoples, the great urban civilizations, that constantly competed with and lashed out at the Hebrews living on their borders. When the Jews finally settled in a country of their own and began to write their laws, it is not surprising the pig should have been associated with enemy nations and the sacrifice to alien gods.

Similarly, prior to the rise of Buddhism in India, Hinduism had no strict prohibition against beef eating. The arrival of Buddhism in the sixth century B.C. confronted the older religion with a competition of faiths. Early Buddhism itself was not at first firmly vegetarian, and it appears what ensued was a kind of dietary arms race, in which each of the two religions developed stronger and stronger proscriptions against meat-eating as a way of proclaiming its spiritual superiority to the other. The less widespread avoidance of chicken by Hinduism may be a reaction to the invasion of Islam, which brought with it a taste for domestic fowl.

As already noted, the eating of horseflesh was customary in Europe during pre-Christian times, especially in the North. Among Germanic and Scandinavian tribes the horse was sacred to Oðin, the chief Germanic god, and to Frey, the god of fertility. When Christianity achieved political power in these countries, it took a variety of steps to stamp out cultural references to paganism, such as changing the names of the week (which is why the Germans call Wednesday—meaning "Woden's, i.e. Oðin's, day,"—*Mittwoch*, "midweek day"). One such religious prohibition was directed at the sacrificing and consumption of horseflesh. In 732 A.D. Pope Gregory III ordered the Germans to quit eating their horses, and similar proscriptions, some ecclesiastical, some civil, spread unevenly over Europe, and then into America, where a number of states outlawed the sale of horse meat. Although horse is still consumed in Iceland and France, it continues to have connotations of low status and uncleanliness.

More fundamentally, early Christianity encouraged vegetarianism and the practice of ritual fasting on bread and water, in part to distinguish itself both from the debauchery and luxury of the Roman society and from competing forms of Jewish asceticism. Early Christians fasted on Wednesday and Friday (later Tuesday), while Judaism's fast days were Monday and Thursday. By the time of Constantine's conversion at the beginning of the fourth century, the church strongly condemned the gluttony associated with Roman paganism, and recommended a continual diet of cereals and vegetables, with meat reserved solely for the sick and for guests.

The religious ambiguities of meat appear in the distinction English speakers make between living animals and their consumable flesh. A cow slaughtered and cooked for the table is transformed into beef; pig becomes pork; deer arrives as venison. On the one hand, this linguistic fastidiousness can be explained as the result of the Norman invasion of 1066, which installed a French-speaking aristocracy over an Anglo-Saxon peasantry. The finer things in life, like good food, naturally gravitated toward a Norman-French vocabulary, while the cruder realities, like barnyard animals, remained Anglo-Saxon. But more is probably at work here. The fact that a living, breathing animal would appear gross and vulgar, as opposed to a side of meat on a platter, takes place against a religious backdrop where beasts have come to symbolize the carnal and unspiritual aspects of humanity. What made a boorish Norman-French warlord turn up his unwashed nose at a pig was less the physical nature of the creature than the symbolic burden of the opposition between flesh and spirit, nature and God, that had slowly infiltrated Western thought.

If meat avoidance somehow separates our identity from rival groups, it also breaks down barriers within our society. Meat is the great gastronomic separator. It divides predators from prey, the rich from the poor, the powerful from the weak, even males from females. From the earliest times to the present, the consumption of animal flesh signaled prestige and power. Whether a person ordinarily eats sirloin steak or ground beef is a shorthand for defining his economic status. Meat functions like money; in fact our word "fee" comes from the Germanic *fexu, "cattle," with the ultimate Indo-European root *pek, "cattle" or "sheep," from which we also get the word "pecuniary." The semantic relationship between meat and currency derives from the fact that for thousands of years people calculated their wealth in terms of livestock.

Meat is also closely linked to gender differences. Societies throughout the world, especially hunter-gatherer cultures, forbid or restrict females from consuming certain kinds of animal flesh. "Only the males in the priestly line may eat of [animals sacrificed as sin offerings]," states the divine prohibition in Leviticus. Even in modern Western societies, the eating of beef by women was considered somewhat gauche if not unnatural well into the nineteenth century, a sentiment that probably still lingers and can be seen in the eating habits of women in public. The word "beef" has become a virtual morpheme for "male," as in the word "beefcake" to describe erotic male photography as opposed to its female counterpart, "cheesecake"—a mere animal by-product.

If meat equals maleness, it also connotes a particularly masculine form of political and military power. In the Bible, the prospective triumph of Israel over its enemies suddenly brings to mind unrestrained meat-eating: "When the Lord thy God shall enlarge thy border, as he hath promised thee, and thou shalt say, I will eat flesh, because thy soul longeth to eat flesh; thou mayest eat flesh, whatsoever thy soul lusteth after" (Deuteronomy 12:20). Several millennia later, most politicians running for executive office attempt to appear conspicuously carnivorous, blazoning their meat eating through associations with hunting, fishing, and ranching. When President Bush was not at the White House, he was at Kennebunkport, fishing. Reagan, sporting a cowboy hat, would take off for his "ranch." Clinton and Carter both drew attention to their duck-hunting Southern roots. Theodore Roosevelt's political persona and his big-game hunting jacket were all but indistinguishable.

Vegetarianism in the symbolically predatory context of national leadership suggests political weakness: the passivity of Gandhi, the weirdness of Hitler. For almost every Western country, and America in particular, steak has overtones of nationalism and national power that citizens want their chief executive to embody. During the 1984 presidential campaign, one of the slogans of candidate Walter Mondale was "Where's the beef?," implying a lack of substance to Reagan's political promises. The phrase came from a commercial for fast-food hamburgers. The remarkable crossover of this slogan, from the realm of ground beef to presidential politics, could only take place because a prior symbolic order existed in which meat and power are one.

The ritual avoidance of meat, whatever its origins, has the ultimate result of metaphorically putting aside the substance of our estrangement from one another, the symbolic currency of class, gender, and political dominion. The dead bodies of animals, by their very absence, become the table around which we reaffirm who we are and why we belong together.

The duality of meat, uniting and dividing, shines some light upon the imponderable nature of Holy Communion. For those who practice it, the sacrament constitutes a communal meal affirming the spiritual unity of believers with one another and with God. Curiously, however, to represent his flesh, Jesus did not choose actual meat, but bread. During the ritual, through the mystery of transubstantiation, the communicants partake of a flesh that divides believers from nonbelievers, the saved from the unredeemed; and yet the substance actually consumed is not this discriminating flesh at all, but rather bread, a food available to all and a metaphor for our common humanity. The simultaneous presence and absence of divine flesh in the Eucharist, the interplay between the divisiveness of meat and the universality of grain helps shape the sacrament into the powerful ritual it is for many Christians.

The Flathead tribe have a story about Coyote and a cannibal giant. Coyote was walking one day when he met Old Woman. She warned him not to continue in the direction he was going lest he run into a giant who devours everything. With his usual bravado, Coyote shrugged off the warning and went on his way, picking up a branch he planned to use to club the giant to death. His path took him to the mouth of an enormous cave. He went in, whistling merrily.

After walking awhile into the cave he began to meet people and animals of all different types lying on the ground half dead. "What's the matter?" he asked them. They explained they were starving to death, because they were inside the stomach of the giant and could not get out. Never at a loss, Coyote took out his hunting knife and began cutting off pieces of the giant's fat and flesh to feed everyone trapped in the giant.

Then Coyote found the giant's heart and stabbed him to death. When the giant opened his mouth to take his last breath, Coyote and all the giant's victims escaped. The last creature to get out was the wood tick, which Coyote barely managed to pull through the giant's teeth. That's why wood ticks are flat.

The giant is us. Or at least the part of us that recognizes no limits, accepts no responsibility for the community, takes without asking, devours without thinking of the consequences. It is the human ego bloated into a colossus. The story admonishes us: Coyote is not to be eaten—not due to any quality of his flesh, but because our carnality requires limits. The same can be said about Pig among Moslems and Jews. Cow among Hindus. Chicken among African Somali, Kikuyu, Kamba, Rundi. Camel among Ethiopian Christians. Dog among Zoroastrians. And Pangolin, Marmoset, Firebellied Toad, and the rest of prohibited beasts that at times make up the very flesh of religious thought.

CHAPTER SIX

Sacrifice

When gods and men parted, sacrifice was created.
—HESIOD

Classical religions exist for us as images of immaculate stone. We see them embodied in the perfect lines of the Parthenon, the stark dome of the Roman Pantheon, the inscrutable blankness of the Wailing Wall. These remnants of earlier faiths inspire a sense of balance, repose, and purity that belies the fact that most places of worship in antiquity were reeking, bloody slaughterhouses.

Animal sacrifice was an "all pervasive reality of the ancient world." We have banished the practice to a dark unremembered space in modern civilization, but the temples that today stand as shrines to art and serenity would, if we could go back and see them in operation, strike us as the equivalent not of modern places of worship, but abattoirs. Their priests had to know both the spiritual mysteries of the cult and the techniques of butchery. Such was the scale of institutionalized blood sacrifice for most of religious history that an alien reviewing a videotaped recording of human religion down the ages might sum up worship on this planet in three words: they kill animals.

Perhaps no change more sharply distinguishes the modern mentality from the ancient. When we look at animals—to the extent we look at them at all in this era of vanishing and invisible beasts—we see pets, objects of entertainment and study, units of production. A

Roman citizen certainly experienced these same qualities; the Romans had no sentimentality about living creatures, as demonstrated by their massive and cruel slaughters of exotic wildlife in the arena. But there would have also been something extra, a recognition that animals were in touch with the gods, and could be used to intervene on behalf of humans. When Caligula appointed his racehorse Incitatus consul, it appalled every sane Roman citizen, but it had a disturbing logic to it for a society in which spiritual well-being visibly depended on the massive shedding of animal blood.

Despite the fact that they considered animals sacred and made killing certain creatures a capital offense, the ancient Egyptians sacrificed literally millions of beasts, including cats, snakes, mice, gazelles, cattle, baboons, falcons, beetles, ibises, crocodiles, and dogs, apparently for the purpose of using their embalmed carcasses as votive offerings to the gods, or as a means of cursing enemies. At Tuna el-Bebel, the Egyptians built a trilevel necropolis covering thirty-seven acres, the first level of which alone contained over four million mummified animals. During the nineteenth century, so many cat mummies were exhumed from the Middle Egyptian town of Beni Hasan el Shuruq that European importers measured them not by the count, but by the ton. An estimated three hundred thousand embalmed felines were unearthed and sent to Liverpool alone, where they were ground into powder and used in English gardens as fertilizer. Occupying a less productive land, the Greeks were stingier in their oblations, but they still gave us the word "hecatomb," meaning the offering of one hundred oxen to the gods, and individuals seeking divine favor brought to local temples an endless parade of doomed domestic fowl and other small beasts. The Romans hardly engaged in any social act without solemnizing it with an animal sacrifice. The Temple in Jerusalem was daily spattered with the warm blood of doves, sheep, and bulls. For the parishioners of the ancient religions, worship would have held associations not with the scent of incense, but the smell of burning flesh.

While details varied from sect to sect, the basic elements of ritual animal sacrifice appear remarkably stable over time and place. To symbolically purify themselves, the participants bathed, changed their clothing, and in some cases abstained from sex for a period of time. The animal also was cleaned and decorated, sometimes lavishly. In Homer's *Odyssey*, Nestor gilded the horns of a sacrificial cow before breaking its neck in order to make it more pleasing to Athena. After the offering was led to the altar, the priest might wash himself again and sprinkle the victim with water. In many ceremonies, the participants might ritually taunt the animal, pelting it with harmless objects such as grain. Then the priest, making the invocation appropriate to the rite, would take out a knife or an ax, accompanied by the rising wail of the participants. As the weapon was poised over the hapless creature, the ceremonial shrieking would grow louder and louder, reaching a crescendo as the knife slit the animal's throat or the ax fell on its spine. If the animal was small, such as a bird or a cat, the priest might peremptorily break its neck with his bare hands. The animal's blood streamed out over the altar or was gathered into a bowl to be spattered over appropriate areas of the temple. Then the carcass was butchered, its entrails (especially the liver) inspected for auguries, and selected cuts roasted as a burnt offering to the god. The remaining flesh was prepared as a meal for the participants or in some cases restricted to the temple priests. On particularly solemn occasions, the entire animal would be burned in what the Greeks called a holocaust.

This minor drama of life and death recurred day in and day out for millennia in holy places throughout the ancient world. The faces of the divinities changed, from Zeus' paternal beard to Moloch's bovine likeness to Yahweh's formless, fiery *Sh'kinah*—the Presence or glory of the Lord. The purpose of the rituals varied as much as religious ceremonies do today. But beyond the mere formalities, the spectacle of the slaughtered beast touched a deeper aspect of human existence and in culture after culture unfolded into the central metaphor of humanity's spiritual quests.

Animal sacrifice is woven into the Bible from the beginning. Cain kills Abel out of envy for his brother's animal offering, and murder enters the world. The first thing Noah does after surviving the Flood and reaching dry land is to build an altar and sacrifice one of every "clean" animal he had gone to such laborious lengths to save from destruction. Those who wrote Genesis must have understood this to be the largest sacrifice ever to take place, and they might have imagined the smoke of the burned carcasses blotting out the sun in portentous reprise of the clouds that brought the forty days of rain.

But no story in the Bible embodies the mysterious burdens and rewards of faith as deeply as the sacrifice by Abraham on Mount Moriah. We tend to concentrate on the tremendous, almost unbearable inner conflict and confusion Abraham must have felt when God instructed him to sacrifice Isaac, the patriarch's only legitimate son and the seeming fulfillment of the divine covenant that Abraham would father a great nation. In almost cinematic fashion, we can visualize the knife lifted up over the helpless boy, the tension in the father's face, the seemingly endless pause right before the strike. Then suddenly an angelic voice calls out, telling Abraham he has proven his faith and should not harm his son. But the story does not end there. The angel does not tell Abraham to lay down the knife. As soon as the voice subsides, Abraham sees a ram with its horns caught in a thicket. Without any direction from the angel, he knows exactly what to do. He takes the ram and sacrifices it "in place of Isaac."

This detail is not an afterthought. In rabbinical writings, the ram is said to have been placed in the thicket on the sixth day of creation, just waiting for Abraham to discover it and fulfill his destiny. On a theological level, the substitution of the ram for Isaac may symbolize the moment when religion moved from formalism to ethics by recognizing the horror of human sacrifice and shifting to a system of animal victims. But something less abstract is at stake here. Without the sacrificial ram, the narrative would either have to end in Isaac's death at his father's hand, which would contradict any notion of a gracious deity, or the story would merely fizzle out, like a bad joke, with God appearing to be a capricious and petty puppeteer. He may have told Abraham to sacrifice Isaac, the moral would say, but he never meant it. Any normal person, including the devout Abraham, could not help but react with anger and the feeling that God was toying with his servant. The ram, however, ennobles the acts of both Abraham and Yahweh. Abraham's God *was* serious in requiring an oblation; but Abraham's obedience was sufficient to permit an animal to substitute for Isaac. The ram joins together the opposite realms of divine rule and free will: by taking Isaac's place, it allows the ultimate proof of Abraham's faithfulness and the fulfillment of Yahweh's promise to make Abraham the founder of a great nation. The story unfolding in the Bible depended on bringing these contradictions together. The biblical history of Israel was released to follow its course the moment Abraham loosened the ram from the thicket and led it to the altar.

The Greco-Roman world had its own history-making sacrifice analogous to Abraham's. After Paris had kidnapped Helen, and the Greek host was gathered at Aulis to sail against Troy, Artemis, the goddess of wild animals, became offended when Agamemnon, leader of the Greeks, killed a stag sacred to her. She sent a plague upon the host and frustrated the fleet's departure by calming the winds. The Greeks' soothsayer informed them that before the goddess would re- move her curse, she required the immolation of Agamemnon's own daughter, Iphigenia. Reluctantly, Agamemnon sent for his daughter and prepared her for sacrifice. At the last moment, however, Artemis snatched the girl away in a cloud and left a hind on the altar in her stead.

The story lacks the resonance of the biblical parallel, since Aga- memnon, unlike Abraham, has no claim to piety or moral leadership. His dilemma is purely political and familial, not spiritual. Nonethe- less, for the Greeks and Romans, the sacrifice at Aulis had a signifi- cance as culturally far-reaching as the one on Mount Moriah. Without the immolation of the hind, Artemis would not have let the

Greeks sail; without the departure of the fleet, no Trojan War; and without the Trojan War, a gaping hole would appear in Greek and Roman myth and legend. There would be no Homeric *Odyssey* and *Iliad*, the texts that defined Greek morality and religion during the Golden Age and produced a cast of heroic characters that filled the stages of Greek tragedy. There would be no legendary Trojan diaspora, which according to Roman mythmakers led to the founding of Rome by Aeneas. There would be no *Aenead*, which embodied the Roman Empire's sense of historic destiny.

Socrates brought a new, transcendental meaning to animal sacrifice, ironically at the very moment he forfeited his own life for the humanistic values of Athens. After drinking the cup of hemlock, his lifelong dialogue on truth and beauty faded to an end with these enigmatic last words: "I owe a cock to Asklepios; will you remember to pay the debt?" This odd request holds a rich paradox that summarizes his philosophy and defies understanding outside the context of animal sacrifice. In a reversal of the usual ritual, Socrates is saying that his friends should sacrifice a rooster to Asklepios, the god of medicine, on the philosopher's behalf, not because the god healed him, but because he did not. Death, asserts Socrates in reversing the meaning of sacrifice, is a greater state of health than life, because only death frees us from this illusory world and returns us to the realm of truth.

In the opening chapter of *Picture This*, Joseph Heller suggests the radical nature of Socrates' final statement by dramatizing the misunderstandings that might have ensued. Socrates' friends, ever faithful but not quite getting the philosopher's point, buy a rooster and deliver it to the only Asklepios they know, a local leather merchant. The authorities become suspicious at this cryptic activity surrounding the death of a convicted subversive. Sensing a plot, they take a bewildered Asklepios in for questioning. The merchant's inability to explain the meaning of the rooster only confirms his guilt in the eyes of the authorities, who summarily put him to death.

While not involving such Kafkaesque extremes, ignorance of

what animal sacrifice meant to the ancient world also leads to misunderstandings about the central elements of Christianity. The church was founded on the image of Christ, the Lamb of God, offering himself up for slaughter to atone for the sins of the world. Jesus, in Christian theology, takes on the role of the sacrificial animals whose blood was shed daily in the Temple. Christians "believe that the sacrificial tradition has reached its ultimate point and climax in the sacrifice of Christ." Under the influence of St. Paul in particular, even the teachings of Jesus became secondary to his function as a sin offering. St. Paul makes the connection explicit, reinterpreting the Jewish laws of animal sacrifice to be a prefiguration of Jesus' crucifixion:

> For the law having a shadow of good things to come, and not the very image of the things, can never with those sacrifices which they offered year by year continually make the comers thereunto perfect . . . But this man, after he had offered one sacrifice for sins for ever, sat down on the right hand of God. [Hebrews 10:1, 12]

This was the figure of Jesus Christ that captured the imagination of Greece and Rome, that inspired the writings of Augustine and Jerome—people who would have seen firsthand the drama of animal sacrifice. If Neitzsche was right when he said that the last Christian died on the cross, that the teachings of Jesus have languished in the shadow of his sacrificial persona, at least part of the reason is the power blood offering worked on the minds of his early followers.

Jewish converts to Christianity apparently continued to practice sacrifice until 70 A.D., when the Romans razed the Temple, the only site where Judaism permitted the ceremony. Thereafter, sacrifice ceased for Jews and Christians alike. As Christianity took root in Europe and paganism withered away, so did the practice of immolation.

The rise of Islam, which limited animal sacrifice to a few ceremonies like *Id al Adha* (the feast commemorating Abraham's sacrifice), also hastened the demise of the institution throughout the Mediterranean world.

Although Christianity disfavored animal sacrifice, it could not prevent it from mutating into other forms. From the ninth century onward, Europe experienced an outbreak of animal "trials" in which creatures such as pigs, wolves, and horses were summoned before civil and ecclesiastical courts to answer for their crimes of murder, destruction of property, consorting with the devil, and so on. As punishment, the animal felons were often hanged or burned at the stake, sometimes after having been dressed up in human clothing. The theory behind these trials is utterly incoherent to modern people, involving a mixture of belief in demon possession and collective guilt. But the dubious theology only thinly masks what was often the real goal of these public spectacles: divine propitiation through animal blood.

The surreal atmosphere of these trials is apparent in the records of the court case brought by the winegrowers of St. Julien, France, in 1545, against the weevils infesting their vineyards. The weevils, defended by Pierre Falcon and Claude Morel, "won" the case, and the court ruled only that public prayers should be recited. However, some forty years later, a new weevil infestation erupted, and a second complaint was filed:

Formerly by virtue of divine services and earnest supplications the scourge and inordinate fury of the aforesaid animals did cease; now they have resumed their depredations and are doing incalculable injury. If the sins of men are the cause of this evil, it behoveth the representatives of Christ on earth to prescribe such measure as may be appropriate to appease the divine wrath. Wherefore we the afore-mentioned syndics, Francois Amenet and Petramand Bertrand, do appear anew and

beseech the official, first, to appoint another procurator and
advocate for the insects in place of the deceased Pierre Falcon
and Claude Morel, and secondly, to visit the grounds and
observe the damage, and then to proceed with excommunication.

The weevils in this second case were represented by advocates
Antoine Filliol and Pierre Rembaud. The lawyers asked for a stay of
the proceedings, arguing that the Bible did not sanction such a law-
suit. After an adjournment of several weeks, the prosecution made its
case, using theological arguments based on the superiority of humans
to animals. The defense replied that animals were subject only to
natural law, not the laws of men. The court also heard the reports of
paid experts who examined the infested fields. A month later, the
lawyers appeared before the court again, with the defense arguing that
no further evidence should be allowed in this case. Meantime, the
winegrowers attempted a compromise: they offered to set aside a tract
of land for use by the weevils if the insects agreed to stay out of the
vineyards, with the proviso that the townspeople would retain mining
and water rights to the weevil sanctuary.

In September, the parties appeared in court to discuss the status
of the settlement. Antoine Filliol, defender of weevils, declared that
he could not accept the plaintiffs' settlement on his clients' behalf
since the land offered was barren and lacked the sustenance his ar-
thropod clients required. The plaintiffs' attorney denied the accuracy
of Filliol's characterization of the land. The court took the matter
under advisement. Regrettably, the final decision reached by the court
will never be known: some vermin (perhaps the weevils themselves,
angry at a negative ruling) destroyed the last page of the verdict.

As an attorney, I'm happy to learn that the courtroom conduct of
lawyers has not appreciably worsened in the last five hundred years.
But I know firsthand that the meticulous due process exhibited in the
St. Julien weevil trial would put to shame the defense most human

defendants receive in our criminal justice system, not to mention in our civil courts. Nor was this case an exception. Some of the best jurists of the Middle Ages vigorously represented rats, pigs, horses, cows, and grasshoppers. But we should not be deceived. The very procedural fastidiousness of these cases reveals the whole thing as a charade, a mere legal formality cloaking a deeper urge to find a scape-goat, a ritual sacrifice for community ills.

We quite properly laugh at these irrational spectacles. At the same time, however, our laughter should be tempered by the fact that we too engage in our own peculiar modes of scapegoating the animal world. The fishing industry in the Pacific Northwest constantly clam-ors for the government to thin the herds of sea lions in the area, pur-portedly because the animals feed on the dwindling number of salmon that return to the region's waterways. Some fishermen have even taken it upon themselves to kill the pinnipeds. And yet, common sense and every scientific study of the matter conclude that the plum-meting salmon population has its origin in excessive dam building, logging in salmon spawning grounds, water pollution, and other human activities. In the calculus of modern sacrifice, the sea lions stand in the place of all the people responsible for the problem who are harder to hold responsible than unarmed and unlawyered sea mammals.

Wildlife officials in this country have a general policy toward predators: when a bear or mountain lion kills or injures a person, it must be hunted down and shot. The usual rationale for the destruc-tion of these animals invokes the idea of protection against future attacks. Very little evidence exists suggesting a predator that attacks a person once will do so again with more frequency than any other creature. This is especially true of mountain lions, which rarely attack people. Nonetheless, a cougar mauling almost always causes animal control officials to swing into action and hunt the guilty feline down. Within a day or two, when they return with a puma carcass, a press release will follow that they believe they got the same animal responsible for the mauling. As if it hardly mattered whether the same or a different cougar were killed, so long as one of the creatures died.

These actions have something akin to the medieval animal trials. The metaphysically insecure rural inhabitants of Europe disguised their form of sacrifice in the byzantine procedures of early jurisprudence. We do the same but couch our expiations in the language of wildlife management. Down deep both reactions express an apprehension that somehow the natural order is threatened when an animal, especially a predator, attacks a human, based perhaps on our notion that we stand at the apex of evolution and should no longer be subject to predation. We have trouble thinking of ourselves as food; that is, as animals.

Our institutional treatment of animals provides all kinds of examples that invite comparison to the blood offerings of antiquity: the mechanized slaughterhouse, the medical research laboratory, trophy hunting. The difference is, we perform these sacrifices without sacrament. It would be glib, however, to suggest that animal sacrifice has simply continued on under different names. In fact, the most striking thing about the practice is how abruptly and completely it fell into disfavor. For several thousand years animal sacrifice was the central ritual of all the diverse religions of Europe, Northern Africa, and the Near East. Then, in a period of just a few centuries, the sacrificial knives were left to rust. Chance circumstances like the destruction of the Temple at Jerusalem and the hostility between pagans and Christians may have triggered the change, but they do not explain the swiftness and thoroughness of its demise. While sacrifice still occurs throughout the nonindustrial world, and even in America, among small sects such as Santeria (the right to do so was upheld by the U.S. Supreme Court in *Lukumi Babalu Aye vs. City of Hialeah, Florida*), most of us are shocked at the thought of killing animals for religious purposes.

The cause of our revulsion says a great deal about our attitude toward animals. To our credit, overt violence toward animals has become something of a taboo in our culture. An unwritten law exists in the film industry, for instance, that you can't shoot a dog in a movie; hundreds of people, yes, but a dog, no. People who violently abuse animals usually receive harsh sentences. But our ethical scruples go only so far. We slaughter millions upon millions of animals every year for food, livestock often raised in deplorably cramped and unsanitary conditions; and as many more die in the name of medical research and consumer product development, which by their very nature are cruel to the victims, whatever the validity of their goals. Let's be honest, our culture doesn't shrink from killing or even mistreating animals, as long as the purpose is (or is imagined to be) some material benefit such as food, medicine, or scientific knowledge.

And that's the key. We don't find animal sacrifice repulsive because it is cruel—the ritual borders on kindness compared to the conditions of life for many animals subjected to mechanized husbandry or vivisection. Rather, our disapproval stems from our belief that it *doesn't work.* If people thought that the immolation of living beasts could bring them prosperity, cure disease, or assuage their guilt, there would be a bloody altar on every street corner in America. Their absence is a tribute to rational thought and religious sophistication, but ironically it also underscores the spiritual marginalization of animals. Abraham's ram? Socrates' rooster? The Lamb of God? The images float by us with as little force as the one-dimensional creatures in a wildlife film.

We circle back to Lévi-Strauss and his epigram: animals are good for thinking. Our culture once worked out the grand religious mysteries of sin and forgiveness, death and resurrection, truth and illusion, through the shed blood of animals. The sacrifice was more than an offering to a deity; it was a method of focusing spiritual themes into a visible act. That was the real sacrifice animals made, the fact that they acted as a bridge to a deeper and more ethical understanding of our spiritual needs, one that thankfully no longer requires blood sacrifice to function. But those insights have become abstract and disembodied, and common religious traditions such as humility and gratitude play no part in how we actually deal with the living world around us. It is not so much that we mistreat animals—though surely recent history has seen the greatest displacement ever of fauna with human artifacts. But rather, we rarely think about them at all.

PART THREE

The Gospel
of Beasts

CHAPTER SEVEN

Wolf's Embrace

Lycanthropy
I comprehend, for without transformation
Men become wolves on any slight occasion
—Byron

Ask a person what historical figure or fictional character he or she would like to be, and you're likely to get an answer only after a long pause for reflection. Ask the same person: "If you were an animal, which would you be?"—and an immediate response will probably be forthcoming. A leopard, a wolf, an eagle, a bear, a tiger, a dolphin: there is an entire bestiary of creatures with which people identify. The reason people can so readily answer this exceedingly hypothetical question about shifting their species is that they in all likelihood have thought about the possibility beforehand. Most of us have singled out a particular kind of animal for special admiration, one we feel close to for reasons not always easy to articulate. Perhaps we once glimpsed the creature in the wilderness, or dreamed about it, or simply became fascinated by its form and habits while watching a wildlife documentary or visiting the zoo. It almost seems as if these animals choose us rather than the other way around.

History abounds with examples of people's special attachment to some animal or other, often of the most unlikely type. Alexander and his beloved horse; the poet Petrarch and his cat; E. O. Wilson's lifetime love affair with ants. I for one, like many people who grow up near the sea, have a long and sometimes painful history with jellyfish, during which time I've developed enormous respect for the power and beauty of creatures normally associated with lack of character and cowardice.

It began during a vacation my family took to the central coast of California when I was a boy. This was in the sleepy resort of Morro Bay, famous for the titanic rock that sits inexplicably in the center of the harbor like some fantastical insurance company logo. As we made the tourist cruise around the rock, I counted a couple hundred jellyfish basking in the water—strange, violet-colored hemispheres as large and delicate as a Southern lady's parasol.

When we got back to shore, I stood on the sea wall lobbing stones at any jellyfish foolhardy enough to float within range. One lucky rock hit a pulsating dome with a plop and the hapless creature turned inside out like a used gym sock and sank into the murk. I could almost hear it gurgling as it went down.

This mean prank must have angered the jellyfish spirits, because several times since then these aquatic invertebrates have almost done me in. Snorkeling off the Aegean isle of Naxos, I blundered into a school of pinkish peach-sized jellyfish the Greeks simply call medusae, after the mythological Gorgon whose hair consisted of writhing serpents and whose gaze turned people to stone (the name stuck and is now the zoological term for the free-swimming phase in the life cycle of the phylum to which jellyfish belong, Cnidaria). Though their sting is relatively mild, their crystalline bodies are virtually invisible, so my face and arms were lashed with burning stingers before I knew what hit me. I flailed, foundered, and probably would have drowned had not the captain of the boat jumped into a zodiac and plucked me out.

Worse was a trip to the Bahamas. There I swam into a school of what looked like crimson and blue party balloons. They were in fact Portuguese men-of-war, which are not individual animals at all, but colonies of medusoids that trail behind them forty feet of tentacles laden with neurotoxins. I got tangled in their stingers and felt what seemed like a carving knife slice around my thighs. Fortunately, again, a friend was there to pull my poor, cringing flesh to dry land.

These and other unpleasant encounters with jellyfish expiated the sins of my youth. You learn to respect an animal that almost kills you several times. And in fact, despite its lowly reputation, the jellyfish is one of nature's most ancient and successful predators, possessing an elegance and simplicity of design that has flourished for half a billion years. One variety, the sea wasp, kills more people each year than the mighty sharks. Another, *Cyanea arctica,* has tentacles trailing up to 250 feet from its purplish-red body, making it the longest animal ever to roam the planet, surpassing even the blue whale. I have, willingly or not, learned lessons of character from this underappreciated species, including the virtue of avoiding unnecessary harm, appreciating friends in need, recognizing the precariousness of life. I now feel grateful toward these noxious invertebrates.

In researching this book, I often encountered similar stories, with people relating their feelings of closeness toward some wild creature, usually a large predator of the canine, feline, ursine, or raptor variety. These emotions inhabit a cultural underground brimming with animals whose associations are contrary to the conventional wisdom of zoology and theology, and accordingly rarely if ever receive serious examination. Jungian analysis may be the exception, but it deals with animals almost exclusively as symbols of the emotional self, usually involving passion and sexuality, all of which may be valid and insightful, but it tends to pass over how animals and religious experience relate. Not surprisingly, then, our society has no interesting explanations, no compelling narratives about this underground bestiary of ours, the psychological affinity to the creatures out there and the creatures within.

In contrast, describe the same experiences to an Ojibwa medicine man, and an entire cosmology comes into focus. The animals that seem to call to us in dream visions (or in televisions) are, we might be told, *nigouimes,* guardian or helping spirits that either belong to animals or take their shapes. Most animistic cultures would proffer a similar reading, using their own local names for the guardian spirits— *nagual,* bush soul, *ié-kyla, ämägät*—and perhaps adding the suggestion that the relationship should be explored, contemplated, pursued, as an important part of a person's spiritual growth, since everyone, not just shamans, has a *nigouimes.* What is particularly interesting is that beasts of prey are the exemplary spirit guardians worldwide and across time, just as they are the fauna most often mentioned in response to the question about choosing a zoological alter ego.

But leave aside shamanism and faraway cultures. Even Chaucer and his contemporaries, Christians and good Catholics all, would have considered a dream about an animal or an encounter with a wild beast a significant matter with spiritual implications, one that could and should be interpreted through the application of symbolic thought. Wulfstan, the eleventh-century Archbishop of York, and one of the great sermonizers of his age, used to sign his homilies with the name *Lupus,* Latin for "wolf," a pun to be sure on his name (which means either wolf-stone, wolf's toe, or wolf's branch), but at the same time a powerful acknowledgment of the ancient Germanic tribal tradition in which the wolf was a quasidivine animal, worthy even of a theologian's respect. At a time when the wolf was a potent symbol of the outlaw and the devil, the clergyman could not have used his *nom de bête* (and his mother would not have christened him Wulfstan) unless an affinity with the wolf also had favorable associations Anglo-Saxon society understood and honored.

Only recently has the mystical pull of the animal world fallen from its status as a meaningful event and landed in the cultural broom closet. Like electric current through a wire, the alternation between the significant and the banal is what drives the workings of culture, and this is a case in point. Our religious self has in the past been clarified and strengthened through stories about the many ways humans and animals interact, not merely physically, but paradigmatically, mythically. Indeed, for primal societies, animal/human narratives embody virtually the entire corpus of sacred history. Modern religious discourse, in contrast, offers only an embarrassed silence on the topic. I was never told a Coyote story in Sunday school, and the countless fantastical zoological visions of saints and mystics in every religious tradition rarely if ever appear in church, synagogue, or mosque. We have exiled such matters to fairy tales for children, away from the serious business of faith. Perhaps we have grown too sophisticated for these metaphors. Or more likely, perhaps, official religion has some reason to be anxious about them.

So estranged are we from our affinity with animals that we have almost forgotten how to read animal narratives, and aspects of our culture with essentially religious motifs go unrecognized right before our eyes. An example is the werewolf legend, a man-animal reproduced endlessly in film and popular culture as a figure of horror, but in fact representing our own dark version of a Coyote story.

For late twentieth-century Americans, the image of the werewolf is inseparable from the figure of Lon Chaney, Jr., his tormented persona fleeing from one monster movie to the next seeking in vain surcease from the affliction of lycanthropy, an end he only achieves through violent death. The meaning of the werewolf genre is condensed into the one moment we all remember from these black-and-white films, the painful transformation from man to animal, shown through close-ups of Chaney's puffy, kindly face turning progressively bestial, hirsute, and vicious. Then the wolf man rushes out and slaughters someone. Beyond the thin supernatural conventions, the psychological theme is clear: the lupine characteristics symbolize the animal nature in all of us, depicted here as base, savage, irrational, murderous, and just waiting to erupt. It is no coincidence that the heyday of the werewolf movie was the 1930s and 1940s, when madness seemed about to overtake civilization, and nations that purported to be the most culturally refined had their hands steeped in blood.

But the werewolf has an older, more overtly religious provenance, one quite distinct from the dangerously tormented creature of horror films. In sixteenth- and seventeenth-century Europe, an outbreak of lycanthropy suddenly became a problem for local authorities. On January 18, 1573, in Dôle, France, one such wolf man was brought to trial in a proceeding not unlike dozens of others that took place during the century. An account of the trial included the following description:

> Gilles Garnier, lycophile as I may call him, lived the life of a hermit, but has since taken a wife, and having no means of support for his family fell into the way, as is natural to defiant and desperate people of rude habits, of wandering into the woods and wild places. In this state he was met by a phantom in the shape of a man, who told him that he could perform miracles, among other things declaring that he would teach him how to change at will into a wolf, lion, leopard, and because the wolf is more familiar in this country than the other kinds of wild beasts he chose to disguise himself in that shape, which he did, using a salve with which he rubbed himself for this purpose, as he has since confessed before dying after recognising the evil of his ways.

Garnier's alleged depredations included killing a twelve-year-old girl and partaking of her flesh, which he found so much to his liking that he brought portions home to his wife. He also killed a young boy, whom the court noted with fastidious Catholic disgust he devoured "in spite of the fact that it was Friday." After publicly admitting his crimes and repenting his sins, Garnier was found guilty of murder and lycanthropy, dragged through the streets, and burned alive.

This was the typical career of the werewolf in the late Middle Ages and Renaissance. The lurid details were often obtained through torture by inquisitors who knew exactly what they wanted, which may explain the consistency of the stories. The important thing to notice is that unlike the modern wolf man, who is afflicted with a curse not of his own desire or making (almost always the result of a werewolf bite), the historical "lycophile" willingly and purposely seeks the power to transform into an animal. Usually, he—and it almost always is a he, just as most witches were women—receives his shape-shifting abilities from a mysterious diabolical figure he encounters in the woods. The figure promises wealth and power (measured rather unambitiously in terms of healthy livestock and the like), in return for the performance of various acts against Christianity and the church. The ability to turn into a wolf is part of the deal, most often requiring the use of a magical salve or wolfskin provided by the mysterious benefactor. After the man is inducted into lycanthropy, he spends nights "coursing" through the woods, randomly attacking children and livestock, though avoiding men and groups of people, since unlike the modern version, the medieval werewolf was by no means invincibly strong and didn't require a silver bullet to be dispatched.

In many of these trials, neither the accused werewolf nor his prosecutors seem quite sure if the criminal physically transformed into an animal or merely acted in a bestial and unnatural manner. There is an ambiguous, dreamlike quality to the confessions, no doubt the result of prolonged torture, but also suggesting the mystical nature of the supposed metamorphosis. This question was a matter of some scholarly debate. Paracelsus, the famous Swiss alchemist, and French philosopher Jean Bodin offered what they considered irrefutable proof of actual transformation; while contrariwise in his 1597 work *Daemonologie*, King James I of England concluded that werewolves were the sorry victims of melancholic delusions, though he did generously concede that sorcerers could transmute themselves into the form of cats, hares, and weasels. The fact that wolves went extinct in Britain long before James took the throne may have influenced his opinion. Other scholars reasoned that a werewolf used a kind of mass hypnotism to deceive people into thinking that he had changed forms. King James' opinion, of course, won out over time, and courts found it increasingly expedient to institutionalize people suspected of shape-shifting, rather than burning them.

Until it was downgraded to a mental illness, lycanthropy in this incarnation played out the central themes of Christianity. It was the physical manifestation of willful apostasy and sin. The transformation from man to beast enacted the rejection of God's order, a turning from the divine image of the human form toward the bestial and grossly physical. Finally, the inevitable public confession and repentance of the werewolf confirmed the inner truth of the faith, where even those who made deals with the devil could be forgiven by God, though one hastens to add not by men. In this sense, lycanthropy was in this period another confirmation of divine truth, like the Apostles' Creed or the Mass, taking flesh-and-blood form for all to experience and dread. Just who merited the sanction of divine truth in these cases, the persecutors or the accused, has become obvious over time.

But there is an even older, more curious tradition. Originally werewolves were not ravening outcasts, but powerful guardians of society, culture heroes in touch with holy powers. Among the Norse, there existed warrior cults that went by the names úlfheðinn ("wolf-jacket") and berserker (bear-shirt). They were skilled fighters, supposedly impervious to pain, whose wild, maniacal attacks, preserved in our phrase "to go berserk," struck fear in the hearts of their enemies. The superhuman strength of berserkers may in fact have been drug-induced, like the ecstasies of shamans in many cultures, brought on by the ingestion of hallucinogenic mushrooms, perhaps fly agarics. The literature repeatedly notes the curious habit of berserkers gnawing on the edge of their shields just before going into their war frenzy. This may have been an act of intimidation, like the Confederate soldier's rebel yell. Or it might have been the way berserkers, having rubbed their shields with an elixir known only to them, secretly ingested the substance that triggered their battle fury.

Later literature portrays wolf-jackets and berserkers as mercenary boors who misuse their warrior skills to bully farmers and other decent folk. There is little doubt, however, that in the distant Germanic past, they constituted the vanguard of tribal defense, akin to the Cheyenne or Pawnee Wolf Soldiers—or our Navy Seals, for that matter.

The Pawnee tell the story of Bear-Man, a chief who took on his ursine qualities while in his mother's womb, because she listened to a story about an abandoned bear cub. Bear-Man was killed in an ambush, but the bears resurrect him, teach him their ways, and turn him into the greatest of warriors. Like Bear-Man, the animal namesakes of the berserkers and wolf-jackets were no mere mascots, but more like totems or *nigouimes* from which the warrior derived supernatural powers, including the ability not only to survive battle, but to cast spells, prognosticate the future, and compose poetry. According to legend, the more gifted of such warriors had the power to shift shape and fight their battles in animal form.

Perhaps the most celebrated Norse hero was Bothvar Bjarki, whose name means "War-Wolf Little Bear." According to the sagas, he lived up to his name by going into a trance and appearing on the battlefield in the form of a great warrior bear. Egil Skallagrimson was a berserker who embodied Iceland's defiance against the rule of Norwegian kings. Virtually unbeatable in battle, he was also one of Iceland's most gifted poets, and a practitioner of *seiðr*, the Old Norse equivalent of sorcery. Egil did not purport to turn into an animal, although he would enter into the berserker's frenzy which mimicked the behavior of a wild creature. His grandfather, however, was named Kvöldulfr, "Night Wolf," and he apparently was a full-blown werewolf.

Like all warriors and sorcerers, however, the berserkers and wolf-jackets had a dark, dangerous side. Egil was a champion of Icelandic independence, but he was also a violent homicide who could fly into a rage and kill without reason. But the fearsomeness of the werewolf in this tradition only confirms its metaphoric and metaphysical importance, not a uniformly negative reputation. Ultimately, the Norse tradition of wer-beasts has its roots in animistic beliefs that associate shape-shifting with spirituality and transcendence. "To behave like a beast of prey . . . ," notes Eliade, "betokens that one has ceased to be a man, that one incarnates a higher religious force, that one has in some sort become a god."

Despite overwhelming odds, the favorable, shamanistic thread of shape-shifting wound it way down the centuries, emerging into view here and there, even in the lycophobic years of the Middle Ages. As already mentioned, it survived in numerous given names such as Wulfstan ("Wolf-Stone"), Rudolf ("Victory-Wolf"), Bernard ("Bear-Bold"). It lives on in literature, from *Beowulf* (bee-wolf, i.e., a bear) to the movie *Dances with Wolves.* It is why comic superheroes nowadays take the form of Spiderman and Wolverine.

In the Old French romance *William of Palermo,* translated into English at the behest of Sir Humphrey de Bohun in 1350, we glimpse this older tradition. The brother of King Apulia, envious of the heir apparent, plots to kill the king's son, William. While the boy William is at play, a werewolf kidnaps him and carries him to a forest near Rome. Unlike most werewolves, William's kidnapper harbors benevolent motives, acting only to protect the boy from his uncle's murderous henchmen. The man-animal takes care of the child and they become friends:

> The wer-wolf embraces the king's son.
> With his fore-feet,
> And so familiar with him
> Is the king's son, that all pleases him,
> Whatever the beast does for him.

In reality, the werewolf is Alphonso, heir to the Spanish throne, transformed by his stepmother, Queen Braunde, as part of her scheme to make her own son Braundinis king. After numerous plot twists common to romances, William grows up with the werewolf's help, becomes a skilled soldier, marries the daughter of the Emperor of Rome, defeats Braundinis, and forces Braunde to return Alphonso to his human shape.

The fact that a kindhearted wolf man could appear as the protagonist in a medieval romance demonstrates that lycanthropy consisted of several religious strands, some negative, some positive, well into historical times.

This brief history of lycanthropy shows the curious trajectory of shape-shifting in Western civilization. From a manifestation of protective spiritual power and creativity, the werewolf became a representative of corrupt, sinful humanity, and then a victim of pathology and madness, devoid of religious content. Since he was a victim, even the wolf man's symbolic meanings finally became suspect, since we tend to require the embodiments of our hopes and fears to take action rather than merely suffer. Lycanthropy does not resonate with us anymore; werewolves seem remarkably mild horrors in a world of genocide and serial murderers who look like the guy next door. Ultimately, the wolf man passed into the realm of farce. Chaney's last depiction of the tormented shape-shifter was in *Abbott and Costello Meet Frankenstein,* which included the following exchange, the silver bullet that killed the genre:

CHANEY: "You don't understand. Every night when the moon is full, I turn into a wolf."

COSTELLO: "You and fifty million other guys."

The theme of shape-shifting lives on, however, in different forms, appropriately enough. Our literary transformations from man to animal now are the work of science rather than the devil, of genetic engineering gone bad, not the supernatural. The werewolf has been displaced by the mad scientists of *The Fly* (both the Vincent Price and Jeff Goldblum versions) and *The Island of Dr. Moreau,* men who willfully if tragically tamper in things better left to providence. These instances seem to circle back to the sensibility of the werewolf trials, where transgression against divine law is made manifest in the melding of animal and human identities.

If the werewolf and berserker have any important resonance today, it is in a purely secular, highly derivative context. We glimpse him in the stereotype of the rock star, who is expected to act in an unrestrained, frenzied manner. Constantly held in check by rules, customs, and ethics, we long to see rock musicians live out our darker desires, take drugs, engage in promiscuous sex, grow their hair long, commit minor felonies, appear half naked in public, and generally thumb their noses at society. The Who trash their instruments, Jimi Hendrix sets his guitar on fire, Ozzy Osborne bites off the head of a live bat, the Sex Pistols spit at their fans: to all this violent and vulgar behavior, the crowds applaud precisely because it disregards the rules of civilized society. The reason rock music falls into this mode, repeating the same antisocial behavior year after year, has less to do with the propensities of any individual than the fact that we demand performers to play a public role akin to a berserker. Even the names of groups suggest a shape-shifter connection: the Beatles, the Animals, the Birds, the Turtles, the Eagles, the Monkees, Toad the Wet Sprocket, Whitesnake, Ratt. It is no coincidence that modern industrial society, perhaps the most regulated form of humanity in the history of the world, should have created rock and roll, an island of animality in an ocean of control.

We project similar if less intense expectations on actors and comedians. Think of Bobcat Goldthwaite setting Jay Leno's chair on fire. For us, these performances are the flesh-and-blood embodiments of creativity, independence, even sexuality. We hope to increase those qualities in ourselves by experiencing what they have to give in the unrestrained space of art. And we have similar contradictory feelings of awe and distrust as the proper Scandinavian burgher did to wolf-jackets: we lionize performers, but would probably prefer our daughter not marry one.

The conflicting feelings invoked by the shape-shifter perhaps help explain the silence of modern religion toward the affinity between humans and animals. In religious context, sexuality easily spills into lust; creativity, irrationality; independence, disobedience. Official religions have always sought clear rules to define their faith, from the Ten Commandments to the religious loyalty oaths. Animal metaphors do not fit into this text- and linguistic-based form of religion, since they constantly threaten to overflow the meanings we give them, to erupt out of symbolic control.

The Chinese epic *A Journey to Heaven* depicts the gradual evolution of beasts into men, and then into saints worthy of paradise. Each animal brings its own quality to the drama: the monkey its ambition, the horse its endurance; even the indolence of the pig plays a part in the ascent of creation toward spirit. The story's vision of spiritual history has a lesson for us today. We piece together our spiritual identities not from rules dropped from heaven, but from the menageries of qualities that the world down here provides. Parts of our character are like the wolf, the bear, and the swan, and in regarding that likeness we better understand our own souls.

Early Christianity knew this. In the *Physiologus* (which by the way never mentions wolves), animals are good for faith, just as they are good for thinking, according to Lévi-Strauss. Our spiritual nature needs not only divine texts, but the fertile, dangerous relationships we have with animals, to reveal with each attraction and disapproval our identities as religious beings. This is the profound sense in which William of Palermo embraces his werewolf benefactor and regains his kingdom. Embracing our deepest thoughts toward animals, we stand to gain no less.

CHAPTER EIGHT

The Hobbyhorse of Jesus

Teddy bears still have their picnic in the woods, and animals reassume their
awesome nature in nightly dreams.
—JULES CASHFORD

Toys are enigmatic objects. Perhaps the strangest artifacts we humans create. And the most perplexing thing about them is that they should in any way perplex us, since nothing more familiar, domestic, and benign accompanies us through life, literally from cradle to grave, as the shapes, sounds, and colors of toys.

Yet the very intimacy of toys sometimes gives us pause. They are associated with a part of our identities that fades into the background with the passage of childhood. Call it innocence, the Platonic pure soul, the Romantic unfettered imagination—whatever it is, the pangs of its absence can unexpectedly leap out at us from the happy form of some insignificant plaything. For this reason, to an adult eye, toys sometimes seem to harbor half-buried meanings—you might almost say a life—belied by their innocent forms. No wonder people enjoy stories about toys that come to life, whether as the dancing Nutcracker, Woody the talking cowboy, or the homicidal doll, Chuckie. Narratives about living toys relate what many of us feel whenever we open an old box in an attic and find a dusty teddy bear or Raggedy Ann staring back at us as if about to speak after a long silence.

Just as a person cannot hear the exact timbre of his own voice because the organs of speech lie so close to the inner ear, so the toys that support vast emotional meanings for us during youth seem to defy understanding after we become adults. When I was a boy growing up in Southern California, I used to make toy boats out of Popsicle sticks and sail them down a small irrigation ditch near my home. Since then, I have traveled most of the world's oceans, and rafted some of the largest, wildest rivers on earth. But I have never sailed on bigger waters than I did as a boy alongside that ditch, watching those fragile Popsicle-stick boats float away. My rational mind tells me this makes no sense, but in the clash between reason and play, toys win.

For children, toys populate not just physical space, but an alternate universe of the imagination. They are our most personal possessions, the tools by which we comprehend our limitations and possibilities. As we mature, however, that relationship subsides, and our toys, like broken seashells washed up on dry land, remain behind as mere artifacts from the lost worlds of childhood. Usually, they evoke in us only the sadness and joy of nostalgia, rather than any awareness of what these bits of plastic, wood, and cloth once meant. Unaccustomed as we are to examining the playthings strewn at our feet by our children, we may not even notice the remarkable fact that most toys (and the earliest toys found in history) take the form of animals.

The existing studies of toys, such as they are, never try to account for this zoological connection. Instead, they usually conclude that toys arise out of two childhood needs: identification with the adult world, and the desire to nurture. Thus, the toy industry produces Hotwheel cars and baby dolls, soldiers and miniature tea sets, Rock 'em Sock 'em Robots and Operation (the goofy game for dopey doctors). While this explanation has its appeal, it fails to account for most of our animal toys, and hence, most toys in general. Children do more than just nurture stuffed animals, or subject plastic menageries to mock-adult treatment. They ride their toys into imaginary worlds, speak through them, play out dramas, engage in conversations, befriend them. It would be only a slight exaggeration to say that one of the deepest and most enduring emotional relationships most Western people have in their lives is an attachment to a teddy bear or some other stuffed creature.

To understand this unexplored affinity between animals and toys, we must travel to the ancient Persian province of Elam, to the city of Susa, the "city of lilies," during the reign of King Utash-Gal, eleven hundred years before the birth of Christ. There, on a morning in late spring, a group of citizens gathered at the site chosen for a new temple—dedicated perhaps to Ishtar, goddess of fertility. To celebrate the laying of the temple's cornerstone, the townspeople brought pottery, jewelry, and small votive objects. The event may have looked something like a scene from a Breughel painting, with all classes of society, from satraps to pickpockets, mingling and making merry. As the ceremony reached its climax, one by one the participants handed their offerings to a priest, who flung each gift into a recess over which the massive baked brick cornerstone would be levered into place.

One person, perhaps a little girl urged on by her proud parents, brought to the priest a small figurine carved of white limestone and resting on a wheeled platform with a string attached in front. Perhaps the figure represents a porcupine or a hedgehog. Perhaps it is a piglet. In any case, it took its place alongside the other pious objects to await holy burial.

Almost three thousand years pass before the carved hedgehog sees the light of day again. Unearthed by archaeologists, it is proclaimed to be the oldest confirmed toy ever found. Presumably, the little Elamite girl held the string and pulled the hedgehog behind her through her city's lily-lined paths, just as children today have pull-toys in the form of wheeled dachshunds and ducks.

But is this hedgehog really a toy? Archaeologists have to hedge their bets: they admit that the little rodent might instead be a fetish, a sacred object representing some animal spirit whose meaning to the ancient inhabitants of Susa has disappeared into the desert as completely as the kingdom's lilies.

Mere plaything or divine image? Few objects in the modern world seem to embrace this breadth of possible meanings. The trinket fits into the palm of your hand, yet no one can with certainty situate it on either extreme of social values, the sacred or the juvenile.

When it comes to toys, this ambiguity goes far beyond the little hedgehog of Susa. From the Bronze Age come even earlier candidates for the first toy: backed clay rattles with the heads of foxes, dogs, and birds. Most archaeologists conclude these were ritual burial objects, but for all we know they could have been made to pacify a fidgety baby while its mother did the wash. Similarly, most experts believe that the small wooden crocodiles and lions, complete with movable jaws, made in Egypt from about 1000 to 500 B.C., were probably children's playthings. However, given the ancient Egyptians' obsession with gods in animal form and their genuine love of animals, no one can say for sure that these figures did not have some serious religious purpose not unlike a Catholic rosary or a Greek Orthodox icon, which are also deceptively homely objects.

The answer to the question of whether these artifacts are sacred or profane is probably: yes. A toy could have been both plaything and religious object, despite the neat division we feel compelled to make in our culture between spiritual matters and juvenilia. This duality appears in the kachina dolls among the Hopi and the other Pueblo Indians of the Southwest. Kachinas are spirit beings that take many forms—deer, sun, eagle, blue corn, dragonfly, cloud. Many Hopi religious ceremonies involve masked dancers who personify the kachinas appropriate for the season and the ritual. Hopi men also make representations of these spirits, usually from cottonwood root, feathers, and animal horn, as gifts for their children, nieces, and nephews. Prior to a kachina ceremony, each child in a family may receive a kachina doll made especially for him. The parents then hang the dolls up on the walls of their homes, so that the children can contemplate the sacred history embodied in the spirits the dolls represent.

All this sounds rather solemn. But no matter how hard the adults try to stop them, inevitably, Hopi children get at the kachina dolls and play with them just as Anglo children might play with Barbie and G.I. Joe.

If Hopi children can amuse themselves with kachina dolls, then ancient people could probably balance play and piety on the back of a stone hedgehog or wooden crocodile. And the same goes for us. In our culture, toys—especially toys in the form of animals—also often harbor spiritual meanings, though they tend to be more elusive than those found in more religious cultures, and easily become lost in all the plastic and crass marketing of modern times.

In *The Cricket on the Hearth,* Dickens created the character of Caleb Plummer, a toymaker. Caleb makes the following observation, instantly understandable to Dickens' readers (and to Europeans at least as far back as the sixteenth century), but which probably makes little sense to today's audience:

> There's rather a run on Noah's arks at present! I could have wished to improve upon the Family, but I don't see how it's to be done at the price. It would be a satisfaction to one's mind, to make it clearer which was Shems and Hams, and which was Wives. Flies an't on that scale neither, as compared with elephants you know!

Caleb's concern involves the most popular toy of his day, the equivalent of our Teenage Mutant Ninja Turtles or Mighty Morphin Power Rangers. It was a toy Noah's ark. Inspired by the biblical story of the Flood, toymakers began carving miniature versions of the ark at least as early as 1590. The toy usually consisted of a wooden boat, figures of Noah and his wife (usually bent with age) and their fellow travelers, sons Shem, Ham, and Japheth, with their respective wives.

Distinguishing the Shems, the Hams, and the nameless spouses was difficult, which apparently led to many a childhood squabble, as Caleb's comment indicates.

But the heart of the play ark was the animals. Often painted in bright colors, three or four hundred beasts (including offbeat creatures like flies, obviously not to scale, to Caleb's chagrin) might accompany a well-made, deluxe ark. Parents encouraged their children to reenact the Flood and other biblical tales using this toy.

In fact, the ark became known as the "Sunday toy," because in strict Protestant homes all children's playthings were put away on the Christian Sabbath except the toy ark. The reason: while the arks, unlike kachina dolls, were not sacred objects in themselves, they did impart spiritual history, and hence had a significance that went beyond their worldly use as playthings.

We live in times much more secular than Dickens' Victorian England could have imagined. Nonetheless, our animal toys retain a patina of spirituality that merely needs to be burnished with religious history to shine again. Consider, for instance, the hobbyhorse.

One of the earliest depictions of this toy appears in a fifteenth-century drawing by an unknown Dutch or German artist. The work shows St. Dorothy, the virgin-martyr who suffered under Emperor Diocletian, watching over the infant Jesus as he rides a hobbyhorse (and inadvertently steps on the saint's robes). The image strikes us as comically discordant; we do not expect to see the sanctity of the Christ Child mingled with a plaything available today on the shelf of any Toys Я Us. It is as if Michelangelo, in painting the Sistine Chapel's Creation of Adam, had portrayed the sublime and mighty hand of God reaching life into the first man adorned with a mood ring.

Ironically, the hobbyhorse is probably the only accurate thing in the whole drawing. St. Dorothy lived three centuries after Jesus, and wasn't likely to meet her Messiah, at least not in this world. The two figures wear anachronistic clothing. The perspective and proportions of the drawing are all off. But the hobbyhorse on which the Christ Child rides was probably as common in first-century Palestine as it is today.

We know, for example, that Socrates was once seen fooling around on a hobbyhorse. So was the Spartan king Aegilias, ostensibly while showing some boys how better to handle a horse, but obviously with an embarrassing amount of childlike enjoyment, since he made everyone promise never to mention the incident (a promise someone obviously didn't keep). The child Jesus, therefore, may very well have played in the dusty streets of Nazareth riding his favorite stick pony: a poignantly humane echo of the fearsome Messiah of Revelation, who appears to John bestriding a white, end-of-the-world steed, smiting the nations with a sword that swings from out of his mouth.

Of course, the fifteenth-century artist who drew St. Dorothy and the Christ Child had no way of knowing the history of hobbyhorses. For this reason his choice of toys is all the more illuminating. It had to derive not from a desire to realistically portray his subject, but from a deeper source he could only have unconsciously sensed: the ancient spiritual overtones associated with the hobbyhorse.

The next time you see a child on a hobbyhorse, particularly a rocking horse, take a moment to observe the remarkable event that unfolds. When a child gets on the toy creature, he leaves the physical landscape of limitations and everyday reality, and enters into a country of the imagination. To what destination exactly is the child riding? In what territory is he traveling? While literally standing still, he makes a mental journal you can almost witness as he stares off into a world invisible to the naked eye. We only need to read D. H. Lawrence's short story "Rocking Horse Winner" to get an idea of how ecstatic, if not frightening, that mock journey can be.

The most familiar adult image obviously analogous to a child on a hobbyhorse is a witch on a broomstick. This is no coincidence. The idea of riding, especially on a symbolic mount, is closely associated with spiritual journeys, for good or ill purposes, throughout history and across cultures. The central role of a shaman involves making a journey to the spirit realm in order to correct temporal problems, such as disease, at their root. In Old Norse mythology, the chief god, Oðin, would make just this kind of sojourn on his eight-legged horse, Sleipnir. Shamans from many parts of the world have similar mystic mounts that carry them to the other world. The Old Norse rune for the letter "R" was called *reið*—"riding"—and had connotations of spiritual travel. By the Middle Ages, through a long process of debasement, Oðin the shaman god, mounted on his furious steed thundering into the land of the dead, declined into the figure of an unnatural hag straddling a broomstick on her way to stir up infernal mischief. Indeed, the origin of the hobbyhorse may not be as a toy at all, but as a shamanistic prop, as it appears in the ecstatic rituals of a number of cultures, including British May Day festivities in the form of Morris dancers.

All this may seem far removed from modern spirituality. But perhaps not. The symbolic relationship between travel, especially pilgrimage, and spiritual growth is known to all societies. In the West it is enshrined in such literary works as Chaucer's *Canterbury Tales* and Conrad's *Heart of Darkness*. But a pilgrimage need not involve physical transport, and the greatest journeys, as the toy boats of my youth prove, can take place within the smallest arc or ark. When a parishioner or member of a synagogue closes her eyes and begins to pray, what occurs is in fact a kind of journey. The most familiar prayer can represent a type of ecstasy, a stepping out of our mundane selves to enter a realm where we focus on the divine in a way we cannot during our everyday comings and goings. The bodily shivers of a Pentecostal, or the davening of an Orthodox Jew at the Wailing Wall even seem to mimic the very motions of a child on a rocking horse.

No one would suggest that children are making shamanic voyages into dreamtime on toy horses. Quite the contrary, the ecstatic shaman, the devout Christian, the pious Buddhist, Muslim, and Jew may owe their religious sensibilities to their childhood rides into the imagination. If we did not learn to negotiate the intangible landscapes of infancy with the help of our animal toys, we might not even know how to make the leap of faith into prayer as adults. Both involve pilgrimages of the mind.

This leads us to the focal point of most of our childhood play: stuffed animals. In the Western world hardly a child's bedroom exists that does not have dozens of these unique possessions. Our babies sleep with them. We give them as gifts to people we love. We call them by names. Several million stuffed animals are bought in America and Europe each year, making them one of the most replicated nonutilitarian objects humankind has ever produced. Yet despite all this, most people don't give a second thought to the throng of animal forms let loose in their homes, their children's rooms, their own beds. Surely these artifacts must tell us something about our relationship to animals.

I should emphasize *our* relationship, because stuffed animals are a very recent development, a unique byproduct of the modern world. One might call them the most unrecognized craze of industrial society. While archaeologists have unearthed cloth dolls almost fifteen hundred years old, no stuffed animal has ever been found that dates before the eighteenth century. It could be that stuffed animals, being mere playthings made of perishable material, simply aren't the type of artifact likely to survive the passage of centuries. But besides the lack of physical remnants, there is a complete absence of early references to stuffed animals in the written records. We can read about children's games going back to the earliest literature: the sixth-century B.C. Greek philosopher Heraclitus mentions the game of jacks as a metaphor for how the gods rule the universe. But since history is silent about stuffed animals until very recent times, we can safely say these strange icons belong uniquely to modern times.

This modernity is perhaps the oddest thing about stuffed animals. A society that has distanced itself from animal creation to a greater

degree than any previous culture has ironically become the most prolific shaper of animal images ever to exist.

Animal images: we shouldn't let the phrase mislead us into thinking that stuffed animals are an attempt to imitate zoological reality.
People have been depicting animals at least since the Lascaux cave
paintings, but very few of these images have anything to do with
realism. We look at Ice Age cave paintings and recognize the figures
as bison, rhinoceroses, deer. Nonetheless, we understand that the
stylized bodies and exaggerated forms are meant to depict something
quite distinct from mere bodily existence. What that something is,
we don't know for sure: the animal soul, a god of some kind, the
power of fertility unleashed with the coming of spring.

The same is true for stuffed animals. Take a look at a teddy bear,
the most popular stuffed animal since the early twentieth century. If
it's a common teddy bear, it hardly looks like a bear at all. The legs
dangle straight under the torso; the arms lie by its side or stretch open
at right angles to the body; the face is more or less flat; no sharp teeth;
no claws. The form is obviously as much human as ursine, but what
does that tell us? How come we rarely make teddy bears that look like
real bears?

Most people know a little bit about the recent history of the teddy
bear. In 1902, President Teddy Roosevelt went to Mississippi to help
settle a border dispute with the state of Louisiana. During his visit,
he took some time out to pursue one of his favorite pastimes, bear
hunting. Seemingly in luck, the President come upon a bear and had
the creature in the crosshairs of his rifle, when he realized the bear
was just a cub. The future candidate of the Bull Moose Party refused
to kill the animal, an act of mercy immortalized by Clifton Berryman,
a cartoonist for the *Washington Star*, who subtitled the incident:
"Drawing the Line in Louisiana."

The cartoon appeared in newspapers all over the nation, and
caught the attention of Morris Michtom, a Russian immigrant who

owned a small toy store in Brooklyn. Mitchtom designed a stuffed bear, with soft movable limbs and button eyes, and put a couple samples in his window with a copy of the cartoon and a label christening the toy "Teddy's Bear." Michtom's creation caught on, and by the end of the decade millions of teddy bears had been produced by toy manufacturers all over the world. Michtom's store, by the way, became the Ideal Toy Company, one of America's largest producers of stuffed animals.

What this well-known story leaves out is the status of stuffed bears *before* Theodore Roosevelt's ursine encounter in the Mississippi woods. Teddy bears existed long before the twenty-sixth president, going back at least as early as the eighteenth century, when they went by the name "Bruin" among English speakers. As late as 1906, an advertisement in the May issue of *Playthings*, a toy industry magazine, read:

THIS IS BRUIN'S DAY—The American line of jointed plush bears is the real thing—Polar Bear, Cinnamon Bear, Grizzly Bear—Baker & Bigler, Sole Manufacturers, 7-0 Bleecker St. corner of Broadway, New York City.

"Bruin" is the name bears often had in beast fables and bestiaries, the fictional bear of moral literature, the bear that had a spiritual lesson to teach, often a harsh lesson. In Aesop's fable of the bear and two travelers, for instance, two men came upon a bear; the faster one climbed a tree; the slower one fell down and played dead. The bear sniffed over the prone man for a while and then departed. The traveler in the tree came down and asked his companion what the bear whispered to him when he put his mouth to his ear. The other man replied, Never again to travel with a friend who would desert him at the first sign of danger.

At almost the exact same time Bruin began showing up in children's cribs, another form of stuffed animals was coming into vogue, perhaps shedding light on the teddy bear's meaning. I am referring to the products of taxidermy, perhaps the weirdest, most macabre practice the West has ever invented.

Taxidermy—the skinning, preserving, and mounting of animals for display—appears to have begun sometime in the eighteenth century. A few isolated examples of stuffed animals appear in history before then: Plutarch, for instance, was known to have affectionately stuffed his beloved pet after its demise. For the most part, however, the historical record is devoid of this practice, even where you might expect to find it. In *Sir Gawain and the Green Knight,* for instance, a fourteenth-century poem that depicts in excruciating detail the stalking, killing, and dismembering of various game animals, no mention is made of preparing the carcasses as trophies. In 1798, Dr. Johnson's friend Mrs. Thrale wrote that while in Venice she saw a long line of people at a sideshow waiting to see a stuffed horse, an incident that suggests taxidermy was still a novelty as late as the nineteenth century.

Taxidermy presumably developed out of trophy hunting among aristocrats who had the time, money, and space to document their recreations. But the practice only really caught on with the rise of the natural history museum. In the late seventeenth and early eighteenth centuries, scientists and collectors began assembling large numbers of zoological specimens. The collections became the core of museums, and these institutions required new methods for preserving carcasses for study and exhibition before an urbanized public increasingly interested in the wonders of nature, especially distant marvels from such places as Africa. The result is the dioramas of bears, lions, zebras, and other large fauna that most of us first experience while on a school field trip.

Having grown up with these displays of gutted and stuffed animals, we don't really fully appreciate the bizarre nature of this art. A contemporary of Shakespeare would likely find the American Museum of Natural History in New York slightly sacrilegious and utterly demented. A contemporary of Chaucer might possibly burn the place down as some kind of temple of death that denied the deeper significance of God's creation. We sense a similar uneasiness with taxidermy when the specimens escape from the museum context. Viewers of the *Addams Family* television series immediately understood that the giant stuffed polar bear and moose head in the living room served as symbols of the protagonists' morbid eccentricities (especially when the creatures growled or trumpeted). Most of us would probably look askance if an acquaintance, even if a hunter, began mounting the entire bodies of large mammals around his house. It just doesn't seem to be a wholesome interest.

Yet taxidermy is seductive. The sheer size and bulk of these imitations usually prevents us from recognizing the fact that taxidermy is just as stylized, just as unreal, as the stuffed animals in a baby's crib. The skin of a grizzly bear, stretched over a frame, fitted with glass eyes, and bearing its canines through plastic lips has as little to do with *Ursus horribilis* as Michtom's button-eyed creation. This is because taxidermy is less about preserving real animals than displaying a philosophical attitude toward animal creation. Prior to and during the Renaissance, animals had meanings. They taught us about God and about ourselves, and to the Renaissance mind, their behavior and forms reflected those moral verities. That, at least, was the story told by religions and mythologies that stretched back to the earliest times. And it is a story we still follow today on some level when we talk to our pets or say a person is as sly as a fox.

By the seventeenth century, however, science began to tell a different story. In this narrative, animals were mere anatomy, soulless matter subject to the brute laws of nature, no more than the sum total of their parts and not much different than machines, a comparison Descartes made, assuring his readers that dogs had no feelings even when they howled in pain, but only physical reactions attributable to their nervous systems. The eternally upright bears and silently roaring lions of the natural history dioramas are perfect monuments to this worldview, lifeless simulacra that can be posed and duplicated at will as the uncomplaining stand-ins for all of the animal kingdom. They are, as it were, the trophies of science.

My point is not to quarrel with the scientific mission of natural history museums. Uncounted millions of people—especially urban people, and especially the generation that grew up before the rise of television—got their first exposure to wild animals through these institutions. As Stephen Gould put it, the fourth floor of the American Museum of Natural history "was the shrine, the principal magic place, the sanctum sanctorum" that convinced him to become a paleontologist. I'm sure many other scientists have similar feelings. I only want to underscore the fact that the fauna exhibits represent only the anatomical aspect of animals (which is no small matter, by the way, and a great leap in understanding from earlier times). And these zoological images fit into the single-minded narrative of animals as soulless matériel, a narrative that has become more or less official in our secular world. But as I have stressed throughout this book, science did not win a complete victory over the earlier understanding of animals. Science never does win a complete victory. Instead, the moral, spiritual aspects of animals went underground, into the most unlikely forms of popular culture. One of these was the teddy bear.

This parallel history in our curious urge to make images of living things suggests the schizophrenia in our attitude toward animals. The modern, dominant view of animals found its narrative in the frozen icons of taxidermy, emphasizing physical verisimilitude, anatomy, biomechanics. The older view melted into the sympathetic, anthropomorphized shapes of stuffed toys, sent off to friendly exile in the play world of children, where they can no longer offend reason by being taken seriously, but where they can comfort us nonetheless. Bruin, Reynard the Fox, Ishtar's (Easter's) sacred rabbit may never have received the imposing, official memorials of the natural history museum, but they exploded into an army of stuffed toys as enigmatic as the painted beasts on the walls of Ice Age caves.

In the end, the moral animals of the Middle Ages and Renaissance may have gotten the better deal. As our understanding of ecology has grown, and as science has slowly freed itself from the nineteenth-century mania for collecting and universalizing, the natural history diorama begins to look increasingly outmoded, if not tawdry. When most of us can watch detailed documentaries on the complex lives of wild animals virtually every night on cable television, a stuffed lion standing before a painted African sunset seems a pitiful end to the king of the beasts, not a great moment in science. Moreover, taxidermy is simply archaic as a teaching tool, like giving a Viewmaster to a kid who is used to video games.

The next time you go to a museum of natural history, take along a teddy bear and go to the grizzly bear diorama. More than likely the museum specimen will stand upright and angry, frozen in a timeless threat it can never carry out, while your stuffed animal, with its big round head and dangling limbs, will stare back at you pleasantly. You will have before you the icons of two conflicting perspectives toward animals and spirituality that have drifted apart for the last few centuries. Then ask yourself which one of these two bears means more to you.

In the clash between reason and play, stuffed animals win.

CHAPTER NINE

Not Naming Bears

. . . a cat must have three names . . .
—T. S. ELIOT

The English language does not have a name for "bear." This remark will naturally strike most people as a contradiction in terms, the literary equivalent of Magritte's painting of a pipe entitled *This Is Not a Pipe.* My sentence appears to enact its own negation. But in fact, English and all the other Germanic languages do in fact lack a word for the genus *Ursus.* The nouns "bear" and "bruin" are circumlocutions meaning "the brown one." They are an attempt specifically not to call the animal by name. The direct Indo-European word for the animal, *rks,* was rejected by Germanic tribes sometime in distant prehistory, though it has gotten into the language in a roundabout fashion through Greek in the noun "arctic," the land under the constellation of Ursa Major, the Great Bear.

The euphemistic etymology of "bear" conforms to a linguistic practice well documented among tribal people: the use of indirect terms to refer to animals considered taboo. Creatures powerful enough to have taboo status might become angry if addressed by their real name, just as we feel perturbed when total strangers call us by our first name. Animistic cultures sought the solution to this problem in coining oblique, honorific titles that talk around the animal's true name, as a token of respect. Anthropologists sometimes refer to these "safe" names by the Tongan term *noa* names.

English is just one of many languages with *noa* names for bears. Lappish, Ainu, Inuit, and dozens of other cultures have all developed elaborate euphemisms for the animal: "wintersleeper," "unmention-able one," "four-legged human," "forest master," "old man," "divine little dear thing who resides among the mountains," and the most pragmatic, "that's him." Beowulf, the hero of the Anglo-Saxon epic poem, not only has bearlike qualities (such as crushing his enemies with a bear hug), but also what appears to be an ursine *noa* name: Beowulf means "bee-wolf," i.e. "the plunderer of honey," a bear. The prominence of such euphemisms goes hand in hand with the impor-tant role bears play in the indigenous rituals of these cultures. Anthro-pologists have long recognized the existence of a circumpolar bear cult encompassing numerous northern groups that consider the animal a spirit guardian of immense power. The existence of our *noa* name "bear" implies that ancient Germanic tribes must have held the ani-mal in similar religious awe, a respect that reaches out from the dis-tant past to leave its mark on modern English vocabulary.

It is a sobering thought to consider that every time we talk about a child's teddy bear, we are reenacting the ritual precaution of animis-tic cults that wandered the frozen roof of the world before the build-ing of the pyramids.

The naming of animals has always fascinated humans. It appears right in the beginning, Genesis 2:19–20, where Yahweh parades the beasts before Adam for him to name. Indeed, the naming of the ani-mals is described in the Bible as the first action ever taken by Adam; the second being his eating the forbidden fruit. Thus, in Hebrew tradition, the names of animals preceded the Fall and constituted one of the few prelapsarian elements to survive Adam's transgression in-tact, since to Christians and Jews alike it was evident that Adam and his progeny until the Tower of Babel spoke Hebrew, just as Deucal-ion, Adam's equivalent in Greek mythology, spoke Greek, and so on.

As a twelfth-century bestiary put it, "Adam did not award the names according to the Latin tongue, nor the Greek one, nor according to any other barbarous speech, but in that language which was current to everybody before the Flood: that is to say, Hebrew." Every Hebrew word for a beast could be seen as a precious fragment of Eden. Every animal was a trace leading back to deep history, when the foundations of the world were established.

The prevailing interpretation of Adam's naming of the beasts views it as a primitive expression of word magic. In this approach, the naming relates back to Genesis 1:28, where God portentously gives Adam and Eve dominion over all other forms of life. By christening the beasts, Adam places them under his power, in the same way that in occult traditions a sorcerer can subdue a demon by invoking its secret name.

Word magic was no doubt known and practiced by the ancient Hebrews. But this interpretation ignores the context of the naming and leads to troubling inconsistencies. Here are the naming verses in full:

> And the Lord God said, It is not good that the man should be alone; I will make him an help meet for him.
>
> And out of the ground the Lord God formed every beast of the field, and every fowl of the air; and brought them unto Adam to see what he would call them: and whatsoever Adam called every living creature, that was the name thereof.
>
> And Adam gave names to all cattle, and to the fowl of the air, and to every beast of the field; but for Adam there was not found an help meet for him. [Genesis 2:20]

The surprising thing about this passage is that, despite a long tradition to the contrary, Adam doesn't name all the animals. The text states specifically, and then repeats itself, that God only brings the beasts of the field and the fowl of the air before Adam (although "beast of the field" is better translated as "wild beast," the terrestrial meaning remains). Sea creatures are excluded from Adam's primeval nomenclature. Now, the text does refer to "every living creature" receiving a name, but given the insistence that only some animals came before Adam's review, it appears the phrase means only that he named every creature that was there, and not the others.

But why this exclusion of fish and sea mammals? With the human dominion theory in mind, the author of the passage could be making a fine point: humans, as land animals, have control over terrestrial creatures, but not those in the sea. The Hebrews were never a seafaring people, and even the most maritime cultures of the time knew that the ocean was an element alien and hostile to mankind. Even the far-sailing Greeks originally called the Black Sea the Axine or "Unfriendly" Sea. But this reasoning only causes more problems. In Genesis 1:28, God *did* give humans dominion over the fish and the sea; moreover, as far as that goes, Adam's denomination of the beasts cannot refer back to the authority given to him over the earth, since Genesis 1:28 occurs *after* the naming. Eve is already present in Genesis 1:28, while Genesis 2:18 loops back before her creation.

And, in fact, Eve is the key to this riddle, because the entire naming ritual involves the search for an appropriate companion for Adam. The text directly frames the naming of the beasts with the divine observation on the one side that Adam should not remain alone, and on the other the creation of Eve. God arranges the naming event not for Adam to assert his hegemony over the animals, but rather the direct opposite, to search for one that would make an appropriate companion for him, a fitting helper, "an help meet." Indeed, the frustration of his quest comes through the language: "but for Adam there was not found an help meet for him."

Returning to the exclusion of ocean life, this explains why Yahweh does not bother to bring sea creatures to the naming. By their very aquatic nature they would not make a good companion for Adam, and therefore they do not make the first cut.

If we put aside the assumption that Adam's naming asserts human dominion over creation, we are free to explore the deeper symbolic meanings of the event, and ask, What does naming the animals have to do with the search for a companion? The fact that God brings the beasts to Adam suggests that the naming constitutes Adam's first introduction to animal creation, that Adam is not just naming the animals but *learning* their names, and through their appellations, their essence. This is what he needs to know in order to evaluate which would make an appropriate companion. He must know the hidden inner character of the animal, not its evident outward form.

Many cultures believe in a direct correspondence between a thing and its name. The name can in a sense bring a subject into being, because words summon the essence of things, as opposed to merely designating their physical existence. This idea lies behind the widely held belief among animistic peoples that a child does not receive its soul until it is christened. This kind of essentialism seems to have been a fundamental belief among the ancient Hebrews also. One of the main techniques Genesis employs to communicate its ideas involves the use of (real or false) etymologies to summarize larger themes, based on the logic that words correspond to essence. For example, the text draws attention to the fact that "Adam" is etymologically related to the Hebrew word for "earth" *(adamah)* out of which he was made and to which he will return. The linguistic relationship emphasizes Adam's humble origins and portends his unfortunate fate. Yahweh himself plays etymologist with Abraham, couching his covenant with him in terms of a name change from Abram ("father is exalted") to Abraham ("father of many"). Jacob was merely a supplanter of his brother *(ya'aqob,* "seizing by the heel"), until becoming the eponymous founder of his nation by taking the name Israel, "the one who struggles with God."

The Bible's etymological essentialism trusts that words, like the animals Adam names, leave footprints that can lead directly back to some original, untainted, perfect designation of what the thing is. Following a similar mind-set, the medieval bestiaries that came in the wake of the *Physiologus* leaned heavily on etymologies, mostly derived from Isidore of Seville's great seventh-century work *Etymologies*, and usually completely wrongheaded. Thus a twelfth-century Latin bestiary states confidently and somewhat incoherently that the bear, *Ursus*, gets its name from *Orsus* ("a beginning"), because mother bears lick their cubs into shape with their mouths *(ore)*, a reference to the ancient belief that bear cubs are born formless. This same bestiary remarks that Adam named the animals "according to the sort of nature which each of them had."

The naming of the animals in Genesis, therefore, constituted the ground zero of meaning for the bestiary etymologists, the point prior to all etymology where noun and the thing nominated were one. In uttering the animals' names, Adam would, from this perspective, be personally encountering the very core being of the beast, the thing that makes it what it is. In other words, what religious thought might term the animal's soul.

If this is so, the naming perhaps originally meant much more than the mere zoological designation of this animal as a coyote, and that animal as a raven. Rather, we have to get rid of the articles, and see the names more as vocatives, as the identification of a personal entity, not a generic noun: Coyote, not just a coyote; Raven, not merely a bird. The naming of the animals takes place not in linguistic history, but in deep history, dreamtime.

In our culture we customarily select personal names for arbitrary reasons unrelated to any inherent meaning the appellations may have. We like the sound, or we want to honor some relative, friend, or celebrity of the same name. In many societies, however, personal names purport to reflect some characteristic considered essential to that individual. For this reason, a person might wait until adulthood before receiving a permanent name, for only then is the course of his or her life clear—Abram becomes Abraham in his eightieth year. Sometimes these essential names come in visions, or spring out of an important quality or event in a person's life. Often as not an animal is involved. The Sioux had Sitting Bull and Crazy Horse; the Icelanders, Sigurd Snake-in-the-Eye and Thorleif Crow. The two cultures were totally distinct, but their way of naming persons derived from the same understanding of nomenclature. Each such name had a story, not just a spelling. The writers of Genesis appear to have understood Adam's naming to be more like these vocatives than the zoological classification modern readers usually project onto the passage.

Adam's intimate experience of nonhuman creation through the naming harmonizes with the rest of Genesis. Yahweh establishes the rule of strict vegetarianism in the Garden of Eden, one that applies to predators as well as humans. The prohibition was so strong that it survived the Fall, and only after the Flood does God permit meat-eating, almost it appears in resigned recognition of the fact that the human race after the Flood proved to be about as wicked as its antediluvian kin (at the first opportunity Noah drinks himself into a stupor, and his son Ham apparently commits some kind of unspecified affront against his unconscious father). Apparently, the writers of Genesis believed that Yahweh originally intended a personal relationship to develop between humans and animal creation, one that never came to fruition.

The naming gives a hint of that grand and evanescent design. If it is more than just arbitrary zoological classification, the naming let Adam bring to light and understand the nature of the creatures, and at the same time, his nature is brought into focus for the first time. He realizes by speaking the animals' names that he is different from them. In the first exercise of self-reflection recorded in the Bible, he concludes that a companion for him does not exist among the wild beasts, something obvious to us, but these events purport to occur in the dreamtime before the origin of family, friendship, women, and sex. Both the animals and Adam begin a process of self-discovery through the naming, a process abruptly curtailed by the designs of one particular animal, the serpent, who promised instant self-knowledge through the forbidden fruit.

Understood in this way, Adam's naming of animals did not just happen once and for all. Rather, as a dreamtime event, it is repeated through time whenever humans and animals relate through language. What my daughter's dog Richard (after Richard the Lion-Hearted) and Nixon's dog Checkers have in common, along with the millions of Spots, Shaggys, etc., is the verbal essentialism of children, who find in an animal's name some quality that summarizes the creature's personality. Freud noted that "children show no trace of arrogance which urges adult civilized men to draw hard-and-fast lines between their own nature and that of all other animals. Children have no scruples over allowing animals to rank as their full equals." As full equals, more or less, they also receive essentialist names from children.

The vocatives we use map the world of our relationships. We give names to pets as if they were part of the family, but not to wildlife, which exists outside the circle of our relationships. Livestock lies somewhere in between: horses often bear personal names, as do some cows, but chickens, pigs, and sheep rarely do. The flexibility of the rule reflects the ambiguous status of farm animals, which appear to us sometimes as servants, sometimes as mere units of production.

The realm of things worthy of names shifts over time. The ancient Greeks, Anglo-Saxons, and Norse used to give personal names not only to people and animals, but to artifacts such as weaponry and jewelry. Long passages in ancient and medieval poetry are dedicated to describing the genealogy of swords or rings, just as if the poet were recounting the biography of a human character. The personification of inanimate objects appears to be a fundamental way of understanding the world in many animistic cultures, which generally perceive a spiritual force in all things, epitomized by the Tongan concept of *mana.* For the late medieval mind, "fox" generically designated the type of animal, but any fox skulking along the hedgerow could also be Reynard, the embodiment of foxiness in fable and folklore. Any rooster caught by a fox could be the vainglorious Chantecleer. Through the ability of the Middle Ages to see the world as a multilayered reality, many animals had a kind of literary doppelgänger, a personification that could occupy the same body as the generic form. It is as if every crow that settled in a vacant lot impressed us as a potential wisecracking Heckel or Jeckel.

But the impression escapes us. If the world of our meaningful relationships is measured by the things we call by name, then our universe of meaning is rapidly shrinking. No culture has dispensed personal names as parsimoniously as ours. We have withdrawn our christening from all objects and most animals, officially limiting personality to humans (and even then denying names to some of them, such as prisoners, who are identified only by number). Like Da Vinci's drawing of a man inscribed in a circle, our world of relationships has metaphorically contracted to the span of a human arm: all the nonhuman world has been excluded as lifeless matter, and animals have become increasingly nameless. Some*thing*, not some*body*.

The verbal narcissism practiced by our culture comes into view through the way we treat computer programs. IBM created a sophisticated chess-playing program with the title of "Deep Blue." When the Deep Blue program gave chess champion Kasparov a run for his money in a 1996 tournament, the program became a celebrity in its own right, with commentators and software experts talking about it as if it were a living being. Deep Blue did this, Deep Blue thought that, Deep Blue made this opening or fell for that gambit. We have given this product of our own minds a personal name and spoken about it accordingly, while many living things, such as cows in a modern mechanized dairy, typically endure a nameless existence.

We have come a long way from Adam's naming of the animals. History experienced another great naming, which took place somewhat removed from paradise. During the late seventeenth century, the Swedish botanist Carolus Linnaeus, frustrated at the lack of a common vocabulary for scientists to describe plants and animals, developed a systematic nomenclature for designating living things, based on a double name, the first being the genus, the second the species. *Canis lupus* for gray wolf, *Ursus horribilis* for grizzly bear, *Homo sapiens* for humans. The nomenclature of Linnaeus' system was confined to the then international language of Latin, which meant that people of different nationalities and tongues could always know they were referring to the same animal. Linnaeus (who appropriately changed his Scandinavian name, Carl von Linné, to its Latin form) understood this was important, because the vernacular terms for animals were so quirky, local, and ill-defined (as they still are), naturalists from different countries, or different cities for that matter, had trouble sharing information about the objects of their study. Linnaeus' elegantly simple solution made the growth of botany and zoology possible.

Thus, Linnaeus succeeded in making the speakers of Germanic languages utter the taboo name of the bear, *Ursus,* which they had so assiduously avoided for thousands of years.

It is difficult to overstate the ambition of Linnaeus' system. Adam purported to name only the birds and terrestrial fauna; Linnaeus' vocabulary defined all life everywhere, whether alive or extinct, whether known or as yet waiting to be discovered in some distant rain forest whose existence the Swedish botanist never even imagined. The key to the system's success is this universality. Unlike the Genesis naming, the naming of relationships and essence, Linnean designation purposely distances us from the animals named, avoiding the distracting traditions that cling to existing vocabularies, avoiding familiar words, avoiding history. Spoken in a dead language, the Linnean names themselves usually have no apparent meaning to the speaker, no etymology that can trace the animal's lineage or qualities, and often the name of newly discovered species goes to the scientist who "discovered" it, essentially displacing the animal's name with a human's.

The Linnean system was never intended to replace the vernacular vocabulary for animals; rather it was supposed to run parallel to it. The language of everyday life used the vernacular; the Linnean system applied to zoology. The first was local and historical; the latter universal, scholarly, and timeless. But the unruly vernacular has succumbed to Linnaeus, intentionally or not. As a matter of sheer quantity, the Linnean system applies to extinct and newly discovered species, which usually have no common name and which greatly outnumber vernacular animals. Our entire vocabulary for dinosaurs, for instance, consists of Linnean categories, *Tyrannosaurus rex* being the one that always comes to mind.

And while Linnaeus' designations continue to grow, Adam's dreamtime naming dwindles. As an experiment, the readers of this book should step outside into a backyard or open area and count the number of plants and animals they can identify by name: ragweed, carpenter bee, Stellar's jay, and so on. If they are typical urban dwellers, the number will probably not exceed half a dozen. In contrast, an aboriginal Australian can easily give the names of scores of creatures throughout a far-flung landscape. Because animals seem so distant from our lives, they increasingly slip into namelessness. It would not be surprising if, in the next generation or two, urban children knew more Linnean names for types of long-extinct dinosaurs than the common names of the songbirds flying just outside their windows. We often even call ourselves *Homo sapiens,* as if the word "human" raises problems of definition better left unresolved.

Vicki Hearns (who by the way uses the term *Homo sapiens* more than once in her book *Adam's Task,* just as I have) tells an anecdote about a linguist who was trying to record the language of a nonliterate, agrarian culture. During an interview with a peasant, he pointed to the man's cow and asked: "What do you call that animal?" Instead of giving the generic term, the peasant answered with the equivalent of our pet name "Bossie." The linguist tried to get around the miscommunication by asking, "Well, what do you call your neighbor's animal that moos and gives milk?" "Why should I call my neighbor's animal?" was the peasant's reply.

The story embodies our culture's confusion about what naming is appropriate to animals. We have a choice. On the one hand, we can use language to establish relationships with living creatures, to elicit their meanings and history, and in this way enhance our own identities. This is the Adamic naming, in which, in Gary Kowalski's phrase, "animals not only have biologies, they have biographies." On the other hand, we can continue to follow Linnaeus, designating animals as creatures out of context and out of contact with us. With Linnaeus, we gain certainty and control, but at what cost?

Back to Adam, brooding in his unshared paradise, in search of a mate. When Yahweh brings the animals and Adam speaks their names, the first man acknowledges their *mana*. This ability, to perceive the spiritual in the material, is the essence of religious thought. It was the first act of worship by humanity, and not, I hasten to add, by *Homo sapiens*.

CHAPTER TEN

Vixens

Spider Woman brought not only the sun to the Cherokee,
but fire with it.
—FROM A CHEROKEE STORY

At some point in our history, female animals went bad. The terms we use for the feminine form of beasts more often than not have unpleasant associations, so much so that many have evolved into the ugliest insults against women in the English language. A bull symbolizes strength and virility, but a cow suggests sloven stupidity. Foxes may seem tricky to us, but vixens embody seductive duplicity at its worst, to the point that when the term "fox" became a sexual compliment sometime in the 1950s or 1960s, the feminine form of the word could not be rehabilitated, and the masculine designation was applied to women also. A boar's reputation for courage and tenacity earned it a place in medieval heraldry; while sows wallow in our vocabulary of contempt. Black widows dominate our imagination as symbols of danger (especially sexual danger) to such an extent, we never even bothered to name the male of the species, except as the oxymoronic "male black widow." She-wolves and bitches, tigresses, harpies, and shrews, all combine to make our feminine bestiary overwhelmingly negative.

In writing this book, I set aside several days during which I recorded every reference to female animals I came across in songs, on television, during conversations, or reading. Not one of these days passed without one or more derogatory remarks finding their way to my list.

Although the English lexicon for female animals is quite small, misogyny works its way into zoological categories in other, less obvious ways. Upon seeing a hunted cetacean breach for air, whalers throughout the eighteenth and nineteenth centuries shouted "thar she blows," without ever worrying whether the sea mammal called for the feminine pronoun. The whale might just as likely have been a male for all the whalers knew, and nothing in the appearance of cetaceans would inherently suggest any particular gender. Not only whales, but sport fish, hunted rabbits, and a variety of other game animals have also acquired the feminine pronoun in specific contexts, whether they are male or female. We should ask why.

André Joly studied the gender of animals in the English language and concluded that female pronouns apply to animals often not to designate sex but rather human control:

> In fact, *she* has acquired a very specific function in Modern English: it is expressly used to refer to an *animal regarded as a minor power.* This accounts in particular for the "professional" use of *she.* Sportsmen, whalers, fishermen are in special relation to the animal. Whatever its size or strength, it is regarded as a potential prey, a power that has to be destroyed—for sport or food—hence a dominated power.

Game animals, creatures selected to be caught or killed, become female in our culture's discourse, regardless of their gender, through a process in which both animals and women collapse into the category of prey.

The association between animals and the feminine has not always been so unflattering. A more reverential attitude marked the earliest human commentary on the gender of animals: the cave paintings of the Upper Paleolithic or Ice Age. Among the numerous animal images in these works, pregnant beasts often appear, sometimes in the context of vegetable symbols and other signs of nature's bounty. The famous pregnant mare of Lascaux, for instance, which even seems to be depicted with the ambling gait of a gravid animal, is overlapped by long feathery objects, once thought to be spears, but more likely representations of grain or other vegetation, suggesting a composition that celebrates the mysteries of fertility embodied in the pregnant animal. André Leroi-Gourhan, the French scholar of Paleolithic culture, analyzed thousands of such figures and signs found in cave paintings, and concluded that they broadly fit into feminine and masculine categories, with female images placed at "the special heart and core of the caves" as if to emphasize their centrality. While no one knows for sure what significance the cave images held for early humanity, the prominence of pregnant creatures and the care with which they were depicted indicate that at the very least their importance went beyond the quest for meat into the spiritual contemplation of renewal, the fruitfulness of nature, and the cycle of life.

A number of anthropologists believe that for thousands of years the mysteries of nature's fecundity took the form of goddess worship and stood at the center of religion, imparting a special awe toward female existence. The Mother Goddess was venerated as the giver and supporter of life, and her powers were especially manifest in females of all species, human and nonhuman alike. As a result, women seem to have held positions of high status, if not preeminence, in Old World cultures from the Paleolithic to the Bronze Age, where the matrilineal descent of property and name was apparently common. In contrast to the negative associations of today, this reflection of nature in culture enriched the way women were viewed, rather than providing a word hoard of invective.

The hypothesis goes that the primeval reign of the Mother Goddess came to an end in the Iron Age, through the invasion of Indo-

European herding cultures, with their distant male sky gods, their patriarchy, and their "fury of fire and sword," as Joseph Campbell put it. Ultimately the monotheism of a male deity transformed the former reverence toward the life-giving power of the female into the sacrilege of worshiping the creation over the creator. Simultaneously, as the different forms of the Mother Goddess and her sacred animals declined into demons and chattel, women's status in many Old World cultures deteriorated to the point that females became the possessions of their fathers and husbands.

This reconstruction of religious history has its problems. Unlike the divinities of Greece, Rome, and Israel, the Mother Goddess had the failing of being preliterate, so that her existence cannot be directly confirmed, but only inferred from fragments of pictorial art and oblique allusions in later texts. More important, the enthusiasm for a matriarchal past tends to glibly pass over the amorality of ancient religions, and the violent excesses such an ethical void can create, or at least silently tolerate. The ethical commitment that monotheism, and in particular Judaism, brought into existence ultimately liberated both men and women in most Western countries from the more obvious forms of oppression, even if its historical forms have been unkind to the feminine gender in humans and animals.

But if some kind of mythological drift from Mother Goddess to monotheism did occur, many non-Western religions still remained anchored in the old ways. Most, if not all, Native American cultures have mythic cycles in which the divine protagonist takes the form of a female animal spirit: Bear Mother among the Haida, White Wolf Maiden among the Zuñi, the Lakota Sioux White Buffalo Calf Woman, the Cherokee Spider Woman. Invariably, the feminine animal spirit represents a force for good, even cultural heroism. In the Bear Mother stories, for instance, which appear in numerous cultures (including Old Norse), a woman is kidnapped by a bear in the form of a man, who takes her to his village to be his bride. In her new life among the bears, the woman learns their "songs," at the same time teaching the bear spirits about human society. The woman usually gives birth to several children by her bear husband who grow up to become leaders or warriors. Eventually, she returns to human society, often after having attained the ability to transform herself into a bear. Restored to friends and family, she teaches the ways of bears to men.

To the extent such positive female animals survive in our culture at all, they have become the denizens of fairy tales and fantasy, Goldilocks' Mama Bear, Mother Goose, and the Big Bad Wolf dressed up like grandmother.

Nonetheless, reverence for female animals died hard even in Western civilization. Feminist scholars have often argued that the depiction of Eve's creation in Genesis provided the religious and philosophical rationale for marginalizing women. Eve's existence is "ontologically inferior" because Yahweh not only makes her after Adam, but derives her substance from the body of his prior masculine creation in a kind of secondary genesis twice removed from the divine image. Whatever the merit of this criticism, the same undertones of feminine inequality do not arise in the creation of the sexes among the beasts. Yahweh makes male and female animals contemporaneously, and bids them to multiply, even before the creation of humanity. Although no mention is made of gender, the subtext suggests that the responsibility, and hence the divine power, of propagation will fall disproportionately on female creatures. If Adam is ontologically superior to Eve, having appeared first, then animal gender has some kind of priority over the sex differences in humans, and female beasts stand preeminent in the divine plan for diffusing life over the earth.

The *Physiologus,* respectful as always toward the animal kingdom, displays its own system of gender, which seems to reflect an older reverential tradition. The author depicts a number of animals, especially birds, as female by nature, most of which are given a favorable symbolic meaning. Using the feminine pronoun throughout, he likens the turtledove to Christ, the church, and faithful wives; the ostrich to humanity in search of religious truth; the vulture to sinful men capable of being saved by grace. But his greatest praise falls on the roe, who dwells in the high mountains and "sees from far off all who approach her, and she knows whether they come with guile or with friendship":

> The roe represents the wisdom of God who loves the prophets,
> that is, the high mountains toward which the Prophet has raised
> his eyes . . . Thus, the roe feeds in the valleys just as our Lord
> Jesus Christ feeds in the Church, since the good works of
> Christians and the gifts of the faithful are the food of Christ . . .
> The roe, however, leaps over the prophets, bounding over the
> hills (that is, the apostles). She has keen vision signifying that
> the Savior sees everything that is done.

In the unrelentingly patriarchal theology of the early Middle Ages, before Mariolatry even appeared on the scene to soften its masculine edges, this passage stands out as a radical departure from orthodox Christian imagery by likening Christ to a female animal hurdling over the earthbound heads of male prophets and apostles. Elsewhere, Christ is symbolized by a stag, a lion, a peacock, or a unicorn; but as far as I know, this is the earliest portrayal of Christ through an overtly feminine symbol. Pope Gelasius might have had this very iconoclastic roe in mind when he added the *Physiologus* to the growing list of banned books in the fifth century.

The association between women and animals goes deeper still. From the beginning, the human imagination all around the world seems to have envisioned nature as feminine (I am unaware of any mythological system in which nature or the earth is masculine). The Mother Goddess appeared as perhaps the earliest expression of this tendency to see the natural world in terms of gender, but long after she had fallen from grace, we still talk about Mother Nature, Mother

Earth, virgin territory, fertile land, the rape of wilderness by greedy men. Husbands marry wives, and husbandry cultivates plants and animals.

But if nature and animals have in this sense remained feminine, even if only through the innuendo of language, their female status has taken on different meanings at different times, falling under the spell of prevailing myths and ideologies. While the Mother Goddess was all in all, as early as St. Augustine, Eve became associated with nature, matter, and the beasts in contrast to the mind and spirit represented by Adam. The resulting schism between passive, sinful feminine nature and redeeming masculine humanity made mischief for the next fifteen hundred years, as writers such as Carolyn Merchant and Susan Griffin have powerfully documented. As embodiments of the fallen world, wild animals and women needed to be controlled by reason and the orderly, domestic civilization reason supposedly produced. In this system of thought, there was no room in the Western world for freethinking women or free-roaming wolves, females with property or animals with rights. Mainstream religion retreated into a way of talking that discounted all animal life and half the human population. The feminization of animals, therefore, played a part in a cluster of problems that mark today's spiritual restlessness.

Few people today hold the view that females and nature are corrupt, or that wild animals are allied with Satan. Nonetheless, we bear the legacy of these associations, not only in our speech, but in the unexamined motivations of our society's most powerful institutions. Many of the "predator control" programs in this country are neither economical nor rational, but they continue to destroy animals, year after year, in what can only be seen as the lingering influence of a vanished theology where wild beasts embodied evil. An example comes to mind close to home. While I was writing this book, a mountain lion was shot by predator control officials when it wandered into a foothill neighborhood not far from where I live. The cougar weighed a pitiful seventeen pounds, and could hardly have threatened a large tomcat, much less a person. Coming on the heels of a ballot initiative in my state to renew sports hunting of cougars, the shooting seemed almost a parody of the big-game mystique, and a symbol of our boorish hostility toward wild things.

Significantly, a similar irrational hostility appears in the disturbing undertone of misogyny in many Hollywood films. The motif of the dragon lady, the femme fatale, is of course a valid artistic device, but an unrelenting contempt for women comes out in films like *Basic Instinct,* where females seem invariably subject to homicidal tendencies or casual rapes. The fact that such films often succeed at the box office suggests our society has deeper spiritual problems than we probably want to admit.

The vocabulary we use, whether words or images, is more than just the sum total of linguistic artifacts that happened to get passed down to us. It coarsens or refines the possibilities of our thought. Our attitudes toward feminine animals affect the status of women, and vice versa, so that a common insult directed against a woman boils up from religious and social conflicts set in motion before the foundation of history. We might want to remember that God watches all things, and if the *Physiologus* is right, God may take the form of a roe deer, likely to frown upon the thoughtless depreciation of the feminine and the feral.

CHAPTER ELEVEN

Wild and Tame

To confront this wild unreasonableness of nature is to
look god in the eye and relent.
—STEPHANIE MILLS

Just as animal gender has had metaphysical resonance through the ages, so too has the distinction between wild animals and domesticated animals. So fundamental are the categories of wild and tame that children usually learn them well before they become familiar with more than a handful of the beasts that fit into each. Like most of our concepts dealing with animals, the contrast is "good for thinking," and from it inevitably unfolds some of our most powerful spiritual metaphors.

Not only Christianity, but Judaism, Islam, and virtually every organized religion on earth employs the symbolism of the path in describing the essence of their teachings. The Tao means just that: the way. Jewish prophets walk the path of righteousness. John the Baptist strove to make the paths straight for the coming Messiah. Christian evangelists hope to save souls who have become "lost," that is wandered from the road to redemption. In discussing this metaphor of the path in the Bible, Northrop Frye shows how deeply it abides in the basic narrative of the text:

> There is, in the first place, the miraculous highway, the path
> opened through the Red Sea, the original type of all paths of

salvation. A passage in Isaiah (11:16) foretells the extension of this miraculous path to bring the lost people of Israel back from Assyria. In the account of the Exodus the Red Sea crossing was followed by a long period of wandering in labyrinthine and frustrated directions. This image remains in the background, set against a contrasting image of a straight highway of God through the desert (Isaiah 40:3).

We seldom look behind this vocabulary of peregrination and direction, yet it can touch us only because a culture like our own sees a strong distinction between the wild and the domesticated. We have carved out two spheres of activity: the civilized realm, where we and our animals live; and the wilderness, where uncontrolled beasts and disorder dwell. We require paths to negotiate travel from one civilized habitation to the next through the dangers and confusion of the wilds, and this condition blossomed into a central image of the spiritual life. The spiritual conflict between civilization and the wild appear in all its concentrated symbolic power in the first stanza of Dante's *Divine Comedy*:

> *Midway in our life's journey, I went astray*
> *from the straight road and woke to find myself*
> *alone in a dark wood.*

For the medieval mind, and for our culture as its heir, the connotations of this geography explode with meaning before we even know where the poem is leading.

Indigenous peoples typically do not make a hard distinction between the domestic and the wild, with the result that these symbolic possibilities do not materialize. The Bororo of Brazil, for instance, like most primal cultures, lack the word for wilderness, since they see themselves as embedded in nature, and are always already "home," even if away from their village. In such a worldview, a person cannot get lost except in the trivial sense of temporarily missing a destination, as when we miss a floor on an elevator. For this reason, most primal societies do not talk about religion as a path, since the question would arise, Who needs one? (The obvious popular exception is Black Elk's sacred cosmology of the "Red Road" as the proper way for humans to relate to nature and each other, but Black Elk, it should be remembered, was a devout practicing Catholic as well as a Sioux spiritual leader.)

Our sacred vocabulary, in contrast, constantly draws on the differences between the two realms of wilderness and civilization. As mentioned in the Introduction to this book, the lovely Twenty-third Psalm gathers its power to describe the intimacy between God and humanity through the imagery of the shepherd and his flock. Just outside the borders of the text, however, lurk the wolf, jackal, lion, and other beasts of the wilderness who threaten the defenseless sheep and are consistently associated in the Old Testament with disorder and the demonic. The looming proximity of the wild beasts is quite literal—they appear just before in Psalm 22:21: "Save me from the lion's mouth: for thou hast heard me from the horn of the unicorns." The beasts of the wilderness never show their faces in Psalm 23, but their near presence drives the logic of the author's thankfulness and awe toward God's care and deliverance. The divine shepherd guides his flock out of the wastelands, where the "valley of the shadow of death" no doubt seemed more than a mere abstraction for a seminomadic people, into a domesticated pastureland, and ultimately the urbanized "house of the Lord."

Most of us have made a pilgrimage of one sort or another. Mine involved walking alone across Iceland, with the help of a raven. While studying in Reykjavik, I decided to hike across the country's interior wastelands, land Icelanders call the *eyðu,* "the empty place," no-man's-land: fifty thousand square miles of uninhabited lava fields, glacier rivers, and volcanic ash so inhospitable NASA practiced the moon landing there in the sixties. I don't know why in particular I wanted to make the trip alone. It was probably a combination of misplaced machismo and a desire to distance myself from a bad situation I was in at the time. It meant all the more to me knowing that among the Old Norse the *eyðu* was a kind of sacred geology, like Jerusalem's Via Dolorosa for Christians. The interior wastelands were the last refuge for outlaw heroes like Egil Skallagrimson and Grettir the Strong, who could not make their peace with a corrupt society. After walking a few days under a midnight sun, I found myself in the heart of the emptiness, perhaps the only human, not to mention vertebrate, within a fifty-mile radius. I think I was able to understand there the awesome loneliness of the desert hermits.

Late one night while I lay wide awake in my tent, I heard the unearthly vocalization of a raven. It swooped down, its black body preternaturally large against the lingering red sun, and landed near my tent, apparently attracted by any sign of life in its journey to who knows where. The presence of the bird startled and pleased me all at once. The raven, I recalled, was Oðin's messenger, bringer of victory in war, but also death. I threw bits of cheese on the black sands for the ambiguous bird to gobble up.

I can't adequately relate what passed between us, the only two living things in the middle of nowhere, except to say I had the urge to seize the animal—out of fear or a desire to possess it, I can't say— and it struck me that if I turned an ankle and died of exposure, this very scavenger might in a few days be picking at my flesh.

Then without any notice, this mythological grackle hopped off to gain flight speed, and flew away. Needless to say, it never did have an opportunity to scavenge my carcass. But for whatever reason, when crows gather in a nearby schoolyard or on telephone lines, I look at them with a great deal more respect than I did before, as if I somehow knew them personally. I welcome their wild inexplicable presence in the midst of our self-satisfied civilization.

The dialogue between wild beasts and domestic life I experienced is a mainstay of biblical imagery. In the New Testament, it becomes the guiding metaphor for understanding the nature of the new covenant. John the Baptist announces Jesus' redemptive office with the words "Behold the Lamb of God, which taketh away the sins of our world" (John 1:29). Jesus alludes back to the perilous wilds behind Psalm 23 when he sends his apostles out to preach: "Go your ways: behold, I send you forth as lambs among wolves" (Luke 10:2). He gives his followers power over snakes and other wild creatures. And ultimately, becoming a Christian is portrayed in the surprisingly quiet metaphor of kine submitting to their husbandman: "Take my yoke upon you, and learn of me"(Matthew 11:29). Rather than some breathtaking mystical vision, knowledge of Christ appears here as the palpable cattle that willingly till the fields under their master's guidance.

These metaphors may seem dead to us, but for an agricultural people, who probably never went a day without encountering a large domestic animal, they must have had an immediacy as vivid as jet aircraft have in our culture. They are able to bear their spiritual symbolism because of the particular associations that gathered round the concepts of wild and tame.

Domestic animals once implied obedience, order, familiarity, even family. For this reason, we still name pets and some livestock, based on a descending scale of kinship, but wild animals go nameless. The point is brought out in Marshall Sahlins' discussion of the difference between our treatment of dogs and horses:

Dogs and horses participate in American society in the capacity of subjects. They have proper personal names, and indeed we

are in the habit of conversing with them as we do not talk to pigs
and cattle . . . But as domestic cohabitants, dogs are closer to
men than are horses . . . Traditionally horses stand in a more
menial, working relationship with people; if dogs are kinsmen,
horses are as servants and nonkin.

In one twelfth-century bestiary, the entries on domestic animals come
directly after a contemplation on Adam's naming of the beasts, as if
the author wanted to emphasize the connection between the familiarity of names and our kinship with pets and livestock. Even the medieval manuscript illuminations depicting the naming of the beasts
underscore this idea, since they avoid portrayals of wild animals like
lions in favor of horses and goats, and such friendly creatures as birds
and deer.

The symbolic overtones of wild animals carry more ambiguity.
From the classical period through the Middle Ages, beasts held associations of savagery, chaos, and menacing evil, so that a medieval hero
could hardly pass up the opportunity to fight with a lion, wolf, or
dragon to demonstrate his virtue. In the fourteenth-century poem *Sir
Gawain and the Green Knight*, Gawain's travels through the Welsh
forestlands sum up most aspects of this convention in just a few lines:

> *Now with serpents he wars, now with savage wolves,*
> *Now with wild men of the woods, that watched from the rocks,*
> *Both with bulls and with bears, and with boars besides,*
> *And giants that came gibbering from the jagged steeps.*
> *Had he not borne himself bravely, and been on God's side,*
> *he had met with many mishaps and mortal harms.* [ll. 719-725]

Filled with monsters, wolves, and wild men, the natural landscape
stood against the City of God and the other urban metaphors that

dominated the discourse of the early church in discussing right living. Our vocabulary for the wild reflects this moral gulf. The most common word for "wilderness" in Old English was *westen*, which is related to Modern English "waste," as in "wasteland," and which applied just as much to dense forests as deserts. The term did not have to do with the land's fertility, but with the absence of human habitation and control. It was land "on its own." The origin of the word "wilderness" is obscure, despite Webster's certainty that it refers to wild animals: *wilde deor*, wild animal (deer). The term appears first in Middle English, and may have originally meant "self-willed land," which roughly corresponds to the original meaning of wasteland. To this day, the word "wild" describes not only the zoological fact of being feral, but the moral condition of being beyond law and ethics, ignorant of or inured to morality, willful in the theological sense (hence the modern neologism "wilding" to denote a random violent crime spree by youths).

It is no coincidence that the most eloquent vision of universal peace in the West, Isaiah 11:6, evokes not merely brotherly love, but a rapprochement of the wild and the tame: "The wolf also shall dwell with the lamb, and the leopard shall lie down with the kid: and the calf and the young lion and the fatling together: and a little child shall lead them." This vision only inspires because we sense a deep division between domesticated and wild creatures that takes on metaphysical dimensions.

But the interplay of wild and tame was always more complex than evil versus good, selfishness versus submission to God's law. The state of wilderness lent itself to metaphoric contrasts between moral purity and the corruption of civilization: simplicity versus sin city. Away from the distractions of human preoccupations, wild nature offered refuge to the anchorite in search of God and prophets offended by the sins of the world. The Bible taught that God was not to be found in Gomorrah, Nineveh, Babylon, Rome, or the other great centers of civilization, but on remote Mount Sinai or in the still small voice that came to Elijah hiding in his cave. Satan is depicted as tempting Jesus not in the splendor of the local bazaar, but in the wilderness, away from the mundane commerce that threatens to blur the moral principles at stake. Walking down the city streets, God and the devil would have for some reason seemed just a little less sublime in their struggle for humanity's soul.

Early Christianity embraced the spiritual possibilities of wilderness with the monastic movement, the separation of Christians from the world, which meant at that time the city. St. Anthony of Egypt, the fourth-century hermit, is generally considered the reluctant father of Christian monasticism. At age twenty, he left civilization behind to live as a hermit in the desert. Fellow Christians inspired by his piety sought Anthony out, and over the years an oxymoronic colony of hermits formed around Anthony's wilderness retreat. Soon they were sharing meals and prayers under Anthony's guidance, setting the pattern for the rise of the great European monasteries in the following centuries.

Eventually even the company of hermits amounted to too much human society for Anthony. He left his protomonastery and spent the rest of his life wandering the desert, withstanding the temptations of the devil, and seeking God by living simply in nature.

The Christian ascetic tradition initiated by St. Anthony produced a number of incongruously lyrical "praise of nature" texts, not the least of which was one written by Alcuin, the inflexible Anglo-Saxon cleric who emphasized Christian withdrawal from the secular world:

> Beloved cell, retirement's sweet abode!
> Farewell, a last farewell, thy poet bids thee!
> Beloved cell, by smiling woods embraced,
> Whose branches, shaken by the genial breeze
> To meditation oft my mind disposed.
> Around thee too, their health-reviving herbs

In verdure gay the fertile meadows spread:
And murmuring near, by flowery banks confined,
Through fragrant meads the crystal streamlets glide,
Wherein his nets the joyful fisher casts,
And fragrant with the apple bending bough,
With rose and lily joined, the garden's smile:
While jubilant, along thy verdant glades
At dawn his melody each songster pours,
And to his god attunes the notes of praise.

Modeled partially on St. Anthony's asceticism, a wilderness so-journ became almost a rite of passage for attaining sainthood, and a whole body of literature grew up around the relationship between holy men and wild animals, such as St. Jerome and his lion. The *Physiologus* participates in this tradition. Of the fifty or so animals described in the book, not one is domesticated. No dog, horse, or sheep appears, despite their well-established history of symbolic meanings. The author apparently believed that while wild animals may embody universal truths, livestock and pets had become so as-similated into the mundane existence of human society that they had nothing of consequence to teach, or at least that their significance had been exhausted and did not require further interpretation. Paradoxi-cally, truth about the human condition was to be found in the realm of wild nature, not the dwellings of men.

The spirituality of wild nature was more than just a literary fad. Celtic monks practiced a form of Christian asceticism that associated spirituality with remote wilderness, even outright inhospitable terri-tory. It was considered a deeply religious practice for devout Irish men of God to build a coracle—a small wood-framed boat stretched with leather, and about the equivalent of a large kayak—and row it straight out into the North Atlantic without destination or provisions. These devotees felt that by placing themselves completely in the hands of God's mercy they could better purify their faith. It may have done that, but it also meant that communities of Celtic monks indisputably reached Iceland and Greenland, and perhaps even North America, before the end of the first millennium. The great monasteries of the Celtic world, centers of learning during the darkest years of the early Middle Ages, were often built on windswept, wild islands like Iona in the Hebrides.

This rehabilitation of wilderness and wild beasts reached a high point with the Romantic movement, where they acquire the sheen of redemption, distilled into Thoreau's famous statement that "In wildness is the preservation of the world"—the complete inversion of the savage symbolic landscape in which Gawain sallied forth.

If one literary text could embody this sensibility, it might be William Blake's "The Tyger." Blake's numinous feline, burning bright in the forests of the night, as most English speakers know, fills the narrator with questions about the deity who could make such power and intensity. "Did he who made the Lamb make thee?" he asks, confused at how the divinity who created the predatory tiger could have also made the gentle domesticated creature that stands for Christ and his teaching of universal love. If a reconciliation is possible, it may be hinted at in the depiction of the tiger Blake engraved along with the poem. The engraving shows a harmless-looking, winsome feline that actually has a slight smile on its muzzle. The creature looks more like a pussycat than the radiant apocalyptic predator celebrated in the poem. Since elsewhere Blake shows his tremendous artistic ability to produce startling, violent images, this innocuous tiger must have been an intentional commentary on the poem, casting doubt on the strong distinction between the wild and the tame made by the speaker. Blake seems to be saying that from a human perspective nature is filled with contradictions, but a more comprehensive, divine vision understands the complementary relationship between the wild and the tame.

The Romantic vision of wild animals has won out in popular culture. Very few people still believe that wilderness represents the fallen world of savagery and sin. America became the first country in history to officially recognize the value of wilderness by passing the Wilderness Act of 1964, and we have enacted statutes to protect endangered species. People of all different backgrounds and faiths recognize the beauty and cultural importance of wild creatures such as eagles, mountain lions, and grizzly bears.

At the same time, domesticated animals, especially livestock, have lost much of their status as kindred due to the mechanization of animal husbandry. For many, domesticated animals have become symbols of the worst traits of civilization. "The pathos of the over-fat pig, white rat stripped of nuance, and dog breeds with their congenital debilitations," suggests Paul Shepard, "signals to us an aspect of the human condition."

Nonetheless, we cannot escape the fact that attempts to redeem the status of wild animals, despite their widespread appeal, have often been visions without power, and the wild has succumbed to the tame in our culture in a profound sense. Belying our laws and protestations, we have exiled wilderness to a few small enclaves, and a person can easily travel from the Atlantic to the Pacific seeing hardly anything except a domesticated landscape. That same person could probably go through life without ever encountering a wild animal in its natural habitat.

Although the physical exile of the wild is plain to see, with human artifacts replacing nature everywhere, the animals of the mind, as John Berger points out, cannot be so easily ostracized. "Sayings, dreams, games, stories, superstitions, the language itself, recall them. The animals of the mind, instead of being dispersed, have been coopted into other categories so that the category *animal* has lost its central importance." Through nature films and zoos, the citizens of modern industrial society probably view more specimens of wild creatures than previous generations back to antiquity. But these constitute only an ersatz experience of the wild, a mere representation of animals, as artificial and lifeless as the dioramas in museums of natural history.

Wild animals have become spectacles in our culture. Millions visit zoos every year to see Blake's tiger or Gawain's serpents, but the institution is a monument to the impossibility of such an encounter. Framed by walls and other artificial props, isolated from interactions with other species, alienated from their habitat, zoo animals are mere reproductions of wild beasts, neither domesticated nor feral, but shadow puppets. Doug Peacock, an expert on grizzly bears, defines true wilderness as the place where something bigger than you can eat you. This is not the space of the zoo. We never meet the true gaze of a wild beast, either as predator or prey or mere neighbor, since all their actions have been rendered void. The relationship is one-dimensional: the visitor gawks, and the animals submit to being objects of observation. I know from experience that you observe a bear in quite a different manner when you know it can see you and can do something about it, like turn and attack.

Nature films, whose popularity has exploded in recent years just as the disappearance of the very animals they depict increases, produce a more subtle if not insidious form of marginalization. Natural history documentaries of wild animals purport to show the creatures interacting with their environment in a natural manner. We supposedly meet predator, prey, and biological curiosities in all their beauty and freedom. How can the camera lie, after all? But the camera always lies when it comes to encountering the wild. As with zoo visitors, film viewers become pure observers of the wilderness spectacle, with nothing at stake except the time invested to watch the images move across the screen. Aspects of an animal's life that have no interest to us, but may dominate their existence, get edited out by people who understand that for such films to be shown, they must sell, and to sell, they must cater to the desires of the viewers. In the editing process, only images of the more spectacular events—chases, mating dis- plays, mothers defending their young—make it to the final work. The verisimilitude of the representation tempts us to disregard the fact that nature films are works of art, artifices that show only certain views of the animals under scrutiny. What is depicted may be factual, but it is also distorted.

I am not saying nature films are bad for animals. They may have great educational value, and urban people who view the beauty of animal life, no matter how mediated, may be more likely to realize the need to protect the wild, not only in this country but abroad. When I was a boy, I never missed *Mutual of Omaha's Wild Kingdom* with Marlin Perkins, and can probably attribute some of my interest in wild animals to the program. But think of it: what greater contra- diction ever existed than a show about wilderness sponsored and owned by an insurance company, the embodiment of domestic secur- ity if there ever was one. The show's title symbolized the problem perfectly. This representation of the wild kingdom belonged to an insurance company, dedicated to smoothing over the wildness of na- ture. As a way to encounter the wild, then, nature films inevitably fail through the very form they take, and we must not fool ourselves into accepting an edited image of a jaguar as a substitute for Jaguar. The one is a cultural artifact, no matter how meticulously accurate; the other is a wild being filled with potential meaning.

We no longer associate wild beasts with savagery and the princi- ple of destruction. At the same time, wild animals have been rendered innocuous by our methods of viewing them. The modern gaze rarely falls upon a truly wild animal that can gaze back. As the distinction between the wild and the tame blurs, the spiritual possibilities inher- ent in the contrast diminish.

"Did he who made the Lamb make thee?" We are in a position to answer Blake's narrator. God quite intentionally made both the tiger and the lamb. The difference between the two creatures is the canvas upon which we have portrayed our deepest spiritual conflicts, from the existence of evil to the hope of enlightenment. The world Thoreau insisted wildness could preserve is not primarily the physical landscape, but the landscape of the soul, the realm of dreams, visions, meditation, and ethics that span the gap between the world we live in and the world we desire to create.

CHAPTER TWELVE

Hellhounds

Every Wolf's & Lion's howl
Raises from Hell a Human Soul.
—WILLIAM BLAKE

Prior to the Middle Ages, hell was a rather boring place. In the Old
Testament, the Hebrew word for hell, *she'öl,* means literally "the pit,"
a dreary location without any physical topography to speak of except
that it was underground and unpleasant. Jonah likens his three days
and nights in the belly of the great fish to being in hell, but that is as
close to tangible imagery as Sheol ever gets. In the New Testament,
fire and brimstone are added to the underworld, but nothing else sub-
stantial. The Koran calls hell the "dismal resting-place," without
much further elaboration, except that it has fire and scalding water,
seven gates, and the Zaqqum tree, which bears fruits like devils' heads
as the punitive diet for the damned—an interesting detail that regrettably receives no further elaboration. Greek and Roman paganism
was only slightly more forthcoming about the nether world. As
Homer depicts Hades in *The Odyssey,* it has the geography of nowhere, a dark gloomy place where "senseless dead men dwell, mere
imitations of perished mortals." Although giant vultures meted out
exquisite torture there, and Cerberus, the three-headed dog, guarded
its gate, the main attribute of the classical underworld was listlessness
and entropy, a shadowy semiconscious existence for souls neither in
torment nor in bliss.

That all changed when animals entered the gates of hell in numbers. Our vision of hell as a place teeming with torments and tormentors took shape during the Middle Ages, which invented an iconography of infernal animals to populate the abode of the damned and to do God's punitive work.

While Ælfric insisted that dogs do not suffer in hell, the popular imagination never really believed him. If not in the literal sense, then at least as symbolism, the iconography of the underworld ultimately came to throng with a population of hellhounds, harpies, serpents, and infernal insects. In some ways this chthonic bestiary has never gone away.

Dante guided the West through this zoological perdition. In *The Inferno,* Dante the pilgrim immediately meets with three symbolic animals, a leopard, a lion, and a she-wolf that drive him toward his descent into hell and represent the categories of sins he will encounter. Before even entering hell proper, he finds the first in a long series of animal tormentors: the wasps and hornets that chase and sting the "opportunists," men and angels that sided neither with God nor Satan, and are hateful to both, doomed to rush about the vestibule of hell trying to avoid their vespid punishment. Next he meets Minos, a half-man, half-bull judge of the underworld. Then Cerberus appears, the three-headed hound of hell, who eternally rips the flesh of those guilty of gluttony, one of whom is called Ciacco, that is, the Hog. As Dante descends, he sees beast after deformed beast, the Minotaur, centaurs, harpies, hellhounds, monstrous serpents, animalistic demons with names like Catclaw and Deaddog, all inflicting torture upon the damned. The thieves of the Eighth Circle are literally and painfully transformed into lizards, and even the writhing of sinners boiled in pitch suggests bestial metaphors to the narrator:

As dolphins surface and begin to flip
their arched backs from the sea, warning the sailors

to fall-to and begin to secure the ship—
So now and then some soul, to ease its pain,
showed us a glimpse of his back above the pitch
and quick as lightning disappeared again.

The symbolic structure of the poem clearly emerges through this persistent animal imagery: hell represents the bestial nature of those who turn from God, and the dehumanization of the sinners increases with the severity of the sin, until at hell's frozen core stands Lucifer, goat-like with bat wings, the complete nullification of the divine and human image.

If Dante provided the poetic bestiary of hell, the Flemish painter Hieronymous Bosch gave it visible form. *Musical Hell,* the third panel of his famous *Triptych of the Garden of Delights,* provided the infernal imagery of the late Middle Ages that remains with us today. The painting depicts an orgy of dismemberment and torture inflicted on sinners by packs of deformed hounds, pigs, reptiles, fowl, hares, and demonic man-animal hybrids. A century after its composition, one churchman expressed his wish that many copies could be circulated for the moral edification of Christians. It was hardly necessary: Bosch's nightmarish image of a hell filled with beasts entered the consciousness of Western Christianity, and forever afterward hell became synonymous with the torments of monstrous beasts.

Some animals simply have a stronger grip on our psyches than others. Rats, snakes, spiders, bats, and a few other creatures in particular haunt our dreams and anxieties more persistently than, say, cows or mountain goats. It's well known that the reptile house at a zoo traditionally outdraws all other exhibits. This fauna of the id populated hell, and has never completely succumbed to zoological fact, but rather keeps its unpleasant otherworldly associations.

While the zoological iconography of hell remains in dreams and art, its ideology has clearly lost its hold on our culture. Few people

believe that actual hellhounds and taloned demons roam the nether-
world to punish sinners. Nonetheless, the interesting thing about infernal animals is not any claims about their literal existence, but the
way they have worked their way out of the underworld into our concept of divine justice.

As early as the Sumerian epic *Gilgamesh,* where the Bull of
Heaven ravages the countryside, animals appear as the tools of God's
retribution. In the Bible, Yahweh punishes the Egyptians with
plagues of frogs, lice, and locusts. When the prophet Elisha, newly
appointed by Elijah, left Jericho for Bethel, he was taunted by a group
of children who made fun of his baldness. Somewhat ungraciously,
the inexperienced Elisha curses the children, and immediately two
she-bears rush out of the woods and kill forty-two boys and girls. In
Beowulf, the theft of treasure belonging to a dragon awakens the reptile to burn the hero's kingdom and bring about his death.

Following this lead, the Renaissance interpreted attacks by animals on immoral persons as divinely inspired. It even gave a name to
these retributive animals that purge society of evil (often at the loss of
innocent lives): scourge.

The scourge lives on today. How many of us do not see divine
justice at work when an abused animal turns on its tormentor, or a
wild creature displaced from its habitat strikes back at humanity? Stories of poachers eaten by alligators or lion tamers mauled by their
beasts cannot help but take on moral significance for us, even if intel-
lectually we declare such events to be random. Who (except maybe a
Spaniard) does not secretly cheer for the bull in the bullfight?

And when nature does not provide such narratives, we create
them. One of the many interpretations of Melville's *Moby Dick* portrays Ahab as the representative of the worst instincts of America,
whose greed, obsession, violence, and hatred of nature are crushed by
the cleansing power of the white whale. Arthur Conan Doyle's *Hound
of the Baskervilles* draws its tension from the possibility of a revenging

hound from hell that scourges the Baskerville family for past wrongs, even if the solution to the mystery proves less than supernatural.

I earlier discussed how the symbolic perspective of the *Physiologus* made its way down the centuries into the modern monster movie. The form the fictional monsters take almost always is that of a scourge. Civilization let loose the atomic bomb, and the result is Godzilla or the giant ants of *Them,* who punish society—the guilty and innocent alike—for its trespass into forbidden knowledge. In *Frogs,* one of many harebrained ecological horror films from the 1970s, Ray Milland poisons the Florida Everglades until the reptiles and amphibians rise up to destroy him and his household, in an oblique allusion to Pharaoh and the plagues in Exodus. The war industry seeks extraterrestrial biological weapons, and the result is the carnage in *Alien.* In *Jurassic Park,* the transgression is undisciplined scientific knowledge tampering with the wisdom of evolution. In *The Fly 2* the taboo involves genetic engineering. In these and a hundred other horror films, the plots hold our attention because we have an ingrained cultural understanding of the morality at work with the animal scourge.

We live in a time when popular culture seems to be reveling in depictions of unnatural external threats: the octopus-like aliens of *Independence Day,* or the turgid UFO conspiracies of *The X-Files.* This fictional paranoia can easily be seen as the dark side of our spiritual longings. As the world seems more chaotic and unmoored, we desire a moral universe, we hunger for religious certainty. Unable to find it in traditional creeds that have shut themselves off from the world of nature, we create an antinature of extraterrestrial monsters and mutant beasts. Scourges all, who rather than serving chaos, unwittingly affirm the morality of the living world around us. It is the fact that these fictional creatures are so thoroughly embedded in our physical environment, instead of some abstract realm, that we find so preferable to disembodied doctrines about morality. Monster scourges play out morality right in front of us.

An essential pillar to religion as it has developed in our culture is that the universe not only has an order, but that the order possesses an intelligible moral content. For many intellectuals and nonintellectuals alike, the enormities of the Second World War, and the apparent nihilism of the Cold War, seemed to extinguish the faith that such a moral order exists. God was declared dead in the wake of Auschwitz and Hiroshima. But faith abides in the smallest things. Whatever cynicism we express about the morality of the universe is belied by our continued creation of popular stories about monstrous beasts that punish humanity for its arrogance. If from time to time we need to reassure ourselves of our spiritual resilience under the demoralizing inhumanity of the postmodern world, we only need to watch a horror film, and to the extent we find it satisfying, we know we still believe in a divine order watching over us in the glower of some infernal beast.

CHAPTER THIRTEEN

Cave Paintings

Before I shoot,
whatever the bow does, and the arrow, and I and
the animals, all come true down deep in the earth
—WILLIAM STAFFORD

In 1926, when Dr. Herbert Kuhn delved into the cave of Les Trois-Frères in the French province of Ariègea, he was perhaps the first human to do so in ten thousand years. As he illuminated the walls and saw the cavalcade of animal images colored in mineral oxides stretching before him—a wounded bear, a dying horse, a prowling lioness—he knew more than just decorative art had been born here. It was, he would later write, the "picture of the magic of the hunt."

Kuhn's interpretation of the animal images of the Upper Paleolithic was only the first in a long line. Joseph Campbell argued the animals of cave art "are herds of eternity, not of time—yet even more vividly real and alive than the animals of time, because their ever-living source." Other scholars see "the story of a great primeval goddess told in the caves of southwestern France through the art and rituals that took place inside them." No one really knows the significance of these awesome animal figures, and a definitive answer is lost forever in time. But most students of these images agree that they represent the first undeniable mark of human self-awareness and consciousness of the cosmic spectacle. Whatever their particular purpose, they were first and foremost an expression of spirituality. As such, they tell as much about ourselves as they do about the fauna of the last Ice Age.

John Berger notes that "every view concerning animals is a comment on human history to date." If so, we can then read our spiritual history through the imagery of beasts we have created. The eruption of art in the figures of Paleolithic fauna drove representational art for the next twenty thousand years without a break. Animal images dominated art through the Middle Ages. Indeed, overall, very little change of style even occurred from the cave paintings to the mosaics of Byzantium. Except for a greater sense of symmetry and composition, the horses of Lascaux could have been painted by the same artist who rendered the fresco of the antelopes in Mycenaean Age Thera. The bull and lion of medieval heraldry can be found in more or less the same form as the bas-relief on the Lion Gate of Bronze Age Mycenae, or the animal guardians on the walls of the eighth-century B.C. Palace of Sargon II at Khorsabad, Assyria. The constancy of animal art cuts across time and culture in a way that defies the course of cultural diversity.

Animal imagery made up the substance of spiritual visions for millennia. What began on the subterranean walls of Lascaux and Altamira developed into the complex mystical expressions of the Bible. Ezekiel's profoundly enigmatic visions announce the inexpressible presence of God in his famous description of the celestial wheels within wheels surmounted by four living creatures:

As for the likeliness of their faces, they four had the face of a man, and the face of a lion, on the right side; and they four had the face of an ox on the left side; they four also had the face of an eagle. [Ezekiel 1:10]

Christian iconography interpreted these four wondrous figures as symbols of the four Gospels (Matthew, the man; Mark, the lion;

Luke, the ox; John, the eagle), and many medieval Gospels are accordingly illuminated with these images.

Early Christian art drew on a number of disparate graphic traditions: Hebrew, Persian, Greek, Roman, and Germanic. And yet, despite its eclecticism and ideological squabbles about the status of animals, Christianity produced a style of art that began and remained for much of its history the art of animal images. Beginning with the simple catacomb paintings in Rome and continuing through the ornate Romanesque basilicas, animal motifs made up the main subject of Christian art. The early fourth-century Church of Santa Costanze in Rome, one of the earlier basilicas in Christendom, hardly contains a decorated space that does not have a representation of fauna. The apse, which was the symbolic focus of the church, as it gestured to heaven, shows Christ giving the Law to Peter and Paul, witnessed by four lambs. The mosaic in the vault shows various birds with symbolic meanings, such as the peacock and dove. The sixth-century apse of the beautiful basilica of Sant' Apollinare in Ravenna is dominated by the parade of white sheep that direct their attention to Christ. The Coptic Church in Egypt developed its own style (called Coptic), whose signature was the silhouette of two animals facing one other. The "lacertine" animals discussed in Chapter 3 became the most common decoration of illuminated manuscripts, especially in Northern Europe. By the year 1200, churches, mausoleums, and manuscripts were still being adorned with a symbolic bestiary, regardless of ongoing theological disputes over the existence of animal souls or the reproaches of St. Bernard about the distractions animal art imposed upon the monks.

This vast tradition begins to dwindle in the Renaissance, a fact that should give us pause. We are all familiar with the redemptive role history writing has assigned to this period; the Renaissance is characterized as the force that lifted European civilization out of the gloom and obscurantism of the Middle Ages and toward what we presume it was destined to become: us. This is one story of the Renaissance. But the disappearance of animal imagery tells another. In this narrative of the Renaissance, the era is marked by a desacralization of nature and a growing preoccupation with the human self. Although great leaps in human knowledge took place, the cost was a widening gulf between the individual self and the world it sought to study. While the Renaissance impelled Western civilization toward undreamt-of power and wealth, it also began the marginalization of the nonhuman world, and hence the source of the modern sense of alienation.

By the twentieth century animal images in art had all but completely vanished. The sole subject of art had become the human subject, which was about the search for the human subject, and artistic representation began to funnel down the well of narcissism. The fact that we do not for the most part see animals in our art anymore itself comments on cultural history, their absence symbolizing the rarity of our encounters with the wild and the subjugation of all fauna through either domestication or banishment.

The rare occurrence of animals in art continues this commentary of absence. The best example is Andy Warhol's *Cow Wallpaper*, which enacts the marginalization of the nonhuman. The work consists of rows of identical pink cow heads, pasted on the wall like wallpaper. The image has been called the absurd end of the pastoral tradition in the West. Like the mass-produced Campbell tomato soup cans, the cows reflect a society in which everything is consumed—soup, celebrity, cows, nature, ideas about nature. According to the account of Ivan Karp, even the artistic inception of the images reduced the cows to mere matériel:

> Warhol said that he was using up images to fast that he was feeling exhausted of imagination . . . he said, "I'm running out of *things* . . . Ivan, tell me what to paint!" And he would ask everybody that . . . I couldn't think of anything. I said, "The

only thing that no one deals with now these days is pastoral . . .
My favourite subject is cows." He said, "Cows . . . Of course!
Cows! New cows! Fresh cows!"

The bovine was just a new *thing* for representation, a way to feed our
culture's insatiable desire for new images. It doesn't tell us anything
about the cow; it merely emphasizes the fact that we have become
consumers to the very core.

What Warhol proclaimed, William Wegman enacted. His photographs of weimaraners in human garb and situations are probably the
most widely reproduced images of animals we have in our culture.
Wegman's photographs are of course meant to startle and amuse. The
absurdity of dogs wearing suits or sports gear is a mild form of social
satire: aren't we almost as silly as canines in our behavior. As Ezra
Pound mused: "When I observe the habits of a dog, I conclude that
man is the superior animal. When I observe the habits of men, I do
not know what to think."

But beneath Wegman's whimsy is a deeper, less attractive parable. His bemused pets, decked out like bad imitations of humans, do
reflect the dominant vision of animals in our society. We are a culture
that has assimilated nature into art, consumerism, tennis shoes.

In a highly acclaimed series of prints on endangered animals, pho-
tographer James Balog faced this same evacuation of the natural as
Warhol, but with an attitude of sympathy and sadness. Balog sought
out animals as his subjects as a metaphor for modern humanity's exile
from nature in a consumer society, rather than to fulfill the needs
of that society for artistic consumption. Consciously destroying the
illusion of nature photography, he has created images of rare and endangered species not in their habitat, but in abstract, artificial spaces.
The result is haunting visions of alienation and uprootedness: a sea
turtle on its back on a white table, a rhinoceros enfolded in a bedsheet,

a Florida panther gazing into the camera like a startled orphaned child against an empty background.

Nature photography and film in our culture reinforce the view that animals live in an idyllic state of wilderness. This imagery of paradise feeds our desires to live lives with stronger roots in nature, without requiring any action on our part. Balog's art deconstructs this romantic fiction by showing animals confused, isolated, "exiled from Eden."

If our depictions of animals are ultimately about ourselves and how we relate to the world, Balog's eerie iconography should make us reflect. We look into the hauntingly vacant eyes of the Florida panther, and suddenly see ourselves, the fauna of alienation.

PART FOUR

The Soul's Other Kingdom

CHAPTER FOURTEEN

Saintly Zoology

I propose Francis as the patron saint of ecologists.
—LYNN WHITE, JR.

For almost a thousand years, literature in Europe had one compulsive theme: the lives (and deaths) of saints. Saints' lives as the genre was called, came into existence in the fourth century, taking the wilderness-loving St. Anthony as its subject, and quickly spread across Europe, in both poetry and prose, in Latin and the vernacular, until it represented one of the main products of monasteries, rivaled only by wine and textiles. Given the precious nature of books in the centuries before the printing press (a fine volume might cost $30,000 in today's currency), the blossoming of saints' lives represented not only a literary passion, but a huge capital expenditure.

Then, in the twelfth century, the genre all but vanished in a puff of smoke. Today the hagiography of the Middle Ages is read, if at all, mostly by scholars, and the sensibility of these works seems so alien to our worldview that they are usually studied only as linguistic and cultural artifacts, as opposed to works of art.

Like other cultural obsessions, such as the seventeenth-century tulip craze, the literary preoccupation with saints illuminates society as much by its sudden disappearance as by its curious intensity. The prominence of the genre obviously had something to do with the self-interest and influence of the authors—as the only fully literate people in the Middle Ages, clerics had a monopoly on what constituted the proper subject of belles lettres; not surprisingly the themes they chose often burnished the reputation of the monastic life and the historical figures who played a role in the continuity of their religious orders. But more than cronyism was at work behind the popularity of hagiography. The Middle Ages had a deep and justifiable anxiety about living a Christian life in an age marked by vast armies on the march, Viking depredations, and cultures rising to power and going extinct in a matter of decades. *Guthlac A,* an Old English versified saint's life, captures the angst and pessimism of the times in a few of its opening lines:

> *The world is troubled [literally stirred up];*
> *The love of Christ cools; many tribulations*
> *have arisen throughout this middle-earth.*

The saint offered a more than theoretical pattern for living in the anxious flux of secular history, a model of how to face a hostile, chaotic world with equanimity and faith. When other models of existence appeared—the scientist and entrepreneur, for instance—who could influence nature and human events, the saints lost their literary standing.

Because the genre provided a pattern for living, the individual works all seem remarkably alike, if not downright repetitive, to modern readers. Dozens of different saints from diverse countries and centuries became the protagonists of hagiography, some walking the deserts of Egypt, others occupying the fens of East Anglia, still others suffering in legendary lands of cannibals and monsters. But all follow the conventions of the genre that were set in stone long before most of Europe learned to write. The typical saint's life traces the saint's youth, his path to the ascetic life, his trials and temptations at the hands of Satan, his miracles and healings, his gift of prophecy, a warning of his death, a farewell to his disciples, and then a miracle at his tomb (usually the dead saint's failure to decompose, accompanied by the sweet odor of sanctity). In addition, among the most important events that marked a saintly biography was an encounter with a wild beast.

On some occasions the saint and the beast met in conflict, playing out the archetypal battle between good and evil. The devil in the shape of a black bird tempted St. Benedict and tried to kill him, until the saint made the sign of the cross and the demonic fowl vanished. St. Peter of Verona was celebrating Mass when Satan galloped into the church in the form of a horse and began stamping the saint's congregation. Again, the sign of the cross foiled the devil's plans and the horse evaporated. St. Guthlac fought off demons that took the shape of venom-spitting serpents.

But the appearance of enemy animals pales in comparison with the complex, friendly relationships saints usually had with wild beasts. St. Jerome's faithful lion, mentioned earlier in this book, is a good example. Its relationship with Jerome follows a pattern found in many saint's lives, where the wild beast becomes tame under the holy man's tutelage. After the monks accept Jerome's lion into their monastery, Jerome puts him in charge of the donkey that carries firewood from a grove to the monastery. The lion loyally protects the donkey, but one day, the great cat falls asleep and some merchants steal his charge. The monks assume that the lion has killed and eaten the creature, so as punishment, they order the king of the beasts to take up the duty of hauling firewood. Though wrongly accused, he does so willingly. In the end, the innocence of the lion shines all the more brightly due to this submission to injustice, as the feline finds the donkey, routs the thieves, and brings the equine back to the monastery.

The lion was so important to the legend surrounding St. Jerome that it appears in three quarters of all paintings, graphics, and sculptures depicting the church father. In a number of paintings that show various important moments in the saint's career on one canvas (a common form of telescoped representation in medieval art), the lion is the one constant in each scene, as if the events were seen from a lion's-eye view.

The lion was not alone in Jerome's bestiary. One scholar counted no less than twenty-two species of mammals, thirty-three kinds of birds, four species of reptiles, and six invertebrates, all appearing in artistic renditions of Jerome. This was appropriate for a saint who, legends aside, wrote sympathetically about the animal kingdom: "For just as we marvel at the Creator when we behold not only heaven and earth, sun and ocean, elephants, camels, horses, oxen, panthers, bears and lions, but also tiny creatures—ants, gnats, flies, worms and the like—their forms are better known to us than their names."

Virtually every other saint joined Jerome in having a wild beast as a comrade. St. Aninas lived with two lions in a cave. Marcarius, Mammas, Mark the Silentiary, Theophanes, and Gerasimus were all connected to lions (in fact the story of the donkey and the wrongly accused lion got transposed from St. Gerasimus to St. Jerome). When a wolf devoured one of his oxen, St. Gentius compelled the predator to help him with his plowing. St. Mala and St. Santes of Urbino both lost their donkeys to wolves, who then had to work the fields in their victims' stead. In the most creative use of a wild animal, St. Maidoc ordered a sea cow from the ocean to plow his field.

The authors of saints' lives had an explanation for these close ties to animals. The encounter demonstrated the holy man's power over nature and natural forces. His control over a wild animal was similar to the ability of Jesus to calm a storm (and in fact not a few saint's lives had such meteorological miracles thrown in). In addition, the saint's beast performed a homiletic function. In this orthodox inter- pretation, wild animals represent sinful mankind—willful, unlawful, violent; they become civilized and obedient under the guidance of the saint, just as sinners overcome their baser nature through exposure to the Scriptures. The saint is also the church, with the animals as the congregation. Or the two can represent reason and appetite. And so on. The point is that a special relationship existed between saint and beast in this genre which defined the power of the holy life.

Nevertheless, the clerical explanations ring hollow. The animals of saints' lives are portrayed in particular ways that bring them into the moral realm of God and man. They are a kind of Christian totem, conscious and caring, loyal and humble. This literary choice is all the more interesting in that these works were written exclusively by clerics, men who knew the orthodox theology about the status of animals—even Ælfric, the churchman who insisted that dogs have no soul, wrote numerous saints' lives that included the improbable bestiaries of the genre. Despite their background, these representatives of medieval orthodoxy seemed compelled to see animals in a way that ennobled and humanized.

In his *Life of Cuthbert*, the Venerable Bede, the preeminent scholar of eighth-century England, apparently sensed no deep theological problem in having penitent ravens gesturing for pardon and bringing a gift to the saint after damaging a house. Although there is a long hagiographical tradition of ravens assisting saints, ultimately traceable to I Kings 17, where Elijah is fed by ravens; and although Bede no doubt understood the ravens' extraordinary behavior as part of the obligatory exhibition of the saint's miraculous power over nature—nevertheless, the birds here are given anthropomorphic qualities above and beyond the requirements of miracle-working. Sensing that *some* justification for the human-like chagrin of the birds is in order, Bede quotes Proverbs 6:6 about learning from an ant, and falls back with a thud on the exegetical thinking of the *Physiologus:* "Let no one think it ridiculous to learn a lesson in virtue from birds." For whatever it is worth, the elaborate border of the tenth-century illuminated frontispiece of a copy of this work contains what looks like a squawking raven, suggesting this episode was interesting enough to have caught the illuminator's attention.

How did the readers take all these plowing, penitent, rational animals? To modern readers, the saints' lives have a fairy-tale quality about them, so we can dismiss the matter out of hand without much thought. A medieval audience did not have that luxury. These stories purported to document church history and were not to be taken lightly. Denying the veracity of a saint's miracles could cause a person to be dragged before an ecclesiastical court, or worse. Moreover some saints went beyond merely associating with animals to the point of coming to their spiritual defense. St. David of Garesja protected deer and birds from hunters, proclaiming their special relationship to God: "He whom I believe in and worship looks after and feeds all his creatures, to whom He has given birth."

Where then do the saint's bestiaries belong—in fiction or in doctrine?

We usually discount medieval thought as rigid and unsophisticated, incapable of approaching new ideas with anything but fear. Quite the opposite is true. The medieval way of thinking excelled at holding together inconsistencies, at seeing two or more aspects of the same object, cutting across time, space, and signification. A serpent could simultaneously be a species of reptile, the creature/spirit that seduced Eve into sin, and an emblem of redemption and resurrection (through the sloughing of its skin). The *Physiologus* addresses this very issue, responding to those who wonder how snakes, lions, and other beasts could possibly symbolize Christ given their "unclean" status in the Bible. The author's answer is both deceptively simple and profound: "The creatures are twofold . . . And there are many others among the creatures who have double significances; certain are praiseworthy, while others are blameworthy, according to their different habits and nature." In contrast to this double vision, our culture has been trained to seek out contradictions, and lawyer-like, use them to disprove assertions. The Middle Ages experienced the world less suspiciously and more creatively.

I believe the saints' lives reflect a particular view of animals that existed alongside the strict, anthropomorphic theology of human uniqueness. This saintly view came to mind in the context of holy subjects, such as saints' lives. Theology taught that dogs had no souls, but when the sacred was at issue, medieval authors unconsciously shifted their perception into a kind of Christian dreamtime where, as Jerome's quote indicates, God manifested himself everywhere, even in lions and insects. But beyond this, in the Christian dreamtime of saints' lives, lions cared for donkeys, and ravens asked for forgiveness. The saints' bestiary contained conscious, soul-inspired creatures, who were just as involved in their redemption as the pious hermits.

It was not that one perspective was real and the other fictional. Both were equally true in the medieval way of looking at the world. The theological view reflected the demands of reason and the perception that human existence is very different from that of the rest of the animal world, at least on the surface. The saintly view responded to God's love of creation found throughout the Bible, from Psalm 106, where the wild beasts are said to be in God's care, to Jesus' remarkable statement that a sparrow does not fall to the ground without drawing God's concern. God's largesse, in this view, embraces all of creation, human and nonhuman alike.

In Christian iconography, when Christ died on the cross, all of nature wept. This *natura plangens* convention took the signs and wonders that accompany Christ's death in Matthew 27:46–54—earthquakes, darkness, the rending of the temple veil—and reworked them in such a way that nature acted volitionally. The ultimate purpose of the convention was usually homiletic, a rhetorical way of emphasizing the depravity of those who turn their back on Christ's sacrifice when even dumb nature was moved to respond. Still, the sacred topic again plunged the medieval authors beyond theology into the saintly view where the natural world "is animated, endowed with sensation, feeling, a will of its own; the created world, sorely aggrieved by the sight of its creator hanging from the cross, reacts with violent upheaval and disruption of its natural functions."

The saintly view of animals found its strongest voice in the person of St. Francis. It is unequivocally announced in the egalitarian first line of his famous *Sermon to the Birds:* "Oh, birds, my brothers, you have a great obligation to praise your Creator." For Francis, all creation participated in a spiritual democracy, where animals, human, and even inanimate objects had the duty and the pleasure of celebrating their divine origin. He practiced what might be called a kind of "intersubjectivity" that bound all creatures with the Creator through humility and veneration.

The legend goes that a fierce wolf was ravaging the lands around Gubbio in central Italy. In the manner of saints' lives, Francis preached to the wolf about the sins it had committed. The wolf repented and when it died, it was buried in consecrated ground for its decision to turn from sin to redemption (curiously, in the nineteenth century a wolf's skull was reportedly unearthed in an old graveyard near Gubbio). The story epitomizes Francis' teaching: although the world appears diverse and contradictory, humans and nonhuman existence intersect at the eternal point of God's sovereignty and goodness, the point where people, wolves, and sparrows become spiritual brothers.

Based on his egalitarian approach to God's creation, Francis has been called the greatest spiritual revolutionary of Western history. Perhaps it is more accurate that Francis said nothing new, nothing that the author of a badly written saint's life did not know, he simply proclaimed the saintly view of animals more powerfully and steadfastly than any other Christian holy man. This is why his less intrepid progeny could not bring themselves to condemn his seeming heterodoxy; they knew that he was only taking seriously what nearly a thousand years of saints' lives had repeatedly suggested.

The kindness and kinship toward animals made by Francis and the hundreds of other saints expressed more than mere sentimentality; they were the fruits of genuine spirituality. For almost a thousand years, the saintly view of animals was able to coexist with the less generous theology of human uniqueness. But when it faded from the scene, what remained was not Ælfric's soulless dog, but a new relationship with animals that we live with today. And, as we shall see, it all had to do with a very ancient image of a great chain.

CHAPTER FIFTEEN

Paragon of Animals

To evolution and to comedy, nothing is sacred but life itself.
—JOSEPH W. MEEKER

Our culture once had a single metaphor to describe humanity's relationship with God and nature: the *scala naturae* or "scales of nature,"
or as it was more popularly known in the Middle Ages, "the Great
Chain of Being." In this cosmological vision, the world was a vast
filigree of lower and higher forms, from sponges to Godhead, with
humankind's place higher than beasts and "a little lower than the
angels," as the Eighth Psalm delicately phrases it. The Great Chain
conjoined the humblest creature to the rest of creation and to its Creator, as if space itself were a seamless fabric of unfolding relationships
that draped across the divide between the physical and the spiritual.
The vision of the Great Chain saw the world as an infinitely diverse
but wonderfully complete whole.

The idea went back to Greek antiquity, where it existed more or
less as a dreary philosophical abstraction, a response to the observation that nature abhors a vacuum, a maxim that required something
or other to fill up empty space. But medieval Christianity infused the
Great Chain with a new power that captured not only the interests
of scholars, but the popular imagination. It expressed God's eternal
participation with his creation; it graphically depicted the biblical
statement that humanity had dominion over the rest of the animals;

and, it gave us the security of belonging to the world (however temporary, seen from the drama of the Apocalypse).

If the Great Chain sounds a little like a spiritualized notion of modern ecology, that should come as no surprise. The metaphor played a role in medieval philosophy similar to that of ecology in our time. The Great Chain was a vast symbol of the orderliness and virtue of God's handiwork, and such a perspective fit perfectly into a society in which restraint was the dominant mood, and the idea of progress had yet to be invented. Although medieval Europeans were quite capable of abusing animals and destroying the natural environment, the idea of doing so in a systematic way to bring about "progress" (through animal experimentation to improve surgical techniques, for example) would never have crossed their minds. Thomas Aquinas invoked the Great Chain in an argument that could be made today by a conservation biologist condemning the extinction of animal species brought about by deforestation:

[T]he goodness of the species transcends the goodness of the individual, as form transcends matter; therefore the multiplication of species is a greater addition to the good of the universe than the multiplication of individuals of a single species. The perfection of the universe therefore requires not only a multitude of individuals, but also diverse kinds, and therefore diverse grades of things.

Aquinas, of course, used the term "species" in the philosophical, not the biological sense, but if he had been able to understand animal extinction, he would have probably applied the logic of "diverse grades of things" to biological diversity as rigorously as he did to the realm of concepts. Aquinas, and his contemporaries, would have considered the destruction of an entire link of the Great Chain an incomprehensible sin against God's perfect order.

But even by Aquinas' time, weak links had already begun to appear in the Great Chain. In his book *Of Animals,* St. Albertus Magnus, Aquinas' mentor, attempted (not always successfully) to discuss living creatures without reference to the spiritual realm implied by the *scala naturae,* and confined himself to cataloguing the characteristics actually observed in nature (or putatively observed by travelers or classical natural historians such as Pliny). At one point, Albertus notes that the "crow is suitable for auguries and incantation, but it is not our purpose to discuss such matters here." The statement concedes that there is a symbolic order in which animals proffer deeper significations, a "reading" that can be made of the type the *Physiologus* discovered. But Albertus invites his audience to bracket off this invisible world in order to concentrate only on the visible. In Albertus' simple dismissal of the crow's augury, we can see the glimmer of the seventeenth century and the rise of scientific empiricism.

The Great Chain survived through the Middle Ages, but the Renaissance transformed it from a symbol of human restraint in the face of a perfect order to an emblem of human superiority over the natural world. Drawing on humanity's position in the Great Chain between "dumb beasts" and articulate angels, Renaissance humanism insisted there was an insurmountable difference between *Homo sapiens* and the rest of creation. "Man" became, to quote Hamlet, "the beauty of the world! the paragon of animals!" (though Shakespeare, as if aware of the absurdity of the claim, follows this declaration with an obscene joke at Hamlet's expense). About the same time Hamlet first strutted upon the stage, Sir Francis Bacon expressed the new centrality of humanity more bluntly: "Man, if we look to final causes, may be regarded as the centre of the world; inasmuch that if man were taken away from the world, the rest would seem all astray, without aim or purpose."

The Great Chain broke apart by the end of the Renaissance. Or more precisely, the divine links above humanity were cut off from the natural world, leaving "Man" at the pinnacle of a physical order of things. Eventually, the Enlightenment replaced the metaphor of cosmic links with that of the machine. The world was like an intricate watch, created by an omnipotent Watchmaker, who having crafted it and started its gears turning, no longer needed to participate in its operations. Nonetheless, the cultural residue of the Great Chain still haunts us and is the source of the notion that *Homo sapiens* stands highest in a natural order of "lower life forms," even though the biological sciences and the evolutionary metaphor they provide tell us we should know better.

We are all familiar with the tableau. It hovers there, visible to our thinking, an idea given graphic form in our minds, as much a part of our sense of self as childhood photographs. On the far left (the side from which we read and write texts), in some primordial sea floats a colony of single-celled creatures, protozoa huddled together as if conspiring about what is to follow. To their immediate right, more complicated but still rudimentary forms appear: a worm, an anemone, a jellyfish, a mollusk. Then, to fill this ocean of progress to the brim, a primitive fish swims into existence. Continuing to the right, poised between sea and land, an ungainly creature with a gaping mouth rears up on elongated fins to breathe its first gulp of air. It is succeeded by a salamander-like amphibian, with all four feet moving tentatively forward on dry ground. After that creeps a reptile, large and arrogant, seemingly aware that for a season it has dominion over the earth. Farther to the right, however, a craftier animal, covered with fur and ambling on bearlike paws, takes its place: a protomammal. No bird appears at this point, or if it does, it is an insignificant pair of wings flying high above the mammal—an apparent digression from the orderly procession below.

Now the really interesting creatures make their appearance; the ones we have all been waiting for. First, a monkey and an ape, still on all fours but apparently straining to stand upright. That virtue, however, is reserved for the next in line, a primitive hominid, perhaps an australopithecine, still hirsute and a bit stooped. His successor, a

Homo erectus, stands straighter and more confident as he lumbers into humanness: only his heavy-browed face gives his backwardness away. After that, a Neanderthal walks, often shown holding a club, perhaps to suggest he hasn't quite made it yet to the noble estate of civilized existence. And finally, on the far right, front and center, leading this zoomorphic parade of emerging forms is the being toward which this compressed history of life has been converging: taller than the rest and highbrowed, a fully erect *Homo sapiens* marches. With his back to the remainder of nature, he faces the blankness at the margin of the graphic, striding off into the invisible unknown with the self-assured gait of one who walks in the evolutionary limelight.

This graphic representation of evolution, which we have all seen in high school textbooks, is of course a crude simplification. It is a heuristic, meant to bring home a basic principle of a scientific theory rather than to elaborate on the very complex and subtle lineage of living forms on this planet. Nevertheless, the particular way our culture chooses to present evolutionary theory suggests an ethical and philosophical stance at work, if not in the makeup of the graphic itself, then at least in how it is used and understood by our culture at large.

Would it not be possible to make a graphic true to evolution theory in which, say, a greyhound occupies the coveted far right position? Dogs emerged more recently than humans. If the graphic is ordered chronologically, as it appears to be, then wouldn't this be a more perfect representation?

The incongruity of having a greyhound succeed a human in our alternate evolution highlights an important ambiguity in the tableau. Strictly speaking the graphic only represents *human* evolution, not evolution in general, as any biologist would have already vehemently pointed out. But this unimpeachable, scientifically accurate objection neglects the way in which the graphic is actually used in our society. For a technological culture transfixed by the presumed supremacy of intellect over nature, human evolution *is* evolution for all intents and purposes. The emergence of *Homo sapiens* stands as a symbol for the entire saga of biological adaptation on this planet. Ask people to "draw" evolution and they will probably come up with something very much like our graphic, with a human being at the lead. Hasn't evolution always been "tending" toward humanity, our culture seems to insist, with a steady development in intellect, creativity, consciousness, or some other ambiguous quality which the struggle for survival has apparently lavished on human beings above all else? Even trained biologists use the term "lower life forms"—a directionality that comes straight out of the Great Chain of Being, though stripped of its appreciation of and reverence toward each link in the chain.

In this way, a double meaning emerges: the representation not only has a scientific significance, but a cultural life in which it embodies and reinforces the idea that the human species is the "goal" of evolution. No reputable biologist would condone such a notion, and yet it is undeniably part of our technological culture, with roots that go back to the Great Chain.

A truly accurate representation of evolution would have humans, greyhounds, slimeworts, and all other modern living forms on the right, representing the present, each equally sharing in the unpredictable unfolding of evolution, with their ancestral forms off somewhere in the past, on the left, intermingling promiscuously in a wanton dance of life. Scientists, of course, do use a genealogical table to represent the evolution of life. In a sense, this scientific view of evolution recasts the Great Chain of Being, but instead of linking species through a timeless and perfect hierarchy, it unites them genealogically. In the evolutionary chain of being, all living things are kin.

But universal kinship is not what comes to mind when the word "evolution" is used and it lacks the cultural resonance of the humanized tableau.

We should ask: Why privilege brain size or bipedalism or any of the other traits of humanity, in representing evolution? Couldn't we give the privileged position according to some other quality we see, rightly or wrongly, as central to understanding the evolutionary process? Thus, if we assumed the ordering principle of evolution is the development of fleetness of foot rather than intellect, a cheetah should be the first in line—running well ahead of the pack. If, instead, longevity is that special quality, then bristlecone pine trees, which can live thousands of years and must experience human society the way we do mayflies, would capture the privileged position now held by a hominid. The list could be extended indefinitely depending on the characteristic being promoted, in essence giving each species its privileged moment as the capstone of evolution, and thus requiring as many representations as there are species on the planet. It would be Andy Warhol's fifteen minutes of fame played out on an evolutionary canvas.

The theory of evolution maintains that all living things, under the pressure of natural selection and domestication, have developed from past forms and are more or less related genealogically depending on the closeness of a common ancestor. This is to say that there is really no basis for putting any life form at the forefront of evolution: elephants are no more developed than toadstools, salmon are no less advanced than seagulls, cabbages have as much status in the scheme of life as kings. To be sure, we are more closely related genealogically to chimpanzees than to lichen, but that doesn't mean lichen lags behind either humans or chimpanzees in the history of life. Chimps and humans can make tools, but lichen can photosynthesize and we can't; chimps and humans have high IQs; but lichen can dissolve stones. The useless comparisons could continue indefinitely. Although it may hurt our species' ego to be likened to lichen, from an evolutionary perspective at least, we cannot produce any biologically aristocratic titles and insist upon our privileged status.

The popular representation of evolution has become a cultural icon for a purpose altogether ulterior to, in fact at variance with, the explication of a scientific theory. What it presents is a story, a narrative, with a fictionalized version of humanity: the character of "Man," or as Muir called him, "Lord Man." We have turned evolution into the monologue of "Man."

The theme of this monologue is that "Man" is a distinct entity among all the other species of this planet. There is "Man" and then there is nature, the realm of "lower" forms, from which "Man" has emerged and separated himself. But this unique creature is not only superior to other life forms; he is their consummation, the goal toward which they have been striving during the past three and a half billion years of organic history. "Man," so the story goes, is the aim of evolution, its telos. And therefore, this paragon of animals, this demigod of creation, has a sort of cosmic sanction bestowed upon his activities. This man's history *is* nature; it is the principle behind the order of things, as Bacon argued, and his intellect with its devices can rightfully supplant the natural world and its unrefined denizens.

While evolutionary theory stands in exact contradiction to the superiority of humanity (and was vigorously denounced by religious authorities as a result), its representation, it seems, has very much been captured by this idea. Thus, a theory that demoted humanity from semidivine status into the swelter of biological forms has strangely come to serve the purpose of promoting the biological and moral superiority of humanity. A biological category has become a moral imperative.

Each religion has its own way of dealing with evolutionary theory: rejecting it, accepting it, modifying it, retelling it. My point is not to argue the issue of the theory's truth, but to highlight the misuse of the fictionalized version of the theory as a metaphor for human existence, a metaphor many religions themselves embrace in placing humanity above the rest of animal creation. Moreover, the fictional character of "Man" no longer merely dwells in the story of evolution, but rather he has installed himself in all the institutions of our culture, including our religious institutions. "Man," as the morally superior center of the world, has banished the saintly view of animals, has marginalized the rest of creation, has monopolized the conversation about spirituality in a way early Christianity, Judaism, and Islam would not have understood—indeed would probably have considered an expression of the ultimate sin of pride. Regrettably, it is this fictionalized character who is often preached from the pulpit, not so much in an explicit manner, but by the exclusion of the rest of creation that marks most of our culture's discourse. Our language of spirituality, unlike the saints' lives, seems willfully and ungenerously to exclude everything except this self-involved "Man."

In *The Order of Things*, Michel Foucault argued that our modern view of humanity as the sovereign of all possible knowledge, ethics, and values is a recent invention, a result of the Enlightenment and the distinct way it arranged and categorized knowledge. What if, he wonders, the way we have come to understand the world were to change, perhaps in the wake of some monumental event, perhaps through the reevaluation of our values? Foucault concludes the book with this premonition:

> If those arrangements were to disappear as they appeared, if
> some event of which we can at the moment do no more than
> sense the possibility . . . were to cause them to crumble . . . then
> one can certainly wager that man would be erased, like a face
> drawn in sand at the edge of the sea.

Could it be that "Man" as we have understood him to be, as the zenith of evolution, as the biological and ethical centerpiece of nature, as the only creature blessed by God, is an extravagant fiction we can no longer afford, not only due to the havoc his story has wreaked on the environment, but the poverty he has caused in our souls? To change the Foucauldian stick figure we have become, we require a spiritual vision, and here again suddenly the animals that provided the first metaphors for religion emerge from twilight, like Paulinus' redeeming sparrow.

CHAPTER SIXTEEN

Peaceable Kingdoms

Not just people
Not even just buildings,
but all that keeps happening.
—WILLIAM STAFFORD

Visions. Spirituality is first and foremost about vision. I do not necessarily or even primarily mean the kind of personal mystical visions
that saints and seers sometimes have, private illuminations of the divine that both fascinate and perplex. I refer simply to a purpose and
direction that a spiritually aware life must have, and that an inspired
religion must promote or risk fading into irrelevance.

Most religions express a hope for a better world, a foretokened
bliss that takes many forms. For Judaism, it is the reign of the Messiah. Christians look forward to the new Jerusalem prepared like a
bride for Christ's second advent. The Koran promises the faithful a
Home of Peace in the gardens of paradise. But whatever the details,
the vision of a better world always calls for neighbor to help neighbor,
for violence to end, for egoism to give way to love. Inevitably, the
expression of this hope seems to be expressed in the image of a new
relationship between animals and humans, and a redemption of nature from violence to cooperation.

Our culture sums up the complex longing for a harmonious world
in one phrase: "the lion shall lie down with the lamb." The image, if
not the exact phrasing, comes from Isaiah and involves more than just
these two species:

The wolf also shall dwell with the lamb, and the leopard shall lie down with the kid; and the calf and the young lion and the fatling together; and a little child shall lead them.

And the cow and the bear shall feed; their young ones shall lie down together; and the lion shall eat straw like the ox.

And the sucking child shall play on the hole of the asp, and the weaned child shall put his hand on the cockatrice' den.

They shall not hurt nor destroy in all my holy mountain: for the earth shall be full of knowledge of the Lord, as the waters cover the sea. [Isaiah 10:6–9]

This powerful vision of humanity at peace with creation, and creation at peace with itself, can be taken literally or metaphorically, depending on one's theology. But what cannot be denied is the impact the image has had on our religious imagination. The striking picture of predator and prey reclining in friendship, and a child casually playing with a venomous snake does not merely embody our hopes, it clarifies them, it informs us that something has gone wrong with our relationship to the world around us that cannot be described with purely philosophical terminology.

The vision of a peaceable kingdom cuts across cultures and time. A fragmentary Sumerian poem about the paradise of Dilmun, written at least a millennium before Isaiah, describes a similar bestiary at peace:

The land Dilmun is clean, the land Dilmun is most bright.
In Dilmun the raven utters no cries,
The ittidu-bird utters not the cry of the ittidu-bird,
The lion kills not,
The wolf snatches not the lamb,
Unknown is the kid-devouring wild dog,
Unknown is the grain-devouring . . . ,
The dove droops not the head,

In the paradise envisioned by the Old Icelandic *Saga of St. Matthew,* animals again define the harmony that is to come. "If a man asks the water for fish," the saga explains, "it will provide various kinds at his feet."

The peaceable kingdom, where humans and nature live in harmony, entered the vocabulary and iconography of the West. Alongside the infernal vision of *Musical Hell* in his *Triptych of the Garden of Earthly Delights,* Bosch created the equally striking *Garden of Eden* and filled it with all types of strange and beautiful animals dwelling in a lush landscape (though typical of the medieval mind-set, he shows a cat devouring a rat, and a bird eating a frog to foreshadow the Fall that has yet to occur). Some four hundred years later, the Quaker artist Edward Hicks draws on a similar animal iconography in painting his many versions of *The Peaceable Kingdom.* One version, *The Peaceable Kingdom of the Branch,* has the words of Isaiah written around the border. Several of the paintings in this series show in the background a meeting between Pilgrims and American Indians, as if Hicks were appropriating the far-off biblical ideal into the history of the new nation as a goal that is both eternal and yet constantly before us.

A half-century later, the peaceable kingdom emerges in a different context. The French artist Henri Rousseau painted *The Dream* and other works showing men and women seemingly transported to primeval jungles filled with exotic wildlife. *The Dream* depicts a nude woman on a couch in the middle of a lush forest harboring a menagerie of docile monkeys, elephants, birds, and lions, all seemingly looked over by a man standing in their midst, playing a horn. The artist explained that the work meant no more than the title indicated—it was about a woman who falls asleep on a couch and dreams she is in the jungle. But the juxtaposition of humans and animals, predators and prey in a serene landscape points beyond the subject matter to a vision of harmony that transcends the world as we know it, a harmony only encountered in dreams. It is Isaiah's communal vision as the personal reverie of a weary industrial citizen.

Our culture tends to attribute these and other expressions of hope for a peaceable kingdom to naïveté and sentiment. They certainly can and have been used as a kind of philosophical escapism from the rigors of a world constantly in conflict. But we must be reminded that visions of natural harmony are at the core of our religious beliefs, from Genesis to Revelation, expressed in the Bible and most other sacred texts, played out through a hundred saints' lives, embodied in religious art and in the pious interpretations of the *Physiologus*. The tableau of the lion and the lamb at peace convinced our civilization while still in its infancy that there was more to the good life than prosperity and empire. It challenged the fiction of "Man" as the center of the creation. It made us dream. If visions of natural harmony are mere naïveté, then we should ask, What does our culture offer as a replacement?

The declaration by Jesus that the kingdom of heaven was within was taken by Western religious thought as a cosmic invitation for in-wardness, for turning away from creation. A false distinction thus arose between the religious and the scientific sensibility. But, if Warwick Fox is correct about the core of Christianity being the blessing of creation, then exploring the kingdom of heaven within us paradoxically turns outward again toward the peaceable kingdom foretokened in Genesis. For many centuries, the official gaze of religion has stopped at "Man" rather than looking into ourselves as humans whose meanings only come to light in the larger landscape of swallow flight and cricket song.

The spiritual aridity that marks much of modern culture has many causes. This book has looked at just one: the marginalization of animals, which has led many of our sacred metaphors to crack and fade, leaving humanity in a world without a firm grasp on its spiritual self-identity as part of a greater creation story. Everywhere "Man" has replaced creation with his own artifacts, both physically and intel-lectually. We wonder why the sacred appears absent from our lives, yet everything that saints, seers, and prophets once invoked to express humanity's relationship with the divine seems to be receding in the face of Man's talkative centrality. We wonder why our spiritual vocabulary has shrunk into sanctimony and dogma, yet many of our religious institutions have become monologues about humanity without even a mention of the animal world that inspired our sacred texts and gave their names to the very letters of the Bible.

But the power to refresh our spiritual insights still resides in our bestiaries, both the animals of nature and the animals of the mind. The beauty of wild creatures has never stopped amazing us. The Twenty-third Psalm still moves and Isaiah's peaceable kingdom still beckons. Our own religious history teems with the clamor of significant beasts that tradition or sheer neglect has eclipsed from view. Since the rise of science, Western culture has undertaken the discovery and cataloguing of the earth's remarkable zoological diversity. Perhaps the time has come for us to embark upon a different kind of journey of discovery, the rediscovery of the meaningful fauna that leads from the visible to the invisible, from knowledge to virtue, from "Man" to our humanity.

Maybe then we can be included in the praise of that almost forgotten book: "Rightly, therefore, did Physiologus compare the ways of animals to spiritual matters."

I live in the Coachella Valley, a part of the Sonoran Desert. As I finish this book, spring has come around again to the desert. At dusk you can see once again bats with baby faces take flight and the great chevrons of geese moving overhead, attended by their strange clarinets and the music of deep history, as they travel the invisible path they have followed for aeons. Overnight an oleander bursts into pink by the wall, where a lizard creeps out of hiding to sun itself. The same lizard seen by a second-century monk on his way to morning prayer, when there came to him a vision of his salvation.

Each creature follows its own course oblivious to me. And yet together they seem to make up an intelligible whole that concerns me in ways I have not even begun to fathom.

Notes

·

INTRODUCTION

p. 1.   Epigraph. John Berger, *About Looking* (New York: Pantheon Books, 1980), p. 5.

p. 2.   *Bishop William of Wykeham . . . good discipline.* Quoted in C. I. A. Ritchie, *The British Dog* (London: Robert Hale, 1981), p. 64.

p. 2.   *One distraught nun . . . terrifying them.* Ibid., p. 64.

pp. 5–6. *His love for God's creation . . . should not be harmed.* See Julien Green, *God's Fool: The Life and Times of St. Francis,* trans. Peter Heinegg (San Francisco: Harper & Row, 1987), p. 217.

p. 8.   *In the Great Code . . . its controlling modes of thought.* Northrop Frye, *The Great Code: The Bible and Literature* (New York: Harcourt Brace Jovanovich, 1982), p. 54.

p. 9.   *in flies a sparrow . . . we know not. The Conversion of King Eadwine,* Book II, Chapter 10. My translation.

p. 10.   *The Prophet told of a woman . . . Eden at her disposal.* Quoted in Javad Nurbakhsh, *Dogs from a Sufi Point of View,* trans. Terry Graham et al. (New York: KhaniQahi Nimatullahi Publications, 1989), pp. 28–29.

p. 14.   *Animals are good to think.* Claude Lévi-Strauss, *Totemism,* trans. R. Needham (London: Merlin Press, 1962), p. 89.

p. 15.   *For millennia, animals were . . . creatures of childhood, nightmare and dream.* John Berger, "Animal World," *New Society,* November 1971.

CHAPTER ONE

p. 19.   Epigraph. William Blake, "Auguries of Innocence."

p. 22.   *And when the ass saw the angel . . . he said, Nay.* Unless otherwise
              indicated, I use the Authorized King James Version of the Bible
              throughout this book.

p. 24.   *The elegant phrase . . . created in his creatures.* Quoted in Gary
              Kowalski, *The Souls of Animals* (Walpole, N.H.: Stillpoint Publish-
              ing, 1991), p. 105.

p. 24.   *Not satisfied with simple homicide . . . the philosopher's death.* For a
              summary of the idea of the world soul in medieval thought, see
              Roger D. Sorrel, *St. Francis of Assisi and Nature: Tradition and
              Innovation in Western Christian Attitudes Toward the Environment*
              (New York: Oxford University Press, 1988), pp. 9–27.

p. 24.   *Thy whole creation speaks . . . look upon them. The Confessions of St.
              Augustine,* trans. F. J. Sheed (New York: Sheed & Ward, 1988).

p. 24.   *He even says . . . study and reason.* Ibid.

p. 25.   *Hund is sawulleas . . . life forms. Aelfric's Catholic Homilies: the
              Second Series, Text,* ed. M. Godden, EETS s.s. 5 (London: Oxford
              University Press, 1979), no. xviii, 11, pp. 75–76.

p. 26.   *What is the meaning . . . the commandments of God.* Quoted in Rüdi-
              ger Robert Beer, *Unicorn: Myth and Reality,* trans. Charles M.
              Stern (New York: Van Nostrand Reinhold Co., 1972), p. 71.

p. 26.   *Called . . . an animistic revolutionary.* Lynn White, Jr., "The His-
              torical Roots of Our Ecologic Crisis," from *Science* 155.3767 (10
              March 1967), pp. 1203–1207. Reprinted in *The Ecocriticism
              Reader: Landmarks in Literary Ecology,* ed. Cheryll Glotfelty and
              Harold Fromm (Athens, Ga.: University of Georgia Press, 1996),
              pp. 3–14.

p. 26.   *His views . . . praise your Creator.* Trans. and ed. Ewert Cousins,
              *Bonaventure: The Soul's Journey into God: The Tree of Life, The
              Life of Francis,* in The Classics of Western Spirituality (New York:
              Paulist Press, 1978), p. 294. St. Francis' sermon was destined to
              become a favorite subject of manuscript illuminations for several
              centuries.

p. 26.   *For Francis . . . all creatures equally.* Max Oelschlaeger, *The Idea of
              Wilderness: From Prehistory to the Age of Ecology* (New Haven,
              Conn.: Yale University Press, 1991), p. 73.

p. 26.   *Church authorities . . . end up at the stake.* White, "The Historic
              Roots of Our Ecologic Crisis," p. 13.

p. 27.   *In 1967, the publication . . . religion and nature.* White, "The His-
              toric Roots of Our Ecologic Crisis," op. cit.

p. 27.   *Fr. Thomas Berry confronts . . . the natural world.* Thomas Berry,
              The Dream of the Earth (San Francisco: Sierra Club Books, 1988).

p. 27.   *The best-known . . . the rest of creation.* Matthew Fox, *Original Blessing* (Santa Fe, N.M.: Bear and Company, Inc., 1983).

p. 29.   *Strikingly similar mandates . . . a common source.* See *The Torah: A Modern Commentary,* p. 572.

p. 30.   *In his comprehensive study . . . epiphanies of the gods.* Mircea Eliade, *Shamanism: Archaic Techniques of Ecstasy,* trans. Willard R. Trask (Princeton: Princeton University Press, 1972), p. 98.

p. 30.   *Eliade further suggests . . . the irrational souls of beasts.* Ibid., pp. 98, 99; Jon Christopher Crocker, *Vital Souls: Bororo Cosmology, Natural Symbolism, and Shamanism* (Tucson, Ariz.: University of Arizona, 1985); Stephen Dow Beckham, Kathryn Ann Toepel, and Rick Minor, *Native American Religious Practices and Uses in Western Oregon* (Eugene, Ore.: University of Oregon, 1984); University of Oregon Anthropological Papers, No. 31, pp. 21–22.

p. 32.   *Not only men, but animals . . . powers and attributes.* Diamond Jennes, *The Ojibwa Indians of Parry Island, Their Social and Religious Life* (Ottawa: Canadian Department of Mines Bulletin no. 78, Museum of Canada Anthropological Series, no. 17, 1935), pp. 20–21.

p. 32.   *The greatest peril of life . . . taking away their bodies.* Knud Rassmussen, *Intellectual Culture of the Iglulik Eskimos, Report of the Fifth Thule Expedition, 1921–24,* vol. 7, No. 1 (Copenhagen: Glydendalske Boghandel, Nordisk Forlag), p. 56.

p. 34.   *. . . the uncounted voices of nature are dumb.* Quoted in Hans Peter Duerr, *Dreamtime: Concerning the Boundary Between Wilderness and Civilization,* trans. Felicitas Goodman (Oxford: Basil Blackwell, 1985), p. 90.

CHAPTER TWO

p. 38.   Epigraph. Origen, *Commentaries on the Song of Songs.*

p. 39.   *The only unconventional element . . . does the honors.* Herbert Freidmann, *A Bestiary for Saint Jerome: Animal Symbolism in European Religious Art* (Washington, D.C.: Smithsonian Institution Press, 1980), pp. 231–234.

p. 40.   *While the work is more . . . by Jerome and his scribes.* Ibid., p. 233.

p. 40.   *We begin first of all . . . king of all the beasts . . . Physiologus,* trans. Michael J. Curley (Austin, Tex.: University of Texas Press, 1979), p. 3.

p. 43.   *Spiritual things . . . real things.* Quoted in Freidmann, *A Bestiary for Saint Jerome,* p. 26.

p. 43.   *Tell me which bird is best . . . the Holy Ghost.* ("Saga me hwilc fugel ys selust. Ic ðe secge, Culfre ys selust; heo getacnað þone helegan gast.") *The Prose Solomon and Saturn and Adrian and Ritheus,* ed.

James E. Cross and Thomas D. Hill (Toronto: University of Toronto Press, 1982), p. 30.

p. 48. *And so, Jerome's Bible . . . the Physiologus.* In a painting by Bartolomeo di Giovanni in the Yale University Art Gallery, the beast is shown holding open a book, perhaps Jerome's Bible, with his paws.

p. 48. *This belief . . . as Max Oelschlaeger puts it.* Oelschlaeger, *The Idea of Wilderness*, p. 16.

p. 49. *The elephant is not . . . bends his legs. The History of Animals*, Book II, Vol. I, in *The Complete Works of Aristotle, the Revised Oxford Translation*, ed. Jonathan Barnes (New Jersey: Princeton University Press, 1984), p. 792.

p. 57. *As E. O. Wilson points out . . .* E. O. Wilson, *Biophilia: The Human Bond with Other Species* (Cambridge, Mass.: Harvard University Press, 1984), p. 55.

CHAPTER THREE

p. 59. Epigraph. Rainer Maria Rilke, *Sonnets to Orpheus.*

p. 60. *One scholar traces . . . a horned serpent.* Richard A. Firmage, *The Alphabet Abecedarium: Some Notes on Letters* (Boston: David R. Godine, 1993).

p. 61. *Much of the Kabbalah . . . sphere of existence.* David Abram, *The Spell of the Sensuous: Perception and Language in a More-than-Human World* (New York: Pantheon Books, 1996), p. 133.

p. 61. *I am Alpha and Omega . . . a child's primer.* Revelation 21:6.

pp. 61–62. *The Egyptians considered . . . part of their bodies.* Firmage, *The Alphabet Abecedarium*, p. 11.

p. 62. *Wulfias . . . the mysteries of the Kingdom of God."* Mark 4:11.

p. 65. *Or, as in the Irish Book of Kells . . . an illuminated letter.* See J. O. Westwood, *The Art of Illuminated Manuscripts: Illustrated Sacred Writings* (New York: Arch Cape Press, 1988).

p. 70. *In discussing the role of literacy . . . the book on the other.* Jack Goody, *The Domestication of the Savage Mind* (Cambridge: Cambridge University Press, 1977), pp. 37, 109.

pp. 71–72. *As a Zuñi elder focuses . . . now speak to us!* David Abram, *The Spell of the Sensuous*, p. 131.

CHAPTER FOUR

p. 77. *He investigated the matter . . . for the people involved.* Dr. Kenneth R. Pelletier, *Sound Mind, Sound Body: A New Model for Lifelong Health* (New York: Simon & Schuster, 1994), p. 152.

p. 77. *A 1980 study of people hospitalized . . . after their release.* David

Spiegel, M.D., "Family Support: How Friends, Families, and Groups Can Help," in *Mind Body Medicine: How to Use Your Mind for Better Health,* ed. Daniel Goleman, Ph.D., and Joel Gurin (New York: Consumer Reports Books, 1993), p. 338.

p. 77.   *At least that was Dr. Seigel's surmise.* Pelletier, *Sound Mind, Sound Body,* pp. 152–153.

p. 78.   *But when their dogs . . . any anxiety at all.* Spiegel, *Mind Body Medicine,* p. 338.

p. 78.   *Other research shows that pets . . . health care workers.* Pelletier, *Sound Mind, Sound Body,* p. 152.

p. 78.   *Starting with Hippocrates . . . Foucault has shown.* Michel Foucault, *The Birth of the Clinic: An Archaeology of the Medical Perception,* trans. Alan Sheridan Smith (New York: Pantheon Books, 1973).

p. 80.   *The sect studied medicinal roots . . . "pious" and "healer."* See Edmund Wilson, *The Dead Sea Scrolls: 1947–1969* (New York: Oxford University Press, 1969), p. 31.

p. 81.   *Nonindustrial societies often regard illness . . . members of his group.* Jerome D. Frank, *Nonmedical Healing: Religious and Secular,* pp. 231–266.

p. 81.   *A woman who cannot nurse . . . water and swallow.* Elliott V. K. Dobbie, ed., *The Anglo Saxon Minor Poems,* The Anglo Saxon Poetic Records 6 (New York: Columbia University Press, 1942). My translation.

p. 82.   *The magico-religious principle . . . like affects like.* For the "rules" of magic, see Marcel Mauss, *A General Theory of Magic,* trans. Robert Brain (New York: Norton, 1972), pp. 60–70.

p. 82.   *Baganda medicine men . . . drive the creature away.* Frank Hamel, *Human Animals: Werewolves and Other Transformations* (Hyde Park, N.Y.: University Books, 1969), p. 45.

p. 83.   *The worms that represented . . . the man became a monk.* Ibid., p. 46.

p. 83.   *Even the Bible . . . the curing of the Garasene demoniac.* See Matthew 8:28–34; Mark 5:1–20; Luke 8:26–39.

p. 84.   *Still others have . . . "confused," "rambling," and "bizarre."* John Meier, *A Marginal Jew: Rethinking the Historical Jesus,* Volume II: *Mentor, Message, and Miracles* (New York: Doubleday, 1994), p. 650. In a parallel story, St. Regulus, archbishop of Arles and Senlis, was also confronted with a demoniac, whose demon requested to enter a nearby ass. The bishop consented, but the ass saw what was coming and made the sign of the cross, forcing the demon to go elsewhere.

p. 84.   *But, as John Meier points out . . . magical healer, or shaman.* Meier, *A Marginal Jew,* pp. 576–595.

p. 84.   *Jesus himself . . . lead people to faith.* John 9:3–5.

p. 85.   *Living creatures beyond . . . process of self-definition.* K. Thomas,

Man and the Natural World: Changing Attitudes in England 1500– 1800 (London: Allen Lane, 1983), p. 40.

p. 89.   *Walk into the Cluny Museum . . . The Lady of the Unicorn.* See Beer, *Unicorn: Myth and Reality.*

p. 90.   *According to John Berger, the gaze . . . are seen by him.* Berger, *About Looking,* p. 3.

p. 91.   *Eye of newt and toe of frog . . . Like a hell-broth boil and bubble. Macbeth,* Act IV, scene 1.

p. 91.   *And at the very time the play . . . creatures on the gallows.* See E. P. Evans, *The Criminal Prosecution and Capital Punishment of Animals* (New York: E. P. Dutton & Co., 1906).

CHAPTER FIVE

p. 94.   *To uncap the cartridges, the gunners . . . considered impure.* Frederick J. Simoons, *Eat Not This Flesh: Food Avoidances in the Old World* (Madison, Wis.: University of Wisconsin Press, 1961).

p. 94.   *The Mau Mau revolt . . . how about eating that?* Credo Mutwa, *My People, the Writings of a Zulu Witch-Doctor* (New York: Penguin Books, 1977), p. 175.

p. 94.   *In the second century B.C., Jewish resistance . . . forced into his mouth.* I Maccabees 1:47; II Maccabees 6.

p. 95.   *To this day, Chaldean Christians . . . pregnancy and nursing.* Simoons, *Eat Not This Flesh,* p. 11.

p. 96.   *Since people rarely get sick . . . parasites seems minuscule.* Ibid., pp. 37–40.

p. 97.   *Nonetheless, believers hallow . . . requiring a rationale. The Torah: A Modern Commentary,* p. 809.

p. 98.   *Anthropologist Frederick Simoons notes . . . one religion or nation and another.* Simoons, *Eat Not This Flesh.*

p. 101.   *Only the males in the priestly line . . . prohibition in Leviticus.* Leviticus 6:22.

p. 101.   *Even in modern Western societies, the eating of beef . . . women in public.* Carol J. Adams, *The Sexual Politics of Meat: A Feminist-Vegetarian Critical Theory* (New York: Continuum, 1990).

p. 103.   *That's why wood ticks are flat.* Based on a tale reported by Louisa McDermott in 1901, printed in *American Indian Myths and Legends,* ed. Richard Erdoes and Alfonso Ortiz (New York: Pantheon Books, 1984), pp. 223–225.

CHAPTER SIX

p. 104.   Epigraph. Hesiod's *Theogony,* quoted in Anne Baring and Jules Cashford, *The Myth of the Goddess: Evolution of an Image* (New York: Viking Arkana, 1991), p. 162.

p. 104.   *Animal sacrifice was . . . the ancient world.* James Serpell, *In the Company of Animals: A Study of Human-Animal Relationships* (New York: Basil Blackwell, 1986), p. 167.

p. 105.   *During the nineteenth century, so many . . . by the ton.* Juliet Clutton-Brock, *Cats: Ancient and Modern* (Cambridge, Mass.: Harvard University Press, 1993), pp. 36–37.

p. 105.   *An estimated three hundred thousand embalmed felines . . . English gardens as fertilizer.* Anwar Iqbal, "Egyptologist Unwraps the History of the House Cat," *Chicago Tribune*, Friday, August 7, 1987.

p. 107.   *But no story in the Bible embodies . . . Abraham on Mount Moriah.* Genesis 22:1–24.

p. 108.   *At the last moment, however, Artemis . . . altar in her stead.* See Euripides' *Iphigenia at Aulis.*

p. 109.   *I owe a cock to Asklepios . . . the debt?* Plato, *Phaedo,* trans. R. Hackford, in *Plato: The Collected Dialogues,* ed. Edith Hamilton and Huntington Cairns (Princeton: Princeton University Press, 1982).

p. 110.   *Christians "believe that the sacrificial tradition . . . the sacrifice of Christ."* Andrew Linzey, *Animal Theology* (Urbana and Chicago: University of Illinois Press, 1994), p. 105.

pp. 111–12.   *Formerly by virtue . . . to proceed with excommunication.* Evans, *The Criminal Prosecution and Capital Punishment of Animals,* pp. 38–51.

p. 112.   *Regrettably, the final decision reached . . . last page of the verdict.* Ibid., pp. 38–51.

CHAPTER SEVEN

p. 119.   Epigraph. Byron, *Don Juan,* Canto IX, 20.

p. 121.   *Jungian analysis may be . . . religious experience relate.* See Clarissa Pinkola Estés, *Women Who Run with the Wolves* (New York: Ballantine Books, 1992).

p. 121.   *The animals that seem to call . . . belong to animals or take their shapes.* Lévi-Strauss, *Totemism,* p. 18.

p. 122.   *What is particularly interesting . . . choosing a zoological alter ego.* See Mircea Eliade, *Rites and Symbols of Initiation: The Mysteries of Birth and Rebirth,* Willard R. Trask, trans. (New York: Spring Publications, 1994), p. 72.

p. 124.   *Gilles Garnier . . . dying after recognizing the evil of his ways.* Letter from Daniel d'Ange to the Dean of the Church of Sens, quoted in *Human Animals,* p. 57.

p. 126.   *Or it might have been the way berserkers . . . triggered their battle fury.* Shield-biting became stereotypic berserker behavior. Like the ready-to-draw stance of gunfighters in Old West legends, shield-biting put normal men into a panic. In *Grettir's Saga*, the great Icelandic hero Grettir turned the gesture to his benefit in laconic Norse fashion. When Grettir was faced with a berserker who began biting his shield as a prelude to his war frenzy, the Icelander calmly walked up to the warrior and kicked the bottom of the shield, slicing it through the befuddled berserker's head.

p. 127.   *The Pawnee tell the story of Bear-Man . . . the greatest of warriors.* White Wolf Woman, pp. 99–101.

p. 127.   *Perhaps the most celebrated Norse hero . . . a great warrior bear.* Hrolf's Saga.

p. 128.   *To behave like a beast of prey . . . some sort become a god.* Eliade, *Rites and Symbols of Initiation*, p. 72.

p. 128.   *The wer-wolf embraces the king's son . . . Whatever the beast does for him.* William of Palermo, ed. W. W. Skeats (1869).

Chapter Eight

p. 132.   *Epigraph.* Jules Cashford, *The Myth of the Goddess: Evolution of an Image* (New York: Viking Arkana, 1991), p. 28.

p. 133.   *Instead, they usually conclude . . . desire to nurture.* Nancy Carlsson-Paige and Diane E. Levin, *Who's Calling the Shots: How to Respond Effectively to Children's Fascination with War Play and War Toys* (Philadelphia, Pa.: New Society Publishers, 1990).

p. 134.   *Presumably, the little Elamite . . . dachshunds and ducks.* Emanuel Hercík, *Folk-Toys* (Prague: Atia, 1951); Carl Gröber, *Children's Toys of Bygone Days*.

p. 137.   *In fact, the ark became known . . . except the toy ark.* Gröber, *Children's Toys of Bygone Days*, pp. 106–109.

p. 137.   *Consider, for instance, the hobbyhorse.* I use the term "hobbyhorse" to refer both to pole horses and rocking horses. Pole horses (a carved or stuffed horse head stuck on a pole) are one of the most widespread and oldest toys in the world, though they are no longer very fashionable in the West.

p. 138.   *The child Jesus . . . out of his mouth.* Revelation 19:11–16.

p. 139.   *Shamans from many parts . . . to the other world.* Eliade, *Shamanism*, p. 466–470.

p. 139.   *Indeed, the origin of the hobbyhorse . . . the form of Morris dancers.* Eliade, *Shamanism*, p. 467.

p. 140.   *One might call them . . . industrial society.* See Berger, *About Looking*, pp. 20–21.

p. 141.   *The future candidate . . . "Drawing the Line in Louisiana."* Gröber, *Children's Toys of Bygone Days*, pp. 111–112.

p. 142.   *THIS IS BRUIN'S DAY . . . New York City.* Quoted in ibid., p. 114.

p. 143.   *Having grown up with these . . . bizarre nature of this art.* It is something of a misnomer to call modern natural museum specimens "stuffed animals." Taxidermists originally stuffed their specimens with excelsior. By the nineteenth century, however, they had devised a method of stretching animal skins over clay or wood frames, a procedure still followed today.

p. 145.   *As Stephen Gould put it . . . to become a paleontologist.* Stephen Gould, "Evolution by Walking," *Natural History,* vol. 104, No. 3, March 1995, p. 13.

CHAPTER NINE

p. 147.   *Epigraph.* T. S. Eliot, "The Naming of Cats," *The Complete Poems and Plays, 1909–1950* (New York: Hartcort, Brace & World, 1971).

p. 148.   *Lappish, Ainu, Inuit . . . "that's him."* Stephen Glosecki, *Shamanism and Old English Poetry* (New York: Garland Publishing, 1989), pp. 202–204.

p. 148.   *The existence of our noa name "bear" . . . on modern English vocabulary.* Ibid., p. 202.

p. 149.   *As a twelfth-century bestiary put it . . . to say, Hebrew.* The Book of Beasts: Being a Translation from a Latin Bestiary of the Twelfth Century, trans. T. H. White (New York: Dover Publications, 1984), pp. 70–71.

p. 149.   *By christening the beasts . . . its secret name.* For a discussion of "secret names," see Isaac Asimov, *In the Beginning . . .* (New York: Crown Publishers, 1981), pp. 97–99.

p. 150.   *Even the far-sailing Greeks . . . "Unfriendly" Sea.* Edith Hamilton, *Mythology* (New York: Mentor Books, 1969), p. 67.

p. 152.   *Thus a twelfth-century Latin bestiary . . . are born formless. The Book of Beasts,* p. 45.

p. 152.   *This same bestiary remarks . . . each of them had. The Book of Beasts,* p. 70.

p. 153.   *The Sioux had Sitting Bull . . . Thorleif Crow.* See *Njal's Saga.*

p. 153.   *The prohibition was so strong . . . against his unconscious father.* Genesis 9:20–27.

p. 154.   *Freud noted . . . full equals.* Quoted in Richard Tapper, "Animality, Humanity, Morality, Society," in *What Is an Animal?* (London: Unwin Hyman, 1988), p. 50.

p. 158.   *"Why should I call my neighbor's animal?"* Vicki Hearne, *Adam's Task: Calling Animals by Name* (New York: Vintage, 1986), p. 140.

p. 158.   *This is the Adamic naming . . . they have biographies.* Kowalski, *The Souls of Animals,* p.107.

CHAPTER TEN

p. 159.   *Epigraph.* Erdoes and Ortiz, eds., *American Indian Myths and Legends,* p. 155.

p. 159.   *She-wolves and bitches . . . overwhelmingly negative.* The only clear exceptions seem to be the lioness, doe, and lady bird beetle, all of which have positive connotations.

p. 160.   *In fact . . . a dominated power.* André Joly, "Toward a Theory of Gender in Modern English," in *Studies in English Grammar,* ed. André Joly and T. Fraser (Paris: Éditions Universitaires, 1975), p. 273.

p. 161.   *André Leroi-Gourhan . . . emphasize their centrality.* André Leroi-Gourhan, *The Treasures of Prehistoric Art,* p. 144.

p. 161.   *A number of anthropologists believe . . . toward female existence.* Joseph Campbell, *Occidental Mythology* (New York: Viking, 1991), pp. 21–22.

p. 161.   *The hypothesis goes that the primeval . . . as Joseph Campbell put it.* Ibid., pp. 21–22.

p. 165.   *The resulting schism between passive . . . have powerfully documented.* Carolyn Merchant, *The Death of Nature: Women, Ecology, and the Scientific Revolution* (New York: Harper & Row, 1980); Susan Griffin, *Women and Nature: The Roaring Inside Her* (New York: Harper & Row, 1978).

CHAPTER ELEVEN

p. 167.   *Epigraph.* Stephanie Mills, "The Wild and the Tame," in *Place of the Wild,* ed. David Clarke Burks (Washington D.C.: Island Press, 1994), p. 54.

pp. 167–68. *There is . . . God through the desert (Isaiah 40:3).* Frye, *The Great Code,* p. 160.

p. 168.   *Midway in our life's journey . . . a dark wood.* Dante, *The Inferno,* trans. John Ciardi (New York: New American Library, 1954), Canto I, lines 1–3.

p. 168.   *The Bororo of Brazil . . . away from their village.* See Crocker, *Vital Souls.*

p. 169.   *Save me from the lion's mouth . . . the unicorns.* Other translations render "unicorn" as simply "wild beast."

p. 171.   *He gives his followers power over snakes and other wild creatures.* Luke 10:19.

pp. 171–72. *Dogs and horses . . . as servants and nonkin.* M. Sahlins, *Culture and Practical Reason* (Chicago: Chicago University Press, 1976), pp. 174–175.

p. 172.   *Even the medieval manuscript . . . creatures as birds and deer.* See

British Museum Harley MS 3244, printed in *The Book of Beasts*,
p. 70.

p. 172.   *Now with serpents he wars . . . many mishaps and mortal harms. Sir
Gawain and the Green Knight,* trans. Maria Borroff (New York:
Norton, 1967).

p. 173.   *The term appears first in Middle English . . . meaning of wasteland.*
Jay Hanford Vest, "Will of the Land," *Environmental Review*
(Winter 1985): 321–329.

pp. 174–75.   *Beloved cell, retirement's sweet abode . . . the notes of praise.* Quoted
in Alfred Biese, *The Development of the Feeling for Nature in the
Middle Ages and Modern Times* (1905; New York: Burt Franklin,
1964), pp. 59–60.

p. 177.   *Sayings, dreams, games . . . lost its central importance.* Berger, *About
Looking,* p. 13.

CHAPTER TWELVE

p. 181.   *Epigraph.* William Blake, "Auguries of Innocence."

p. 181.   *As Homer depicts Hades in* The Odyssey *. . . imitations of perish
mortals. The Odyssey of Homer,* trans. Richmond Lattimore (New
York: Harper and Row, 1967), Book XI, 11. 475–476.

pp. 182–83.   *As dolphins surface and begin to flip . . . disappeared again.* Dante,
The Inferno, trans. John Ciardi, Canto XXII, lines 19–21.

p. 183.   *A century after its composition . . . edifications of Christians.* See *The
Complete Paintings of Bosch* (New York: Harry N. Abrams, 1966),
pp. 100–101.

CHAPTER THIRTEEN

p. 187.   *Epigraph.* From William Stafford, "Lescaux," in *Fin, Feather, Fur*
(Rexburg, Idaho: Honeybrook Press, 1989).

p. 187.   *As he illuminated . . . "picture of the magic of the hunt."* Dr. Herbert
Kuhn, quoted in Joseph Campbell, *The Masks of God: Primitive
Mythology* (Harmondsworth: Penguin Books, 1976), pp. 307–308.

p. 187.   *Joseph Campbell argued the animals . . . their ever-living source.*
Ibid., p. 377.

p. 187.   *Other scholars see . . . place inside them. Myth of the Mother Goddess,*
p. 16.

p. 188.   *John Berger notes . . . human history to date.* Berger, "Animal
World."

pp. 190–91.   *Warhol said . . . "Cows . . . Of course! Cows! New cows! Fresh cows!"*
Eric Shanes, *Warhol* (New York: Portland House, 1991), p. 30.

p. 191.   *As Ezra Pound mused . . . what to think.* Ezra Pound, "Meditatio" in *Personae: The Shorter Poems*, a revised edition prepared by Lean Baechler and A. Walton Litz (New York: New Directions, 1990).

p. 192.   *Balog's art deconstructs . . . exiled from Eden.* Sierra volume II, no. 5, Sept./Oct. 1990.

Chapter Fourteen

p. 195.   *Epigraph.* Lynn White, Jr., *Historical Roots of Our Ecologic Crisis,* p. 1207.

p. 196.   *The world is troubled . . . this middle-earth.* Guthlac A, 1137–39. My translation.

p. 197.   *Again, the sign of the cross . . . horse evaporated.* See *Human Animals,* p. 49.

p. 197.   *The lion was so important . . . the church father.* Freidmann, *A Bestiary for St. Jerome.* p. 229.

p. 198.   *One scholar counted no less . . . renditions of Jerome.* Ibid., p. 23.

p. 198.   *For just as we marvel . . . than their names.* Ibid., p. 24.

p. 198.   *When a wolf devoured one of his oxen, St. Gentius . . . plow his field.* Hamel, *Human Animals,* p. 47.

p. 199.   *In his* Life of Cuthbert *. . . damaging a house.* Bede, *Life of Cuthbert,* trans. J. F. Webb (New York: Penguin, 1981), Chapter 20.

p. 199.   *For whatever it is worth . . . the illuminator's attention.* See Corpus Christi College Cambridge Library, MS 183, fo. 1v.

p. 200.   *St. David of Garesja protected . . . has given birth.* Quoted in Andrew Linzey, *Christianity and the Rights of Animals* (New York: Crossroads, 1991), p. 45.

p. 201.   *Still, the sacred topic again plunged . . . its natural functions.* Joseph L. Baird, "Natura Plangens, the Ruthwell Cros and the Dream of the Rood," *Studies in Iconography* 10 (1984–86): 40.

p. 201.   *The saintly view of animals . . . to praise your Creator. Bonaventure: The Soul's Journey into God: The Tree of Life, The Life of Francis,* in The Classics of Western Spirituality trans. and ed. Ewert Cousins (New York: Paulist Press, 1978), p. 294.

p. 202.   *Based on his egalitarian approach . . . revolutionary of Western history.* White, *Historical Roots of Our Ecologic Crisis,* p. 1207.

Chapter Fifteen

p. 203.   *Epigraph.* Joseph Meeker, "The Comic Mode," in Glotfelty and Fromm, eds., *Ecocriticism Reader,* p.161.

p. 204.   *[T]he goodness of the species . . . diverse grades of things.* Thomas Aquinas, *Summa Contra Gentiles,* bk. 3 chap. 71. Quoted in Arthur Lovejoy, *The Great Chain of Being: A Study of the History of an Idea* (Cambridge: Harvard University Press, 1950), p. 77.

p. 205.   *At one point, Albertus notes . . . such matters here.* Albert the Great, *Man and Beast (De animalibus* [Books 22–26]), trans. James J. Scanlan (Binghamton, N.Y.: Medieval and Renaissance Texts and Studies, 1987), p. 216.

p. 205.   *Man . . . without aim or purpose. The Philosophical Works of Francis Bacon,* ed. Robert Leslie Ellis and James Spedding (1905; reprint ed., Freeport, N.Y.: Books for Libraries Press, 1970), vol. 6, p. 747.

CHAPTER SIXTEEN

p. 212.   *Epigraph.* William Stafford, "Our City" in *Fin, Feather, Fur.*
p. 213.   *The land Dilmun is clean . . . The dove droops not the head,* cited in *The Torah: A Modern Commentary,* p. 32.
p. 214.   *The Saga of St. Matthew,* quoted in Gísli Pásson, "The Idea of Fish: Land and Sea in the Icelandic World-View," in *Animal Signifiers: Human Meaning in the Natural World,* ed. Roy Willis (London: Rutledge, 1994), p. 123.

Bibliography

Abram, David. *The Spell of the Sensuous: Perception and Language in a More-than-Human World.* New York: Pantheon Books, 1996.

Adams, Carol J. *The Sexual Politics of Meat: A Feminist-Vegetarian Critical Theory.* New York: Continuum, 1990.

Albert the Great. *Man and Beast (De animalibus* [Books 22–26]). Trans. James J. Scanlan. Binghamton, N.Y.: Medieval and Renaissance Texts and Studies, 1987.

Aristotle. *The History of Animals,* Book II, in *The Complete Works of Aristotle, the Revised Oxford Translation.* Jonathan Barnes, ed. Volume One. Princeton: Princeton University Press, 1984.

Asimov, Isaac. *In the Beginning . . .* New York: Crown Publishers, 1981.

Bacon, Francis. *The Philosophical Works of Francis Bacon.* Robert Leslie Ellis and James Spedding, eds. 1905; reprint ed., Freeport, N.Y.: Books for Libraries Press, 1970.

Baring, Anne, and Cashford, Jules. *The Myth of the Goddess: Evolution of an Image.* New York: Viking Arkana, 1991.

Beer, Rüdiger Robert. *Unicorn: Myth and Reality.* Trans. Charles M. Stern. New York: Van Nostrand Reinhold Co., 1972.

Berger, John. *About Looking.* New York: Pantheon Books, 1980.

———. "Animal World." *New Society,* November 1971.

Berry, Thomas. *The Dream of the Earth.* San Francisco: Sierra Club Books, 1988.

Biese, Alfred. *The Development of the Feeling for Nature in the Middle Ages and Modern Times.* 1905; New York: Burt Franklin, 1964.

The Book of Beasts: Being a Translation from a Latin Bestiary of the Twelfth Century. Trans. T. H. White. New York: Dover Publications, 1984.

Bynum, Caroline Walker. *Holy Feast and Holy Fast: The Religious Significance of Food to Medieval Women*. Berkeley and Los Angeles: University of California Press, 1987.

Campbell, Joseph. *Occidental Mythology*. New York: Viking, 1991.

Carlsson-Paige, Nancy, and Levin, Diane E. *Who's Calling the Shots: How to Respond Effectively to Children's Fascination with War Play and War Toys*. Philadelphia, Pa.: New Society Publishers, 1990.

Clutton-Brock, Juliet. *Cats: Ancient and Modern*. Cambridge, Mass.: Harvard University Press, 1993.

Crocker, Jon Christopher. *Vital Souls: Bororo Cosmology, Natural Symbolism, and Shamanism*. Tucson, Ariz.: University of Arizona Press, 1985.

Dobbie, Elliott V. K., ed. *The Anglo Saxon Minor Poems*. The Anglo Saxon Poetic Records 6. New York: Columbia University Press, 1942.

Duerr, Hans Peter. *Dreamtime: Concerning the Boundary Between Wilderness and Civilization*. Trans. Felicitas Goodman. Oxford: Basil Blackwell, 1985.

Elder, John C., and Rockefeller, Steven C., eds. *Spirit and Nature: Why the Environment Is a Religious Issue*. Boston: Beacon Press, 1992.

Eliade, Mircea. *Rites and Symbols of Initiation: The Mysteries of Birth and Rebirth*. Trans. Willard R. Trask. New York: Spring Publications, 1994.

———. *Shamanism: Archaic Techniques of Ecstasy*. Trans. Willard R. Trask. Princeton: Princeton University Press, 1964.

Erdoes, Richard, and Ortiz, Alfonso, eds. *American Indian Myths and Legends*. New York: Pantheon Books, 1984.

Estés, Clarissa Pinkola. *Women Who Run with the Wolves: Myths and Stories of the Wild Woman Archetype*. New York: Ballantine Books, 1992.

Evans, E. P. *The Criminal Prosecution and Capital Punishment of Animals*. New York: E. P. Dutton & Co., 1906.

Firmage, Richard A. *The Alphabet Abecedarium: Some Notes on Letters*. Boston: David R. Godine, 1993.

Foley, Dan J. *Toys Through the Ages*. New York: Chilton Books, 1962.

Foucault, Michel. *The Birth of the Clinic: An Archaelogy of the Medical Perception*. Trans. Alan Sheridan Smith. New York: Pantheon Books, 1973.

———. *The Order of Things: An Archaeology of the Human Sciences*. A Translation of *Les Mot et Les Chases*. New York: Vintage Books, 1973.

Freidmann, Herbert. *A Bestiary for Saint Jerome: Animal Symbolism in European Religious Art*. Washington, D.C.: Smithsonian Institution Press, 1980.

Frye, Northrop. *The Great Code: The Bible and Literature*. New York: Harcourt Brace Jovanovich, 1982.

Glosecki, Stephen. *Shamanism and Old English Poetry*. New York: Garland Publishing, 1989.

Glotfelty, Cheryll, and Fromm, Harold, eds. *The Ecocriticism Reader*. Athens, Ga.: University of Georgia Press, 1996.

Goleman, Daniel, and Gurin, Joel, eds. *Mind Body Medicine: How to Use Your Mind for Better Health*. New York: Consumer Reports Books, 1993.

Goody, Jack. *The Domestication of the Savage Mind.* Cambridge: Cambridge University Press, 1977.

Gould, Stephen. "Evolution by Walking." *Natural History,* Vol. 104, No. 3, March 1995.

Green, Julien. *God's Fool: The Life and Times of St. Francis.* Trans. Peter Heinegg. San Francisco: Harper & Row, 1987.

Griffin, Susan. *Women and Nature: The Roaring Inside Her.* New York: Harper & Row, 1978.

Gröber, Carl, *Children's Toys of Bygone Days.*

Hamel, Frank. *Human Animals: Werewolves and Other Transformations.* New York: New York University Books, 1969.

Hearne, Vicki. *Adam's Task: Calling Animals by Name.* New York: Vintage, 1986.

Hercík, Emanuel. *Folk-Toys.* Prague: Atia, 1951.

Holistic Approaches to Ancient and Contemporary Medicine. New York: Harcourt Brace Jovanovich, 1979.

Jennes, Diamond. *The Ojibwa Indians of Parry Island, Their Social and Religious Life.* Ottawa: Canadian Department of Mines Bulletin no. 78, Museum of Canada Anthropological Series, no. 17, 1935.

Joly, André. "Toward a Theory of Gender in Modern English." *Studies in English Grammar.* Andre Joly and T. Fraser, eds. Paris: Éditions Universitaires, 1975.

Klingender, Francis. *Animals in Art and Thought to the End of the Middle Ages.* Cambridge, Mass.: MIT Press, 1971.

Kowalski, Gary. *The Souls of Animals.* Walpole, N.H.: Stillpoint Publishing, 1991.

Leroi-Gourhan, André. *The Treasures of Prehistoric Art.* New York: Harry N. Abrams, 1980.

Lévi-Strauss, Claude. *Totemism.* Trans. R. Needham. London: Merlin Press, 1962.

Lewinsohn, Richard. *Animals, Men and Myths: An Informative and Entertaining History of Man and the Animals Around Him.* Translated without attribution. New York: Harper & Brothers, 1954.

Linzey, Andrew. *Animal Theology.* Urbana and Chicago: University of Illinois Press, 1994.

―――. *Christianity and the Rights of Animals.* New York: Crossroads, 1991.

Lopez, Barry Holstun. *Of Wolves and Men.* New York: Charles Scribner's Sons, 1978.

Lovejoy, Arthur. *The Great Chain of Being: A Study of the History of an Idea.* Cambridge: Harvard University Press, 1950.

Mauss, Marcel. *A General Theory of Magic.* Trans. Robert Brain. New York: Norton, 1972.

Meier, John. *A Marginal Jew: Rethinking the Historical Jesus.* Volume II: *Mentor, Message, and Miracles.* New York: Doubleday, 1994.

Merchant, Carolyn. *The Death of Nature: Women, Ecology, and the Scientific Revolution.* New York: Harper & Row, 1980.

Morris, Ramona and Desmond. *Men and Snakes.* New York: McGraw-Hill, 1965.

Morris, Ian. *A Venetian Bestiary.* New York: Thames & Hudson, 1982.

Mutwa, Credo. *My People, the Writings of a Zulu Witch-Doctor.* New York: Penguin Books, 1977.

Nurbaksh, Javad. *Dogs from a Sufi Point of View.* Tran. Terry Graham et al. New York: KhaniQahi Nimatullahi Publications, 1989.

Oelschlaeger, Max. *The Idea of Wilderness: From Prehistory to the Age of Ecology.* New Haven, Conn.: Yale University Press, 1991.

Pelletier, Kenneth R. *Sound Mind, Sound Body: A New Model for Lifelong Health.* New York: Simon & Schuster, 1994.

Phoebus, Gaston, Comte de Foix. *Livre de la Chasse.* Sometime before 1391. Transcribed in Baillie Grohman, ed., *Master of the Game,* by Edward, Second Duke of York. London: Ballantyne, Hanson & Co., 1904.

Physiologus. Trans. Michael J. Curley. Austin, Tex.: University of Texas Press, 1979.

Rassmussen, Knud. *Intellectual Culture of the Iglulik Eskimos. Report of the Fifth Thule Expedition, 1921–24.* Vol. 7, No. 1. Copenhagen: Glydendalske Boghandel, Nordisk Forlag.

Reichard, Gladys A. *Navaho Medicine Man.* New York: J. J. Augustin, 1939.

Ritchie, C. I. A. *The British Dog.* London: Robert Hale, 1981.

Sahlins, M. *Culture and Practical Reason.* Chicago: Chicago University Press, 1976.

Sandar, Donald F. *Navaho Indian Medicine and Medicine Men.*

Serpell, James. *In the Company of Animals: A Study of Human-Animal Relationships.* New York: Basil Blackwell, 1986.

Shanes, Eric. *Warhol.* New York: Portland House, 1991.

Simoons, Frederick J. *Eat Not This Flesh: Food Avoidances in the Old World.* Madison, Wisc.: University of Wisconsin Press, 1961.

Spiegel, David. "Family Support: How Friends, Families, and Groups Can Help." *Mind Body Medicine: How to Use Your Mind for Better Health,* ed. Daniel Goleman, Ph.D., and Joel Gurin. New York: Consumer Reports Books, 1993.

Starobinski, Jean. *A History of Medicine.* New York: Hawthorn Books, 1964.

Tapper, Richard. "Animality, Humanity, Morality, Society." *What Is an Animal?* London: Unwin Hyman, 1988.

The Complete Paintings of Bosch. New York: Harry N. Abrams, 1966.

Thomas, K. *Man and the Natural World: Changing Attitudes in England 1500–1800.* London: Allen Lane, 1983.

The Torah: A Modern Commentary. Commentaries by W. Gunther Plaut and Bernard J. Bamberger. New York: Union of American Hebrew Congregations, 1981.

Vest, Jay Hanford. "Will of the Land." *Environmental Review*, Winter 1985: 321–329.

Westwood, J. O. *The Art of Illuminated Manuscripts: Illustrated Sacred Writings.* New York: Arch Cape Press, 1988.

White Wolf Woman: Native American Transformation Myths. Collected and re-told by Teresa Pijoan. Little Rock, Ark.: August Hope Publishers, 1992.

Wilson, E. O. *Biophilia: The Human Bond with Other Species.* Cambridge, Mass.: Harvard University Press, 1984.

Wilson, Edmund. *The Dead Sea Scrolls: 1947–1969.* New York: Oxford University Press, 1969.

Index